AF657092

PAKISTAN INSIGHTS 2021-22

A Granular Look at Key Issues in Pakistan

PAKISTAN INSIGHTS 2021-22

A Granular Look at Key Issues in Pakistan

Editor

TILAK DEVASHER

Vivekananda International Foundation
New Delhi

PENTAGON PRESS LLP

PAKISTAN INSIGHTS - 2021-22
A Granular Look at Key Issues in Pakistan
Editor: Tilak Devasher

ISBN 978-93-90095-57-5

First Published in 2022

Copyright © Vivekananda International Foundation, New Delhi

All rights reserved. No part of this publication may be reproduced, stored in a retrieval system, or transmitted in any form or by any means, electronic, mechanical, photocopying, recording or otherwise, without the prior written permission of the Publisher.

Disclaimer: The views and opinions expressed in the book are the individual assertion of the Author. The Publisher does not take any responsibility for the same in any manner whatsoever. The same shall solely be the responsibility of the Author.

Published by
PENTAGON PRESS LLP
206, Peacock Lane, Shahpur Jat
New Delhi-110049
Phones: 011-64706243, 26491568
Telefax: 011-26490600
email: rajan@pentagonpress.in
website: www.pentagonpress.in

Printed at Aegean Offset Printers, Greater Noida, U.P.

Contents

MAP OF PAKISTAN

Pakistan at a Glance

Aakriti Vinayak

Area

Total (Land and Water): 881,889 sq km

Province-wise Area

Balochistan: 347,190 sq. km

Punjab: 205,345 sq. km

Sindh: 140,914 sq. km

Khyber Pakhtunkhwa (including erstwhile Federally Administered Tribal Agencies): 101,741 sq. km

International Borders

Afghanistan: 2,670 km

China: 438 km (via Pakistan Occupied Kashmir)

India: 3,190 km

Iran: 959 km

Length of Coastline

1,046 km

Energy

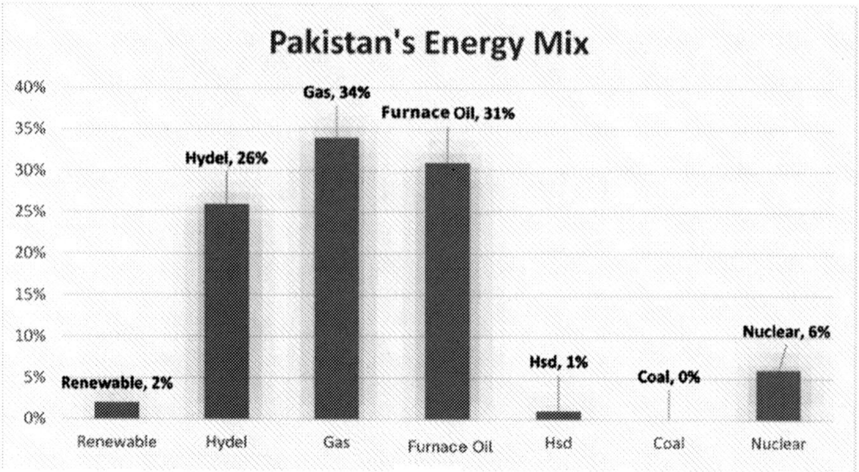

Source: https://en.dailypakistan.com.pk/featured/a-primer-on-pakistans-energy-mix/

(Hsd: High Speed Diesel)

Production of Crude Oil: 2,652,217 barrels

Number of Oilfields: 167 (July 2018)

Production of Natural Gas: 123,749 cubic feet

Number of Gas Fields: 181 (July 2018)

Electricity Generation: Installed Capacity: 2020-21 (July-April) (MW) 37,261, Source: Ministry of Energy, (Power Division)

DEMOGRAPHIC BASE

Population

207,862,518 (2017)

Population Density

242.9 per sq. km (Britannica)

Human Development Index (HDI) (2021): 0.557, Rank 154 (UNDP)

Province-wise Demography

Punjab: 53%

Sindh: 23%

Khyber Pakhtunkhwa (including FATA): 17%

Balochistan: 6%

(Census 2017)

Religion

Muslims: 97% (Sunni 77%, Shia 20%)

Christians, Hindus and Others 3%

ECONOMIC PROFILE

Economy, General

Basic Economic Parameters

Criteria	*Values*
GDP (billion $) [2] (2020)	262.61
GDP growth (annual %) [2] (2020)	-0.9%
Inflation [3] (April 2021)	11.1%
Agriculture (% of GDP) [3] (2021)	19.2%
Industry (% of GDP) [3] (2021)	19.1%
Services (% of GDP) [3] (2021)	61.7%
Exports of goods and services (% of GDP) [2] (2020)	10%
Imports of goods and services (% of GDP) [2] (2020)	17.4%
Gross capital formation (% of GDP) [2] ((2020)	14%
Urban population growth (annual %) [2] (2020)	2.7%
Energy use (kg of oil equivalent per capita) [2] (2014)	484.44
Electric power consumption (kWh per capita) [2] (2014)	471.04
Tax revenue (% of GDP) [3] (2021)	12.1%
Personal remittances, received (billion $) [2] (2020)	26.108
Foreign direct investment (billion $) (2020)	0.8
Net official development assistance received (current US$) (million) [2] (2019)	3005.15

[1] *Pakistan Bureau of Statistics (PBS)*
[2] *World Bank Data*
[3] *Pakistan Economic Survey 2020-2021*

INFRASTRUCTURE PROFILE (Pakistan Economic Survey 2019-20)

Infrastructure

Road Network: 263,775 km

National Highways of Pakistan: 13,000 km

Railways (Track Length)

11,811 km

MILITARY PROFILE (MILITARY BALANCE 2021, IISS)

Defence Budget (Pakistan Rupee (Rs))

2018	*2019*	*2020*	*2021*
1.11 tr	1.40 tr	1.48 tr	1.65 tr

Force Levels

ACTIVE 651,800 (Army 560,000 Navy 21,800 Air 70,000) Paramilitary 291,000

Strategic Forces

Army Strategic Forces Command: 12,000-15,000

Air: 1-2 sqn of F-16 A/B or Mirage 5 may be assigned a nuclear-strike role

Pakistan Coast Guard (Ministry of Interior)

5 Patrol and Coastal Combatants

Frontier Corps (Ministry of Interior)

70,000

Other

11 paramilitary regiments (total: 40 paramilitary bn)

List of Contributors

Dr. Arvind Gupta is the Director of the Vivekananda Foundation, New Delhi. He was the Deputy National Security Adviser and Secretary, National Security Council, Government of India during 2014-17. Prior to that, he was Director-General of the Institute for Defence Studies and Analyses, Ministry of Defence, New Delhi. He is a former career diplomat and has served in the Ministry of External Affairs and Indian missions abroad. Author of five books, his last book *Opportunity for India in a Changing World* was published by KW Publishers Pvt. Ltd. in 2021. Penguin India published *How India Manages Its National Security* in 2018. He has edited several books. He co-edited (with Anil Wadhwa) a volume titled *India's Foreign Policy: Surviving in a Turbulent World* (Sage 2020) and with Arpita Mitra a volume titled *Vasudhaiva Kutumbakam: The Relevance of India's Ancient Thinking to Contemporary Strategic Reality* (Aryan International, New Delhi, 2020). He comments frequently on strategic affairs on national television, and lectures at military academies and universities.

Rana Banerji is a former officer of the Indian Administrative Services (IAS-1972, Assam-Meghalaya cadre). He retired as Special Secretary, Cabinet Secretariat, in October 2009. After retirement, Banerji headed a Task Force on Intelligence Reforms at the Institute for Defence Studies & Analyses (IDSA). He participates in the UN Human Rights Commission Privacy Rights Rapporteur's annual meetings on Accountability & Intelligence Reforms. He has participated in several Track II & Track 1.5 interactions on Indo-Pak relations, Indo-US Security Relations & and Indo-Pak-Afghan Tripartite Dialogue (2010-2015). His focus area of expertise pertains to Pakistan, Afghanistan, Islamic Terrorism.

Tilak Devasher is a Consultant with the Vivekananda International Foundation. He is a former Special Secretary, Cabinet Secretariat, Government of India. During his professional career Tilak specialized in security issues, especially pertaining to India's neighbourhood. He is the author of '*Pakistan: Courting the Abyss*' (December 2016), '*Pakistan: At the Helm*' (June 2018) and '*Pakistan: The Balochistan Conundrum.*' All the books have been published by Harper Collins India. He is currently a member of the National Security Advisory Board (NSAB), Emeritus Resource Faculty at Rashtriya Raksha University and Distinguished Fellow, United Services Institution of India.

Dr. Shalini Chawla is a Distinguished Fellow at the Centre for Air Power Studies (CAPS), New Delhi. She joined CAPS in 2006 and has published more than 100 research articles in national and international journals on a wide range of issues relating to Pakistan and Afghanistan. She has authored five books and lectures regularly at various universities, think tanks and leading institutions of the Indian Armed Forces and Foreign Service. She is actively engaged in India's Track 1.5 initiatives. She received a Commendation and Badge by the Chief of Air Staff in October 2020 for her praiseworthy contribution to the Service.

Amb. Satish Chandra joined the Indian Foreign Service in 1965 and till 1989 was posted in various capacities in Indian missions in Vienna, Karachi, Washington D.C., Algiers, and Dhaka as well as at headquarters. Subsequently, he served as India's Ambassador to the Philippines (1989-1992), India's Permanent Representative to the UN Offices in Geneva (1992-1995) and its High Commissioner to Pakistan (1995-1998). He set up the NSCS in 1999 and headed it as Secretary till demission from office in February 2005 concurrently holding the post of Deputy National Security Advisor from February 2002. Apart from representing India at a variety of multilateral fora such as the IAEA, WHO, ILO, the UN Human Rights Commission, the Disarmament Commission, etc., he served as the President of the Conference on Disarmament during his assignment in Geneva. He was President of the Association of Indian Diplomats in 2010. He has been associated with the Vivekananda International Foundation since its inception in 2009 and is currently the Vice Chairman of its Board of Trustees.

Aakriti Vinayak is a Research Associate at Vivekananda International Foundation, New Delhi. She has completed her Masters in International Relations from Jawaharlal Nehru University and Bachelors in History from Jesus and Mary College, University of Delhi. She has also completed her MPhil from the Department of Political Science, University of Delhi. Her research interests are primarily Pakistani politics, India's neighbourhood and China, and Soft power and cultural diplomacy. Prior to joining the VIF she has worked with the Institute of Chinese Studies, *The Times of India* and the Indian National Trust for Art and Cultural Heritage (INTACH).

Amb. D.P. Srivastava is a Distinguished Fellow at the Vivekananda International Foundation. A former diplomat, he was Indian Ambassador to Iran, the Czech Republic, Libya and India's High Commissioner to Malta. During his tenure in Iran, he led negotiations on Indian participation in Chabahar Port. He has also served in Karachi. After retirement, he served as Senior Advisor to ONGC Videsh Ltd. for a year (2015-16), and Board of Directors of GAIL (2017-20). He holds a post-graduate degree in Political Science and Governance.

Lt Gen (Dr.) Rakesh Sharma (Retd) was commissioned in the Indian Army in 1977, and had a career spanning forty years. He had extensive operational experience in Jammu and Kashmir, North-East and on the western borders. He had trained the Botswana Army for three years, attended the National College in Nigeria, and National Defence College at New Delhi. He was Research Fellow at the Institute for Defence Studies and Analyses (IDSA). General Rakesh Sharma commanded the Fire and Fury Corps in Ladakh, facing both Pakistan and China. He writes regularly for newspapers, military journals and contributes chapters in books. He is currently on the Executive Council of the IDSA and Global Counter-Terrorism Council and Distinguished Fellow with the Vivekananda International Foundation and the Centre for Land Warfare Studies. He is the author of a monograph published by USI, New Delhi, titled *The Determinants of India's National Military Strategy.*

Amb. Gautam Mukhopadhaya (IFS 1980) has served in Indian embassies in Mexico, France, Cuba, the Permanent Mission of India, New York, and the Ministry of External Affairs, India, as well as on deputation with the ministries of Culture and Defence of India. He has been a Consultant on Social Development at the UN, New York, and Visiting Fellow at the Carnegie Endowment for International Peace, Washington DC. He graduated from the National Defence College (NDC) and re-opened the Indian Embassy in Kabul in November 2001 after the ouster of the Taliban. He then served as India's Ambassador to Syria, Afghanistan and Myanmar before retiring from service in May 2016. He is presently affiliated to the Centre for Policy Research as a Senior Visiting Fellow focusing on Afghanistan, Myanmar, India's Act East policy, the Indo-Pacific and the North East of India.

Stop Press

Tilak Devasher

As the book was going to press, major events took place in Pakistan leading to the incumbent Prime Minister Imran Khan losing a vote of no-confidence moved by the combined Opposition. As a result, he had to make way for Shehbaz Sharif who was elected leader of the House and the Prime Minister of Pakistan on 11 April 2022.

The catalyst for the political churning that took place was the fact that the all-powerful army finally had to accept that the person they had 'selected' to run the country was unable to deliver either on the economy or on governance. Despite this, they could have still persisted with him until the next elections in 2023 but for two reasons. First, the establishment, popularly referred to as the 'selectors', started taking flak for supporting an incompetent government and second, Imran Khan bit the hand that brought him to power.

Imran Khan made the cardinal error of trying to meddle in army postings and transfers that the army considers its redlines. Specifically, he tried to resist and prevent army chief Gen. Bajwa's transfer of DG ISI Lt. Gen Faiz Hameed as Corps Commander Peshawar. What Imran Khan wanted was for Hameed to continue as DG ISI so that he could help him to manage the political situation. It is assessed that Imran Khan wanted Hameed to succeed Bajwa as army chief in November 2022 and so be in position when the next general elections were held. For his part, Hameed too, had ambitions of succeeding Bajwa, but could not do so without having commanded a Corps. Ultimately, Imran Khan had to stand down though it is believed that Hameed continued to strategize for him from Peshawar. The incident was the proverbial last straw for the army that, as an institution, jealously guards its internal management and does not brook any interference from politicians.

The fallout of the incident was that the army became 'neutral' and cut Imran Khan adrift politically. The mantra of the civil and military being on the 'same page' faded away and without the army's political management, Imran Khan started fumbling. Since 2018 when the army had cobbled his majority and brought him to power, Imran Khan had depended on it to smoothen the politics of governance i.e. continue to manage his slender parliamentary majority and the passage of essential legislation. So dependent had he become that as a Punjab politician put it colourfully, Imran Khan had got so used to his nappies being changed that he couldn't do so himself! Resultantly, his coalition put together by the army started to break apart. Most of his allies started deserting him, and even some members of the PTI got together with the Opposition. Sensing an opportunity in the army's 'neutrality', the combined opposition introduced a no-confidence motion (NCM) against him in the National Assembly in early March.

Realising that he had lost his majority in Parliament, Imran Khan resorted to a plethora of dodgy, dubious and patently unconstitutional moves to ensure that the NCM did not take place and he continued to stay in power. His inflated ego refused to accept that he could be removed from power democratically. In the process he created a constitutional crisis that could have had serious consequences.

The key gambit used was the allegation of an American conspiracy to remove him from power because he followed "an independent foreign policy." The specific reference was to his visit to Russia that coincided with the Russian invasion of Ukraine. Imran Khan also accused the entire Opposition of being linked to the alleged American intrigue, thereby implicitly terming them as traitors. The allegation hinged on a communication from the USA supposedly warning of dire consequences if the NCM failed but that if no trust motion succeeded, Pakistan will be forgiven. At a rally in Islamabad, Imran Khan dramatically waved a piece of paper claiming it to be the communication.

Since conspiracy theories, especially those involving the USA, have great resonance in Pakistan, Imran Khan thought that this narrative would galvanize his support base generating sympathy, show him as a nationalist fighting for Pakistan's sovereignty, and set the narrative for the next elections. It was a simple yet effective way to distract the people from their economic woes by raising the idea of a foreign conspiracy and diverting attention from his dismal performance of the past three and a half years. In a coordinated move, the Deputy Speaker of the National Assembly rejected the opposition's NCM on the grounds that it was a US-sponsored attempt at "regime change" in Pakistan even though no evidence was presented or debated and prorogued the Assembly. On cue, Imran Khan advised the President to dissolve the National Assembly and call for fresh elections. The President immediately obliged.

As his call for nation-wide protests and his assertion that he would not accept the outcome of the NCM showed, Imran Khan would rather prefer that the whole system collapse than bow out democratically and gracefully. He presumed that the judiciary would accept the *fait accompli* of the dissolution of the National Assembly and settle for the familiar 'doctrine of necessity' used to justify coups in Pakistan, and he could get away with his flagrant constitutional violation.

However, the Supreme Court unanimously held the Deputy Speaker's rejection of the NCM to be unconstitutional, restored the National Assembly and directed the Speaker to conduct voting on the NCM on 09 April. On 'D' Day, Imran Khan again tried his best to stall the proceedings using various ploys. Reports indicate that he even tried to sack the army chief Gen Bajwa and appoint Lt Gen Faiz Hameed in his stead but this did not work too when the bureaucracy did not play ball. If whispers in Islamabad are to be believed, the army had to 'knock' some sense into him. As a result of Imran Khan's antics, the National Assembly was turned into a laughing stock. After several dramatic developments that included the scare of an army take-over, prison vans at the parliament complex, the prime minister being visited by senior army officers, the Supreme Court and the Islamabad High Court opening their doors near midnight, the NCM was finally voted upon at midnight. The Opposition carried the motion with the help of the estranged allies of Imran Khan. This may well be the first time in recent memory that a sitting prime minister was booted out democratically in Pakistan.

Meanwhile, the Punjab provincial assembly saw even greater chaos and mayhem. The house was summoned on the directives of the Lahore High Court to elect the new chief minister, but it witnessed scenes of violence. The PTI MPAs, who were supporting the Speaker, Chaudhry Pervez Elahi to be elected the leader of the house did not want the voting to be presided over by Deputy Speaker Mazari. They believed that he would be partial towards the opposition despite the fact that he had been directed by the High Court to hold the election of the Chief Minister. As a result, MPAs of the PTI and PML-Q physically attacked the deputy speaker. Mazari called the police in defence of the assembly. In the melee Elahi too was supposedly injured. Nevertheless, the voting did take place the next day and Hamza Sharif was elected leader of the house. As in the

National Assembly, in Punjab too, the PTI and its allies were shown to be stopping the democratic process through unconstitutional means.

What Next for Imran Khan?

After his unceremonious ouster from office, an angry Imran Khan who has not reconciled to his democratic removal, has held massive rallies in key cities like Peshawar and Karachi and a smaller one in Lahore. In these rallies, he has hit back at the new government by projecting them as an 'imported government' i.e. the proxies of the USA. He is now in what has been called 'container mode', seeking to mobilise the people with the objective of forcing early elections. Imran's intention is to demonstrate his popularity to the army so as to drive a wedge between the army and the people. In a subtle variation, he has started hinting that Gen Bajwa was responsible for his exit, without naming the army chief. The social media cell of the PTI is busy spreading the narrative of retired army officers being critical of the current army leadership not supporting Imran Khan. In this, he has been banking on the massive crowds that have attended his rallies and his narrative of an American conspiracy being responsible for his ouster. The ouster conspiracy has certainly galvanised the PTI support base. Had Imran Khan's government lasted the full tenure and then gone into elections, he would have found it much harder to bounce back. Evidence of this is the fact that in none of his rallies has Imran Khan talked about his achievements during the last three and a half years because he would be hard-pressed to show any. Instead, the constant refrain is on the American conspiracy that has struck a chord among his supporters.

In reality, the communication that Imran Khan touted as a big conspiracy, was actually a routine diplomatic cable sent by the Pakistan Ambassador in Washington DC based on his conversation with a US official at a farewell lunch that the Ambassador himself had hosted. The army too pitched in with the DG ISPR categorically denying that there was any conspiracy. In fact, the DG ISPR's press conference on 14 April demolished various elements of Imran Khan's narrative. He said that the word "conspiracy" was not used in the statement issued after a meeting of the National Security Committee last month, instead saying that a demarche was issued for the use of "undiplomatic language" which he said "is equal to interference." He also clarified that the USA did not ask Pakistan for any bases after its withdrawal from Afghanistan; it was the PM who went to the establishment for a solution, not the other way around.[1] DG ISPR also indicated that the army chief had no intention to seek an extension.

With DG ISPR stating unambiguously that there was no conspiracy to effect a regime change in Pakistan, the narrative that Imran Khan has been marketing to play the martyr was torn to shreds. Clearly, the army was compelled to do so given the harm that Imran Khan's assertions were causing to the country and to Pak-US relations.

Moreover, a significant blow to the "conspiracy narrative" was delivered by a former PTI Minister Fawad Chaudhry when he told a TV channel that the PTI government was ousted as its ties with the establishment became "strained." He added: "Had our [relationship] with the establishment been good, then we would have still been in government." He said many attempts were made, and he himself tried his best to repair the relationship, but to no avail.[2]

Though for the moment it would appear the PTI would continue using the fabricated conspiracy strategy, Imran Khan has possibly realised that in the light of the ISPR revelations, he would find it very difficult to continue to justify his narrative on this score. Yet, he may be forced to continue on his path because he has gone out on a limb on this narrative. Of course, being the master of U-turns, he could do another one now but it would dent his credibility in the eyes of many of his supporters. Moreover, what else can he offer? He has no positive narrative about his achievements and so has to fall back on negative conspiracy theories. He is, therefore, in search for another narrative to play the victim card that would be converted into a campaign slogan. This could well be the judiciary that Imran Khan has started criticising and since he would not want to take on the army as a whole, he is trying to blame the army chief.

Meanwhile, as the Lahore rally showed, diminishing returns are now becoming apparent. Imran Khan's speeches have become repetitive and are low on substance. Already analysts have started noticing that there is nothing new in what Imran Khan is saying: it is the same words and the same slogans.

Former Ministers of Imran Khan have upped the ante, trying to create an atmosphere of anarchy in the country. For example, Shehryar Afridi, the former minister of state for interior, told his supporters "If suicide was not forbidden (*haram*) I'd go into parliament with explosives and blow it up."[3] Fawad Chaudhry, another former minister tweeted: "We are inches away from full fledged Civil unrest, @ImranKhanPTI has exercised utmost restraint very soon even he won't be able to stop this very angry mob and we'll see country plunging into a civil unrest, imported leaders will not be able to leave country."[4] He also raised the possibility of martial law. Imran Khan himself had warned the disgruntled PTI legislators who were hobnobbing with the opposition that even their children would face the wrath of the people. The former PTI Sindh governor Imran Ismail threatened that they had the power to shut down Karachi on half an hour's notice and "We will take to the streets and teach them a lesson."[5] Adviser Zulfi Bukhari warned, "These are just a few MPAs, imagine if the *awam* [public] goes out of control and takes the matter in their own hands... only solution to calm this civil unrest is ELECTIONS. Let the people decide their own fate. CALL ELECTIONS!"[6]

Meanwhile, the new government headed by Prime Minister Shehbaz Sharif faces major challenges on various fronts.

Among the key political challenges would be when to call for elections—early or let them happen when due in mid-2023. The new government is possibly banking on the hope that Khan will eventually run out of steam, as did the then Opposition's own Pakistan Democratic Movement (PDM). After all, it would be very difficult to sustain the momentum of rallies that inevitably have diminishing returns and in any case on their own cannot force an election. The danger for the government, however, would be that the longer elections are delayed, the more the people will have an opportunity to judge its governance, especially on the economic front, and compare it with that provided by Imran Khan.

Another critical issue would be managing a coalition of disparate parties, each of whom has its own political ambitions that would run counter to those of the PML-N. All these parties would be jockeying to get an advantageous position for the next election where they are likely to contest against each other. With the PTI MNAs having resigned from the National Assembly, the issue will not be so much the management of the government's slender parliamentary majority but sharing the loaves of office i.e. ministerial and other posts, with the coalition partners. Giving them a stake in the government would be the best way of ensuring the survival of the government.

A linked challenge would be to handle the fallout of Imran Khan's rallies and his confrontational politics aimed at forcing the government to call early elections. Imran Khan seems to be convinced that the popular support he has engendered would translate into votes and hence the need to push ahead for early elections. This threat to all parties from a confrontational Imran Khan will also keep the coalition together.

Yet another challenge would be the conduct of President Arif Alvi who, after the new government came to power, has started behaving in a partisan manner rather than as the Head of state. He did not administer the oath of office to

Prime Minister Shehbaz Sharif claiming he was sick just before the ceremony. At the time of writing he has not accepted the advice of the new government to remove Punjab Governor Omar Cheema though he has sworn the second batch of ministers.

The biggest challenge, however, would be the economy. While the longer-term issues would be the escalating fiscal and balance of payments deficits, spiralling debt, dwindling foreign exchange reserves, the devaluation of the rupee, etc., for the common man, double digit inflation, the energy crisis and potential massive hike in the price of petrol and diesel would be the yardsticks by which they will measure the success of the new government. The IMF programme is bound to be resumed but would involve taking tough measures that would have a big political cost.

The economic problem is compounded by the fact that the new government has a very short term of governance—a maximum till August 2023 till the next general elections or a shorter term if elections are held earlier. This would be inadequate to take the tough remedial measures that are required before going to the people to seek a fresh mandate.

An immediate problem is of oil subsidy. Former Prime Minister Shahid Khaqan Abbasi was quoted in *The News* stating that petrol costs the government Rs 171 per litre whereas it is sold at around Rs 150 per litre. Diesel costs the government around Rs 196 per litre but is sold at Rs 144 per litre.[7] If the government did not raise the prices of petrol and diesel, the oil subsidy could cost the country even more than the defence budget. However, if the prices were raised, there would be a strong public reaction. According to Miftah Ismail, the Finance Minister, the subsidy was costing the country some Rs 2.5 billion a day.[8] One reason for this problem was the fact that the Imran Khan government towards the end of its tenure capped the price of petrol and diesel resulting in very heavy subsidies. This was one of the reasons that the IMF bailout program was suspended.[9] The new government, for populist reasons, would find it extremely hard to undo the capping of the oil price and end the subsidy on oil. However, continuing the subsidy would be disastrous.

In foreign policy, an immediate issue would be to restore relations with the USA that have nose-dived due to Imran Khan directly charging it, falsely as it turns out, of being responsible for having him removed from power. Another issue would be the relations with China. The China Pakistan Economic Corridor (CPEC), the flagship project of China's BRI, seems to have plateaued and despite the high sounding epithets, the relations did not progress much during the tenure of Imran Khan. Bringing the relations back on track would have to be a priority for the new government. The advantage that Shehbaz Sharif would have is that even as Chief Minister of Punjab, he had a good relationship with the Chinese, especially with the large number of CPEC projects that he cornered for Punjab. The Sharifs also have a good equation with the Saudis and this would be an important point after the embarrassment of Imran Khan selling the gifts he had received from the Saudi royal family. Finally, the Taliban victory in August 2021 was meant to have been the culmination of Pakistan's 'Afghanistan project' of installing a 'friendly' government in Kabul but the euphoria did not last long. Pak-Afghan tensions on the Durand Line, the issue of the safe havens of the Tehrik-i-Taliban Pakistan (TTP) and their attacks in Pakistan are the issues that have bedevilled relations. Here the army would play a larger role. Any major foreign policy initiative with India is unlikely due to the short term of the government. However, bilateral exchanges will revert to being diplomatic rather than abusive that was Imran Khan's style.

Beyond the immediate political, economic and foreign policy challenges, a critical issue that faces not merely the new government but the country is the fact that Pakistan has become a deeply divided country, even more than it usually has been. From the beginning of his tenure, Imran Khan had rejected the idea of sitting with the Opposition on issues of national interest. On the contrary, he launched a witch-hunt against them on the pretext of accountability. Anyone who questioned the PTI government's policy was termed a traitor. Thus, instead of reaching a consensus with the Opposition on important issues, the PTI government promulgated at least 54 presidential ordinances during its term. Analysts were amazed at the number of ordinances being issued in a parliamentary democracy.

Amplifying the polarisation has been the hateful and provocative comments of former ministers of the PTI and the abusive use of social media by all sides. The political polarisation has been such that *Dawn* reported a seven-year-old girl telling her father that in her class the followers of the Pakistan Tehreek-i-Insaf (PTI) and Pakistan Muslim League-Nawaz (PML-N) have started sitting separately.[10]

An editorial in *Dawn* of 04 April possibly best summed up the role of Imran Khan in the turmoil when it held "Mr Khan has dealt a fatal blow to constitutionalism and given rise to the strongest concerns yet that he may not be suited to hold public office within a democratic order."[11]

Overall, therefore, at the time of writing, there is an element of uncertainty being built up in the country. This coupled with rising prices, a precarious economy and the extreme polarisation does not bode well for either stability or good governance.

22 April 2022

ENDNOTES

1. ISPR Presser: edit in *Daily Times*, Apr 16, 2022, https://dailytimes.com.pk/920193/ispr-presser/
2. Govt ousted after ties with establishment became strained: Fawad Chaudhry, April 21, 2022, https://www.thenews.com.pk/print/952058-govt-ousted-after-ties-with-establishment-became-strained-fawad
3. Abbas Nasir, Hiccups won't derail system, *Dawn,* 17 April 2022, https://www.dawn.com/news/1685412/hiccups-wont-derail-system
4. 'We are inches away from full-fledged civil unrest', says Fawad, *The Express Tribune*, April 17, 2022, https://tribune.com.pk/story/2352888/we-are-inches-away-from-full-fledged-civil-unrest-says-fawad
5. 'Was it a conspiracy or interference?' Imran Khan asks supporters at PTI power show in Karachi, *Dawn*, 16 April 2022, https://www.dawn.com/news/1685299
6. 'We are inches away from full-fledged civil unrest', says Fawad, report in *The Express Tribune*, April 17, 2022, https://tribune.com.pk/story/2352888/we-are-inches-away-from-full-fledged-civil-unrest-says-fawad
7. Ansar Abbasi, Imran Khan's trap for Shehbaz govt, *The News*, April 19, 2022, https://www.thenews.com.pk/print/951508-ik-s-trap-for-shehbaz-govt
8. Hiccups won't derail system, by Abbas Nasir in *Dawn*, April 17, 2022, https://www.dawn.com/news/1685412/hiccups-wont-derail-system
9. Ansar Abbasi, Imran Khan's trap for Shehbaz govt, *The News*, April 19, 2022
10. Ikram Junaidi, 'Growing political intolerance divides already polarised society in Pakistan', *Dawn*, 19 April 2022, https://www.dawn.com/news/1685714/growing-political-intolerance-divides-already-polarised-society-in-pakistan
11. 'Democracy subverted', Edit, *Dawn,* 04 April 2022, https://www.dawn.com/news/1683311

Editor's Note

Pakistan Insights 2021-22 is the third in the Pakistan Insight series being brought out by the Vivekananda International Foundation (VIF) to deepen the understanding of Pakistan. Ideas for the various chapters are based on the discussions held in the Pakistan Study Group (PSG) that was set up in February 2018 in the VIF. The previous two editions—*Pakistan Insights 2019* and *Pakistan Insights 2020*—received widespread acclaim and it is hoped that this edition too will be well received.

During the past year, COVID-19 continued to impose severe constraints. Resultantly, instead of Pakistan Insights 2021, the VIF was compelled to bring out a combined edition for 2021-22. Hopefully, the practice of single year editions will resume from the next one.

Dr. Arvind Gupta kick-starts the discussions by asserting that despite his serious limitations, Imran Khan has managed to survive many challenges that would include COVID, the opposition coming together, a deep persisting economic crisis, deterioration of relations with allies, continuing instability in Afghanistan and the inability to move out of the grey list of the FATF. The reason for his survival is that his benefactors—the military establishment—has continued to back him. So long as they do so, Imran Khan will remain in power. However, there are serious doubts whether he would be able complete his five-year term with the establishment now projecting a neutral stance. Moreover, Imran Khan's dream of transforming Pakistan into a *Naya Pakistan* and realising the ideal of *Riyasat-e-Medina* is far from being fulfilled.

Rana Banerji looks at the internal developments in Pakistan and civil-military relations. His conclusion is that three years into its tenure, the Pakistan Tehrik-e-Insaf (PTI)'s civilian government led by Prime Minister Imran Khan continues to drift, seemingly rudderless and ill prepared, failing to tackle simple and complex issues of governance, despite frequent hand holding or bail-outs by the Military Establishment. A key factor that has continued to hound the government was the issue of legitimacy as well as the process that led to its formation, a thinly-veiled reference to the 'hybrid' support extended by the military. Moreover, the many failures of the PTI government were now being 'linked' by many to the establishment and 'criticism of the 'Miltablishment' (Military Establishment) had increased, for hoisting and propping up an incapable Imran Khan. At the time of writing, this support or 'same page' trust had frayed at the edges.

Tilak Devasher looks at the ethnic fault-lines in Pakistan. Though Pakistan is a cauldron of fault-lines, among them perhaps the most critical for Pakistan are the ethnic ones. His analysis of the four provinces in Pakistan reveals deep-seated fissures and alienation that could explode at any time if the centralizing policies of the Punjab-centric governments continue and the army refuses to countenance any sort of provincial rights. Following the breakaway of East Pakistan in 1971, his chapter assesses how Pakistan fares in keeping its other nationalities together. He highlights that the main general issue triggering ethnic resentment in Pakistan is of identity. Simply stated, into the seventh decade of its creation, there continues to be a debate over the meaning of a 'Pakistan identity.' Apart from ethnic issues of the Baloch, Pashtuns and Sindhis, he flags Punjab's predicament to distinguish between a Punjabi provincial identity and a Pakistani identity, so interwoven have they become.

Dr. Shalini Chawla looks at the growth of extremism in Pakistan. She holds that Pakistan has been unable to reflect on its strategic choices and has failed to accept that the root cause behind rising extremism in society is its belief in radical Islamic ideology and adoption of terrorism as a potent foreign policy tool. Currently, there is a rise in religious intolerance within Pakistan due to the state's sanction of legitimacy to the Taliban's radical ideology in Afghanistan, an indifferent attitude towards the complete breach of civil rights and liberties of the Afghans, strengthening of the religious political groups and Imran Khan's consistent drive for Islamophobia at global platforms. Consequently, the last seven decades have witnessed Pakistan's drift into extremism and its inclination to support extremist ideology. She asserts that religion has been used in Pakistan for nation building, statecraft and strategic security.

Tilak Devasher takes a deep dive into Pakistan's non-traditional security threats based on the acronym that he has coined—WEEP factors—i.e., Water, Education, Economy and Population. He notes that Pakistan faced an emergency situation in all these areas a decade ago and today it should be in a disaster management mode. However, there are no signs that it is. These non-traditional threats actually go to the heart of what is going wrong with Pakistan. A comprehension of such threats is crucial to understand where Pakistan is headed and what threats it could pose for itself and to the region in addition to the traditional military and terrorist threats that it poses. Individually, each of these elements have not only a far-reaching impact on every strata of society but are decisive elements in its security. Collectively, they are a fundamental factor in determining the quality of life, health and longevity of its citizens. The degradation in each of these parameters takes a long time to manifest itself just as rectification and reversing the trends take a considerably longer time.

Amb. Satish Chandra and Dr. Arvind Gupta examine the National Security Policy (NSP) announced by Pakistan in January 2022.

According to Amb. Chandra, Pakistan's National Security Policy (NSP) 2022-2026 was essentially an exercise in image building necessitated by its being in the doghouse internationally because of its abominable human rights record, an economy perpetually in shambles largely due to the prioritisation of military spending over development, dicey democratic credentials, and being a breeding ground for terror. Accordingly, the NSP tries to project Pakistan as a much-maligned peace-loving state determined to pull itself up by the bootstraps by focusing more than ever before on the economy and on human security.

He holds that the NSP disappoints as it is long on rhetoric and short on specifics, fails to transcend the banal, and displays the customary animosity towards India. It is unlikely to lead to any meaningful policy change and is no more than an effort to blunt Pakistan's negative image.

Dr. Arvind Gupta underlines that while the NSP stresses that Pakistan wants peaceful relations with India, it goes on to make the improvement in relations dependent upon a "...just and peaceful resolution of the Jammu and Kashmir dispute" which "remains at the core of our bilateral relationship." He shows how the anti-India rant goes on: India is blamed for "military adventurism", "non-contact warfare", "arms build-up", "belligerence towards Pakistan" and policies of "exceptionalism that undermine the global non-proliferation regime." All this shows that there are no signs of a rethink on Jammu and Kashmir. In the light of such uncompromising formulations, it is difficult to believe that Pakistan's India policy will change in the near future even as it tries to tell the world that it is adopting a new paradigm in its national security approach. He concludes that the target of the document was not so much India as the rest of the world. Through this document, Pakistan was trying to project to the rest of the world that it was a progressive, moderate country with a huge economic potential and not an intolerant, bankrupt, dysfunctional, terrorist-infested country as India would have the world believe.

Aakriti Vinayak provides an analysis of the media in Pakistan showing its evolution and the constraints it faces today. She holds that the media in Pakistan in the last 70 years has remained 'under siege' and 'in chains.' Though liberalisation of the media has mainstreamed it in Pakistan as a stakeholder, the country's transitional and fragile democracy has prevented it from playing a true watchdog role for society. More importantly, Pakistan's chequered political history of long stretches of martial law, the subjugation of representative governments by the deep state, and a brutal domination of the media landscape ownership for most part of the country's existence almost ensures that media independence has been mostly fiction. In fact, the media remains under a state of crisis and stress in Pakistan. She notes how, under the current regime of Imran Khan, the media is going through the worst forms of censorship and crackdown that Pakistan has seen.

Amb. Dinkar Srivastava takes a look at Pakistan's foreign policy in its various dimensions. He holds that foreign policy has enjoyed a large salience in Pakistan's national polity since its inception, something that was unusual for a nascent country struggling with major internal issues. Moreover, there was no external security threat to justify such an inversion of priorities. Despite this, Pakistan's foreign policy had been characterized by the primacy of force over diplomacy. There was an interplay of ideology and interests in its policies on J&K and Afghanistan issues with Kashmir being projected as the unfinished agenda of partition and following a policy of seeking strategic depth in Afghanistan. He notes that it has become difficult for both civil and military leaders to break out of these dogmas that had imposed enormous costs in terms of unsustainable levels of military expenditure that had impoverished the country. In addition, it has also given rise to the radicalisation of society.

Lt Gen Rakesh Sharma (Retd) takes a look at the Pak Army's war fighting doctrine and the role of nationalism and identity in it. He elaborates how, after Pakistan was created, the Army usurped the role of custodian of Pakistan's nationhood and identity. In doing so, it has overthrown elected civil governments, enforced martial law, and dismissed Parliament on multiple occasions. Pakistan's military doctrines have evolved over the last seven decades from 'The Riposte'; 'offensive-defence'; to 'war by proxy' to avoiding conventional war but enlarging their unconventional sphere (hybrid war) under the nuclear overhang;

introduction of the threat of tactical nuclear weapons and full spectrum nuclear weapons.

Amb. Gautam Mukhopadhaya looks at the role of Pakistan in the Taliban takeover of Afghanistan and its aftermath. He traces the evolution of the Taliban from its origins in the madarsas and refugee camps on the Pakistani side of the Durand Line between 1992-96, through its rule in Afghanistan from 1996-2001 (Taliban 1.0), to its relocation in Pakistan after it was driven out of Afghanistan by the USA and the Northern Alliance post 9/11, remaining there from 2002-21, and then regrouping as a radicalised insurgency using suicide and other forms of terrorism (Taliban 2.0), to its new incarnation as a victorious force and new 'government' in Kabul in August-September 2021 (Taliban 3.0). He holds that Pakistan had conducted a covert hybrid war against Afghanistan for over 20 years from the end of 2001 until the eventual military takeover by the Taliban. During this period, there was barely-concealed Pakistani military, technical, logistical, intelligence, satellite and other assistance as also the participation of Pakistani and foreign/regional *jihadi* outfits at key moments of the takeover, most visibly by Pakistani regulars in the Panjsher operation. He concludes that cumulatively, the post-2021 situation in Afghanistan presents a far more complicated picture of Afghanistan in 2022 of a fractured political and military landscape and multiple conflict faultlines. This is quite different than the simple Taliban-Northern Alliance contest of the 1990s or the Western gamble that the Taliban will be able to provide stability and governance in Afghanistan, control drug trafficking and arms proliferation, and prevent the consolidation of terrorist groups.

Finally, the editor tries to do some crystal-ball gazing to predict the future trajectory of Pakistan with the caveat that predicting Pakistan is always fraught with risk, given the number of moving parts. Leaving aside the unexpected, three trends, in particular, are noteworthy and could resonate in the year ahead—the precarious economic situation, civil-military relations and the survivability of the Imran Khan government; and developments in Afghanistan that are impacting Pakistan.

The editor would like to thank Ms. Anuttama Ganguly and Ms. Aakriti Vinayak for their support and help in bringing out this volume.

Members of the Pakistan Study Group are:

Dr. Arvind Gupta, Director VIF
Gen N.C. Vij (Retd)
Amb Satish Chandra

Amb G. Parthasarathy
C.D. Sahay
Lt Gen Ravi Sawhney (Retd)
Lt Gen Ata Hasnain (Retd)
Rana Banerji
Amb D.P. Srivastava
Amb T.C.A. Raghavan
Amb Arun Kumar Singh
Brig Rahul Bhonsle (Retd)
Dr. Shalini Chawla
Sushant Sareen
Amb Amar Sinha
Amb Gautam Mukhopadhaya
Amb P. S. Raghavan
Lt Gen Ranbir Singh (Retd)
Gp Capt Naval Jagota
Tilak Devasher, Convenor

Tilak Devasher
Consultant VIF
Member, National Security Advisory Board
Editor, *Pakistan Insights*

New Delhi, 21 March 2022

Introduction
Developments in Pakistan: An Overview

Dr. Arvind Gupta

The Prime Minister Imran Khan-led government is well into the fourth year of its tenure. Since becoming the prime minister in 2018, he has survived many challenges—COVID, sugar scandal, Pakistan Democratic Movement's (PDM) political rallies, deep economic crisis, deterioration of relations with allies like Saudi Arabia and the UAE, tense relations with India, continuing instability in Afghanistan and the inability to move out of the grey list of the FATF. He has been pilloried as an incompetent, inconsistent, blundering, and incapable prime minister.

Yet, true to his style, Imran Khan has not been on the back foot. He has misused the National Accountability Bureau (NAB) to pressurise his opponents and publicly labelled them as being 'mafias.' He proclaimed in 2019 that "mafias were present in the Federal Board of Revenue and other government institutions, in politics and in newspapers.... Those journalists who had benefited from the corrupt system in the past were now writing against his administration,"[1] he said.

So far, no prime minister in Pakistan has been able to complete his or her term. Imran Khan has lived from one crisis to another. Speculations about whether he would be able to complete his five-year term continue unabated. He enjoys a thin majority in the National Assembly. Rebellion within the ruling party can also derail the government.

One reason for Imran Khan's survivability has been his carefully cultivated relations with the armed forces. It is widely believed that the army helped Imran Khan's PTI to win the 2018 elections. Pakistani opposition parties dubbed the 2018 elections as 'rigged' elections. Some experts describe the current system of governance in Pakistan as a 'hybrid' system. The army takes the key decisions while the elected leaders and the government are held accountable for any mishaps. The army has the dominant role in foreign and security policies. So long as the military establishment backs him, Imran Khan will remain in power. Despite the perceived non-performance of his government, the armed forces have not pulled the rug from under Imran Khan's feet. He is their candidate and remains so. The TINA factor—there is no alternative—is also in play. But, Imran Khan cannot take the continued support of the military for granted.

Politics

Pakistan Democratic Movement (PDM): The inability of the opposition to mount a credible challenge to Imran Khan is another factor for Imran Khan's survival. The opposition has not been able to encash the public discontent with the government. The opposition alliance PDM, after organising some impressive anti-government rallies across the country, lost momentum due to internal contradictions. The Pakistan People's Party (PPP) and Pakistan Muslim League Nawaz (PML-N) were poles apart. For them to remain together on major issues was not easy. Each had its own axe to grind.

The formation of the PDM in September 2020 to oppose the PTI government was a momentous event. It was formed as a movement of 11 opposition parties. It adopted a 26-point charter[2] demanding the resignation of the government which it said had come to power through 'rigged elections.' It asked for "transparent elections" in the country and demanded the enactment of electoral reforms without any role for the armed forces or agencies. It held the 'selected' government responsible for the "fall of Kashmir" and endangering the China Pakistan Economic Corridor (CPEC). It condemned the establishment's efforts to pressurise independent and upright judges through false corruption cases and 'references.' It asked for a new 'accountability' law that would apply to "all institutes and individuals."[3]

The rise of the PDM reminded people of the opposition unity movements of the Seventies and the Eighties, namely, the Pakistan National Alliance (PNA) and the Movement of Restoration of Democracy (MRD) formed to bring an end to Gen Zia's dictatorial regime. Fifteen years ago, the exiled leaders Benazir Bhutto and Nawaz Sharif had signed a 'Charter of Democracy' (CoD) (2006) to oust the Musharraf regime. The CoD did lead to a pro-democracy movement and the eventual ouster of Musharraf. But this time around, the PDM is hamstrung by major friction between the two leading parties on many issues.

Both need to survive and cannot make too many concessions at the expense of their own interests. Even the Charter of Democracy had broken down eventually.

The PDM announced a schedule of public rallies and protests in Gujranwala, Karachi, Quetta, Peshawar, Multan, and Lahore ending with a 'Long March' to Islamabad in January 2021. Many of these rallies were impressive and caused the government much discomfort. But towards the end of 2020, differences arose on whether or not the Members of the National Assemblies (MNAs) should resign from parliament. The PML-N proposed that MNAs should resign but the PPP was opposed. That weakened the PDM's unity. The scheduled 'long march' to Islamabad was deferred indefinitely. Thereafter, differences manifested over who would be the leader of the opposition in the Senate. In April, the PPP decided to leave the PDM. Although the PDM is not officially dead, it has become comatose. It was an interesting experiment in contemporary Pakistan politics. After the brief limelight it enjoyed, its unity was in tatters in 2021. In April 2021, the PML-N decided to form a separate bloc of five opposition parties in the Senate, excluding the PPP and ANP. Advantage PTI thanks to an open split in opposition ranks. The PML-N said that the PDM would adopt a new strategy after Ramzan. With the departure of the PPP, the PML-N may try to assume a greater role in the PDM. But it is difficult to believe that without the PPP, a major opposition party, the PDM, would be effective. However, the combined opposition was able to re-invent itself in late 2021-early 2022 and forge unity to move a no-confidence motion against Imran Khan.

The PDM saga has shown that it is very difficult for the opposition to unite given the core interests of key members that they would like to protect. Anti-Imran Khan rhetoric is not good enough as a glue to unite the opposition.

Further, the army plays an important though indirect role in the elections. Each political party has to bear this factor in mind. An openly anti-army stance is likely to prove counterproductive beyond a point. That may be the reason why, after the release of Shabaz Sharif, the PML-N seems to have softened its anti-establishment rhetoric. Even the PPP would not be interested in being seen as anti-army.

During this period, Imran Khan kept up the pressure on the opposition, using a variety of tactics. He has kept the opposition on tenterhooks by talking about corruption, unleashing the National Accountability Bureau and other methods.

PML-N: The PML-N is at an interesting juncture. Nawaz Sharif is in a London hospital from where he tries to run the show. His charisma remains intact. He tried to motivate the masses by his video-linked speeches and sharp anti-establishment rhetoric. His daughter, Maryam Nawaz, is the heir apparent, taking care of the day-to-day affairs of the party. The PDM platform gave her the visibility of a national leader. She did a credible job. Nawaz Sharif's brother, Shehbaz Sharif, was then in jail. When he was released, the government got busy involving him in a variety of cases so that he could not energize the party. In the meanwhile, Maryam has built her own identity and come out of her father's shadow. She was the one who led the party during the PDM's agitations.

The direction in which the PML-N will evolve is still unclear. What will be the role of Nawaz Sharif who is in exile in London? Will he be able to run the party as before? Will there be a contest between Maryam and Shehbaz for party supremacy? Shehbaz, a consensus builder, maintains his own links with the army. After his release, the sharp anti-army rhetoric which Nawaz Sharif and Maryam had espoused has become dim and barely visible. The party has realised that rubbing the army the wrong way did not necessarily improve the prospects of winning elections. It will have to think of a strategy to win the next elections due in 2023.

PPP: Bilawal Bhutto Zardari, the PPP's young leader, is stepping out of the shadow of his father, Asif Zardari. His differences with Maryam in the PDM led to the weakening of the opposition movement. There are voices in the party that the PPP should soften its anti-establishment stance. The PPP's key concern is to safeguard its turf in Sindh where it rules and to maximise its gains at the centre. This explains its very public spat with the PML-N over the post of the opposition leader in the Senate. The PPP would not like to see its government in Sindh to be destabilised. Therefore, it has to be careful as it has a stake in the current system. That is why it has cooled towards the PDM.

Pakistan Tehreek-i-Insaaf (PTI): All is not well with the PTI. Imran Khan's one-time close confidant, Jahangir Tareen, reportedly the richest man in Pakistan, fell out with prime minister Khan. He has made his own 'forward block' of dissident MNAs in the national assembly as well as in the Punjab assembly. He demanded the withdrawal of all probes against him and associates for financial irregularity. The block holds a potential threat to the PTI's integrity. If Tareen breaks off, the PTI government, which has a thin majority in the NA, would be endangered. It remains to be seen how Imran Khan handles the threat from the rebels. While the party has not split formally, Tareen has flexed his muscle. The PTI's weaknesses have been exposed. The threat to the stability of the government from the Tareen-led 'forward block' may turn out to be more potent than those from the PDM.

Tehreek-e-Labbaiq Pakistan (TLP): The Imran Khan government has often buckled under pressure mounted by religious groups like the TLP who have more than once brought their supporters out on the streets for religious causes. In 2018, Imran Khan had to cancel the appointment of a top adviser because of a furore in fundamentalist religious circles that the latter was an Ahmadiya. To appease the TLP, the government has entered into several agreements with it. When in April 2021 the TLP demanded the ouster of the French ambassador on account of President Macron's allegedly anti-Islam attitudes, the government was in a tight spot. The expulsion of the French diplomat would have landed the government in a major spat with the entire European Union (EU). It tried to deflect the crisis by promising the TLP a resolution in the national assembly. The crisis has been defused but not ended. The growing popularity of the TLP can prove to be a game-changer in Pakistan's politics.

The TLP rose to fame when it demanded the release of Mumtaz Qadri, who in 2011 assassinated the Punjab governor, Salman Taseer, an outspoken critic of the blasphemy law. Overnight, Mumtaz Qadri became a hero of the religious extremists in Pakistan. In 2018, the TLP mobilized its cadres after the Supreme Court ordered the release of a Christian woman, Asia Bibi, charged with blasphemy. The TLP was used by the military to cut into the PML-N vote. But it has developed national political ambitions. In the 2018 elections, the TLP won a significant share of votes across the country. It differs from other Islamic groups, as it is a political party with national ambitions.

The TLP has gained a significant following in the prevailing atmosphere of unemployment, poverty, inequity, and social breakdown in Pakistan. Radical Islam offers refuge to millions of impoverished youth who see no future in the current system. After the death of its firebrand leader Khadim Hussain Rizvi, there were some doubts about the TLP's longevity. But, Khadim Hussain Rizvi's son, Saad Hussain Rizvi, has taken over the reins of the party and has emerged as a leader in his own right. The TLP is a hard line group which, in the past, has "called for the assassination of Pakistan's Supreme Court judges, demanded a mutiny in the armed forces and have vowed to wipe out the Netherlands with nuclear weapons." The TLP's clout in Pakistan's politics cannot be ignored.

Media: Imran Khan has publically claimed that the Pakistani media made a significant contribution towards giving him and his party, the PTI, visibility in Pakistan which helped it to win elections. Yet, increasingly, the Imran Khan regime has become intolerant of criticism. The Pakistani media is under constant pressure from the government, agencies and militants and Islamic radicals. Attacks on journalists, arbitrary arrests, and disappearances are all too common. Media house owners are routinely put under pressure. Programmes are taken off the air arbitrarily. According to prominent journalist Najam Sethi, "Currently, two institutions representing the civil-military hybrid regime are being manipulated to manage and control the media. The ISPR is the Miltablishment boot while PEMRA is the civilian arm of this joint exercise."[4]

Pakistan has enacted harsh laws to suppress the media. Freedom of speech is under threat. Social media is being brought under the control of agencies rapidly. In 2021, the Pakistan government proposed a law called 'Pakistan Media Development Authority' (PMDA) which was stoutly opposed by Pakistan's media fraternity in a joint statement.[5] They termed it as unconstitutional and undemocratic and compared it with Ayub Khan's infamous 'Press and Publications Ordinance 1963.' The Pakistani newspaper *Dawn* wrote editorially, "Make no mistake: the proposed Pakistan Media Development Authority Ordinance...is a declaration of war against journalists. It will, if enacted, erase all critical voices from print, electronic and digital platforms through a system of coercive censorship that will allow only a pliant media to survive... (It) will eviscerate the very rationale for the fourth estate, which is to act as a check on excesses of power and function as a watchdog for the public interest."[6]

There is a sense of fear and uncertainty in the Pakistan media fraternity. In 2020, one of the most prominent media house owners, Shakil-ur-Rehman, was arrested by the National Accountability Bureau and released on bail after eight months of incarceration. According to the Pakistan Press Foundation's 2020 report, "press freedom continued to be threatened with journalists being abducted, killed, arrested, and manhandled with impunity. Women journalists were subjected to threats and harassment online highlighting the gendered nature of attacks on press freedom."[7]

Minorities: The condition of minorities in Pakistan has been a matter of global concern. Increasing Islamisation of society, the draconian blasphemy law, mushroom growth of *jihadi* groups, forced conversions, and daily persecution has generated fear amongst them. At the time of Partition, the minorities made up about a quarter of Pakistan's population. Today, the ratio is about 3 to 4 per cent. According to the 2017 Census, religious minorities constitute about 4 per cent of the population. This includes 1.6 per cent Hindus, 1.6 per cent Christians,

Ahmediyas 0.2 per cent and others 0.07 per cent. Muslims make up 96.2 per cent of Pakistan's population.[8]

According to Pakistan's National Database and Registration Authority (NADRA), in 2012, Pakistan had about 1.4 million Hindus, 1.2 million Christians, 125,000, Ahmediyas, 6,000 Sikhs, and 4,000 Parsis. The declining ratio of minorities in Pakistan's population has compelled the US's USCIRF to designate Pakistan as a "country of particular concern" since 2002. A report compiled by members of the European Parliament in 2019 cited religious violence and forced conversions as the reason for the decline of the minorities population.

Hindus, Christians and Sikhs bear the brunt of the blasphemy law and forced conversions. According to a survey conducted by All Pakistan Hindu Rights Movement, of the 428 Hindu temples in Pakistan, only 20 have survived. The government of Pakistan has promised to restore the temples that have been encroached or forcibly taken. But this is more for optics. Hindu girls are forcibly married off to Muslims and converted. Reportedly, about 30 Hindu women are converted to Islam every month. According to the Pakistan Hindu Council, "religious persecution, especially forced conversions, remains the foremost reason for the migration of Hindus from Pakistan."[9]

Although Mohammad Ali Jinnah, the founder of Pakistan, tried to reassure the minorities that they would be safe in Muslim Pakistan, that was not to be. The efforts towards Islamisation began soon after his death. In 1949, Prime Minister Liaqat Ali Khan introduced the Objectives Resolution which was adopted by the Pakistan Constituent Assembly despite the objections by the minority members. The resolution was made a part of the Pakistani Constitution. It proclaimed Pakistan as an Islamic state based on Islamic ideology and faith. General Zia-ul-Haq speeded up the Islamisation of Pakistan in the Eighties. He also encouraged the setting up of Sipahe Sahaba Pakistan (SSP), an extremist organisation, which targeted minorities and the Shia population. A large number of radical Islamist groups came into existence during Zia-ul-Haq's time. Over time, many of these groups took to terrorism. They spread hate and violence against minorities with impunity. That process continues to this day.

Although Prime Minister Imran Khan has tried to reassure the minorities, they continue to feel unsafe. Farahnaz Ispahani has described the decline in minorities population in Pakistan as "slow genocide."[10]

The problem is that Pakistani laws are inherently anti-minorities. Although the Constitution promises every Pakistani freedom of religion, its various provisions militate against this. The blasphemy law, the Hudood ordinances and the laws on conversion, apostasy, etc., have encouraged systemic persecution and promoted hate and violence. According to Ashok Bhan, "Pakistan should be told to repeal all discriminatory laws and Ahmadi-specific laws, and amend its domestic legislation to bring it in line with international human rights standards, in particular the so-called blasphemy laws, Hudood ordinances, and provisions relating to proselytism, conversion and apostasy."[11]

Economy

For the past many years, Pakistan's GDP growth has remained below 5 per cent, which is considered a bare minimum for overall development. Inflation is a major concern and so is the rising debt burden. The interest rates are high too. This stifles growth. The government has negotiated a bailout plan with the IMF, but it finds the IMF conditions onerous. Remittances from the Diaspora provide some relief. The economy has also been hit by COVID.

The government's delivery record has been below par. The government and its members have been embroiled in various scandals. Its economic policies have been questioned. The promises made by Imran Khan to usher in a 'Naya Pakistan' have not materialised. The country is saddled with a mountain of debt. The Prime Minister has been beseeching the international community for debt forgiveness. There is little money left for developmental purposes after accounting for debt repayments and defence expenditure. A significant part of development expenditure is taken up by a few mega-projects, leaving little for social spending.

The government claims that there has been a notable improvement in the economy since 2018 when the PTI government came to power. For instance, the government has taken credit for a sharp drop in the Current Account Deficit that dropped by nearly 73 per cent, improvement in the credit rating from negative to stable, and improvement in the country's rank on the Ease of Doing Business Index had improved from 136 to 108.[12]

But the real story is different.[13] As Sushant Sareen points out, the country faces several structural problems like high food inflation, debt-ridden energy sector, high tax rates, narrow tax base, and depreciating rupee. The economic growth has been steadily falling "from 5.6 per cent in 2018 to 3.3 per cent in 2019." The country's imports have decreased and exports have not kept pace. Food inflation was in double digits in January 2020. The interest rates rose from 6.5 per cent in May 2018 to 13.25 per cent in July 2019.[14] According to Dr. Pasha, economic hardships have pushed nearly 87 million people in Pakistan below the poverty line by 2021.[15] This is due to the effect of COVID.

One of the highlights of the Imran government's tenure has been negotiating a USD 6 billion, 39-month IMF loan. The loan was considered essential as the government was running into a serious balance-of-payments problem. This was the 13th time that Pakistan had to go to the IMF for a bailout. After the first tranche, the IMF disbursements were halted in March 2020 due to COVID. This put Pakistan in a tough spot. Using the crisis as an opportunity, Imran Khan lobbied hard for the international community for rescheduling the debt of the developing countries. It managed to get US$ 1.4 billion from the IMF under its Rapid Financing Instrument scheme and US$ 2 billion from the G20 and other multilateral institutions in debt relief. What saved Pakistan was the high rate of inward remittances from the Pakistani Diaspora who remitted home more than US$ 2 billion per month on an average. Inward remittances to Pakistan grew at about 9 per cent in 2020, totalling about $ 24 bn.[16]

Pakistan's budget 2021-22[17]

On 11 June 2021, the government presented its third budget since the assumption of power. It has opted for a growth-oriented budget for 2021-22, that provides for higher expenditure on defence and development. In a please-all budget, the government decided not to increase taxes, give salary hikes to government employees but increase the Public Sector Development Programme. The budget for 2021-22 has been kept at PKR 8,487 billion (19 per cent higher than in FY 2020-21). Of this, the Defence Services account for PKR 1,379 billion (16 per cent), interest payments take up PKR 3,060 billion (36 per cent) and PSDP (both federal and provincial) account for PKR 2,135 billion (25 per cent, a rise of 37 per cent from last year).

The government claimed that it had inherited a bankrupt economy in 2018. Pakistan was on the verge of defaulting on its loan repayments. The government asserts that it has succeeded in stabilising the economy. It has been put on a growth path. The GDP growth rate was minus 0.4 per cent in 2019-20 and 3.9 per cent in 2020-21. The projected growth rate for 2021-22 is 4.8 per cent.

Inward remittances recorded an unprecedented high of US$ 29 billion. The government took the credit for having brought the current account from a deficit of US$ 4,657 million in FY 20 to a surplus of US$ 773 million in 10 months of FY 21.

The budget pegs the fiscal deficit at 6.3 per cent for FY 2021-22, lower than in the previous year. As per the Economic Survey, it was 7.1 per cent in 2019-20 and 7 per cent in 2020-21.

Pakistan has suffered from high inflation for the last many years. The inflation was 11.2 per cent in 2019-20 and 8.6 per cent in 2020-2021. The budget targets an inflation rate of 8.2 per cent during 2021-22.

Pakistan registered a trade deficit of $ 22,736 million compared to a deficit of $ 20,599 million in ten months of FY21, an increase of 11 per cent.

The Foreign Direct Investment (FDI) hit $1.55 billion during 10M FY21, a decline of 32 per cent YoY.

During 10 months of FY21, total imports recorded a growth of 8 per cent YoY to $ 48,625 million. Exports were $ 25,889 million, 6 per cent higher YoY.

The budget makes rather optimistic assumptions about revenue in FY 2021-22. The Federal Board of Revenue (FBR) tax revenue target has been set at PKR 5,829 bn, PKR 134 bn less than what has been committed to the IMF. It may be noted that in the last two years, the government has fallen short of the targeted FBR tax collection.

It remains to be seen how the IMF views the budget. The IMF has been insisting upon fiscal prudence and discipline. The government has broken the IMF imposed discipline many times earlier. The predicted current account deficit is higher than the figure negotiated with the IMF. The government is likely to enter into negotiations with the IMF so that future tranches are not affected. The Pakistan government seems to be confident that the upward trend of remittances will continue and provide a cushion to the government.

The budget does not address key structural issues. One is the burden of massive debt. At the end of March 2021, Pakistan's total public debt stood at PKR 38 trillion. The domestic debt amounted to PKR 25.6 trillion (up 13.8 per cent YoY) while foreign public debt was PKR 12.5 trillion. In fact, proposed higher spending may force the government to borrow more, thereby increasing the debt burden. In addition, the problem is of high inflation and the loss-making public sector. The textile sector is suffering badly. The government has been helpless in arresting the growing debt in the power sector. According to the official data, since December 2018, the total circular debt has increased from PKR. 1,415 bn to PKR. 2,266 bn.[18]

FATF: Pakistan is on the Financial Action Task Force's (FATF) grey list since 2018 for not having complied with its recommendations on curbing terror financing and money laundering. It is for the third time that Pakistan has been put on the grey list. FATF is an international watchdog to curb terror financing and money laundering. It has the mandate to determine the financial systems of a country to assess whether it is robust enough to curb terror financing and money laundering. Not implementing the recommendations of the FATF entails major economic and financial consequences for Pakistan.

In its June 2021 meeting, the FATF assessed that "Pakistan will move from enhanced (expedited) to enhanced follow-up, and will continue to report back to the APG on progress to strengthen its implementation of AML/CFT measures."[19] This means Pakistan has shown progress but it will continue to remain on the grey list. The FATF also berated Pakistan in several areas. Pakistan remains non-compliant on two recommendations and partially compliant in several areas.

Pakistan has struggled to come out of the grey list of the FATF. The problem is that Pakistani actions are at best cosmetic. The government lacks the political will to take action against the culprits. While Pakistan claims it has put the regulatory and legal framework in place, it has yet to demonstrate its efficacy and take real action.

COVID: There was much self-congratulation in Pakistan for having tackled the COVID crisis in 2020 and 2021 well. Fortunately, for Pakistan, the first wave of COVID in 2020 was relatively mild. Despite the numerous missteps by the government, Pakistan's overall caseload and the COVID death count was relatively modest. A National Command Operations Centre (NCOC) run jointly by the army and civilian authorities was set up at the apex level to manage the situation. The infection peaked on June 20 and subsided by August.

The second wave in 2021 was more serious. As of 15 May 2021, Pakistan had reported 870,703 cases; 19,336 dead, 776,315 recovered.[20] These figures must be seen in the context of the low testing rate in Pakistan. After peaking in April, the number of daily cases in Pakistan came down, as did the positivity rate.

Prime Minister Imran Khan did not shy away from taking the credit. The fact is he was unsure in the beginning on how to handle the crisis. The World Health Organisation (WHO) chief's statements were quoted for Pakistan's handling of COVID. Pakistani commentators proudly told the rest of the world that the Pakistan model should be emulated by other countries.

There was much gloating in Pakistan over how they handled COVID better than India. The Indian case was studied to draw lessons for Pakistan. The main criticism of India was that the authorities declared victory over COVID too early, dropped their guard, underestimated the ferocity of the mutant and did not prepare the country with adequate vaccines, etc. The point, however, is that in Pakistan too, the authorities were ill prepared and people did not follow the COVID appropriate behaviour. The difference was that Pakistan was spared the spread of the highly transmissible variant that India had been attacked with.

According to an article in *The Nation,* the NCOC became the "nerve centre of planning, execution and supervision. The National Disaster Management Authority (NDMA) was mobilised.... It expanded in record time its operations across the nooks and corners of Pakistan.... The NCOC and NDMA kept evolving the response and structures to adjust to the changing situation. Their round-the-clock functioning and system of feedback for mid-course correction helped the state in flattening the curve and presenting Pakistan as one of the best-managed states in the world...not even a single labourer or worker travelled on foot to his hometown, the public and private transportation system remained functional. The Pakistani system of charity and philanthropy, another major factor that helped Pakistan in the fight against COVID, was the spirit to help the poor and downtrodden.... To conclude, Pakistan in comparison with India has outperformed it in all domains..."[21]

Even if the health impact of COVID in Pakistan seemed less severe than in other countries, the impact on the economy was severe. According to a World Bank paper, "...Half of the working population saw either job or income losses, ... more than two million people (fell) below the poverty line...(and) 40 per cent of households suffered from moderate to severe food insecurity."[22] The long-term impact of COVID on Pakistan society and the economy will be serious.

Education

Pakistan has a young demography. About 60 per cent of the population is between the ages of 15 and 64 years and a third is in the 0 to 14 year range. For the lack of education and skills, it is unable to exploit the demographic potential fully. Prime Minister Imran Khan had promised to overhaul the education system. The spending on education has been meagre, much less than that in South Asian countries.

Low spend on education is a perennial problem. Successive governments have been giving less than 2.5 per cent budget to the education sector which is quite inadequate for building a robust education system for a modern society and economy. According to a World Bank paper, even after a lapse of 70 years and the adoption of more than 25 educational policies, the education system has failed to take the nation out of the increasing economic, political and social quagmire.[23] The Imran Khan government cut the education budget by 37 per cent in 2019. Many publicly funded universities were starved of funds and forced to cut down on new admissions.[24]

In 2017, Pakistan spent only 2.9 per cent of its GDP on education; Nepal allocated 5.1 per cent, and India 4.6 per cent of its GDP on education in 2016. In Pakistan, expenditures actually "decreased to 2.4 per cent of GDP in 2018/19.[25] The Global Human Capital Index (2017), which measures how well countries develop their human capital, ranked Pakistan 125th out of 130 countries, representing 93 per cent of the world's population.[26]

Experts identify key problems associated with the education system in Pakistan as being the lack of an adequate budget, poor policy implementation, inefficient testing system, low quality of teachers, low enrolment, high dropout rates, political interference, outdated curriculum, corruption, mismanagement and supervision, and lack of research.[27]

Further, there is a divide between expensive private sector education and government-funded education. Pakistan has now implemented a common curriculum for class 1 to 5 students. In addition, a large number of children receive education in religious madrassas which give orthodox education. Pakistan has formulated a new education policy the details of which are discussed elsewhere in this book.

Numbers tell a stark story of education in Pakistan. After Nigeria, Pakistan has the highest number of school dropouts. Approximately 22.7 million Pakistani children age five to 16, that is, 44 per cent of this age group, did not participate in education in 2017.

The participation of girls in the education system is low. According to Human Rights Watch, "32 per cent of girls of elementary school age are out of school, compared with 21 per cent of boys. By grade six, only 41 per cent of girls participate in education, compared to 51 per cent of boys. And by grade nine, merely 13 per cent of young women are still enrolled in school.[28] The gross enrolment rate (GER) in secondary education is as low as 43 per cent before dropping down to 9 per cent at the tertiary level—an extremely low percentage by global standards. To put these rates into a regional perspective, the secondary GER in both India and Bangladesh is 73 per cent, and as high as 98 per cent in Sri Lanka (UNESCO statistics). [29]

Madrassas: Education has become a battleground between liberal and religious ideologies. There are about 30,000 madrassas in Pakistan that impart religious education mostly. Many of these are funded by Saudi Arabia and also Iran. An estimated 1.8 million to 3.5 million students study in these madrassas.[30] Many of the madrassas are located in rural areas. They are autonomous. Government control is minimal. In 2001, the government had set up a Pakistan Madrassa Education Board to bring about greater standardisation. But, the efforts to standardise madrassa education have not borne fruit. Religious seminaries have produced radicalised minds. Many noted terrorists and radical preachers hail from these madrassas. Madrassa education imparted in Pakistan is of global concern as they get students from all over the world.[31] The Afghan Taliban were the product of Pakistani madrassa education. Afghan refugees, who came to Pakistan due to unsettled conditions in Afghanistan, studied in these madrassas.

Some of the degrees issued by the madrassas—*shahadatul alia* (12+2), *shahadatul almiya* (12+2+2), and some others are recognised as equivalent to Bachelor's and Master's degrees in Arabic and Islamic studies. The government is trying to mainstream madrassa education. Madrassa-educated students are allowed to sit for federal board exams and also study the national curriculum. It remains to be seen whether this attempt to bring some uniformity in the education system succeeds.[32]

Tertiary Education: Pakistan has presently 209 recognized degree-awarding institutions (DAIs), up from 59 in 2001 to 139 in 2010. Punjab has the highest share of these. Overall participation rates in tertiary education remain low in Pakistan: "The country's tertiary GER stood at only 9 per cent in 2018, compared to 29 per cent in India and 21 per cent in Bangladesh."[33]

The higher education system suffers from many problems. Low budgets is one and autonomy is other. Ironically, the PTI government in its first budget in 2018 had reduced the budget of the Higher Education Council by over a third. The HEC is an autonomous body and a thorn in the side of the government. In 2021, President Alvi issued an ordinance clipping the HEC's wings. It was put under the control of the Education Ministry. The chairman of the HEC resigned in protest. He blamed the government for putting political pressure on him to fall in line.[34]

Skills: For an economy to remain globally competitive, it requires a workforce skilled in new technologies. With a poor base in primary and secondary education, Pakistan faces a serious shortage of adequately skilled workers. Its 3,600 vocational and technical institutions enrol about 400,000 students. These institutions are concentrated mostly in Punjab and Sindh.[35] Short of funds, Pakistan has sought the help of other countries to improve skills and training in the country. A National

Vocational Qualification Framework (NVQF) was set up in 2009 with the help of the European Union (EU) and the governments of the Netherlands, Norway, and, perhaps foremost, Germany, with its internationally recognized TVET system.[36] These are sporadic efforts. Educated Pakistanis continue to seek opportunities abroad. Weak industry and weak economy do not create appropriate job opportunities.

Geopolitical Environment

Thanks to its location and history, Pakistan has a significant influence on the regional environment. Likewise, global and regional developments affect it significantly. Pakistan has also honed the art of leveraging its geostrategic location and making the best of a bad situation. In Pakistani thinking, blaming external factors and countries for its deficiencies comes quite naturally. Since its inception, Pakistan has exploited the USA and now it is the turn of China.

In Pakistan's foreign policy, India, Afghanistan, China, the USA and the Islamic countries have a key role. As the geopolitical environment undergoes a major transformation, Pakistan's foreign policy will also see significant adjustments.

Following the withdrawal of US troops from Afghanistan, the situation in Afghanistan is likely to become unstable. The prospects of a fresh bout of violent civil war in Afghanistan from which Pakistan will not remain untouched cannot be ruled out. The Iran-Saudi rivalry continues though some efforts at reconciliation were made in 2021. China has enhanced its influence in the region. Pakistan's dependence on China has grown significantly. This has reduced Pakistan's space for manoeuvring. Pakistan has made the 5 August 2019 changes made by India in Kashmir as a sticking point in the resumption of bilateral talks.

Afghanistan: Pakistan has always used the Afghanistan situation to its advantage as it has control over the Haqqani group of the Taliban. Most regional countries have convinced themselves that without Pakistan's help and cooperation, Afghanistan cannot become stable. Pakistan has fenced the border to stop the anticipated inflow of Afghans into Pakistan. It remains to be seen how Pakistan leverages its position to its advantage as Afghanistan becomes more and more unstable. Many Pakistani experts feel that the extent of the influence of Pakistan over the Taliban is overstated and that the Taliban cleverly exploit Pakistan for their needs. Pakistan has to worry about the revival of Tehrik-e-Taliban Pakistan (TTP) which carried out over 100 attacks across the Pak-Afghan border between July and October 2020.[37] There are also reports in the Pakistan media that the

TTP is attacking Chinese interests in Pakistan. Further, the link between Al-Qaeda and the Taliban remains intact.

Pakistani analysts try to portray that Pakistan has no control over the Afghan Taliban. Such self-serving analysis ignores the fact that the Haqqani group of the Taliban is under the control of the ISI and that the Taliban regularly consulted Pakistan during the so-called Doha peace talks. The Afghan leadership has repeatedly blamed Pakistan for providing shelter to the Taliban. Pakistan is now worried that instability in Afghanistan may affect it adversely. But it refuses to come clean on why it continues to provide shelter, sanctuaries and assistance to the Taliban who have taken over power and imposed a Sharia rule under an Islamic Emirate.

China: In the last few years, Pakistan has come to depend on China for its survival. The China Pakistan Economic Corridor (CPEC), which encompasses a swathe of energy, infrastructure, connectivity and economic projects, is a defining mark of the China-Pakistan relationship which has become highly strategic. Despite the inherent dangers of Pakistan falling into a debt trap, China's potential US$ 62 billion investment in the China-Pakistan Economic Corridor (CPEC) is seen as a major opportunity to build Pakistan's infrastructure and overcome energy shortages. The chances of Pakistan falling into a debt trap have increased because many of the CPEC projects are turning out to be white elephants.

For China, the CPEC is a means of getting access to the Arabian Sea and Chinese influence in the geostrategically located country. The Gwadar port is critical for China's outlet to the Indian Ocean and to Africa. According to former CPEC Authority Chairman, Lt Gen (retd) Asim Saleem Bajwa (31 May 2021), the Gwadar Port and Gwadar Free Zone would generate economic activities of around $ 10 billion per annum. The China Port Holding Company has constructed four berths costing around $ 300 million. Over 67,000 metric tons of cargo under the Afghan Transit Trade Agreement have been transported to Afghanistan. Bajwa stated that 24,000 MT of fertilizer for Afghanistan from Australia had been sent.[38]

Islamabad Security Dialogue: The Pakistani army is trying to show it is changing with time. Pakistan has launched an annual Islamabad Security Dialogue whose first meeting was held in March 2021. PM Imran Khan, General Bajwa and senior officials addressed the gathering. Gen Bajwa spoke about fresh thinking on national security. He talked about geo-economics rather than geopolitics as being the new paradigm of Pakistan's national security concept. He offered to India to bury the past and make a new beginning but adding at the same time, he expected India to create a conducive environment. On Kashmir, there was no appreciable change in Pakistan's attitude. It wants India to undo the August 2019 changes in Kashmir. That is a non-starter.

Pakistan has been trying to sell the geo-economics concept to the USA, offering a relationship based on economy, trade and technology rather than security. It remains to be seen how successfully Pakistan convinces the world of its new thinking on security, considering that its dalliance with terrorism continues and its position on Kashmir remains as hard as ever.

USA: Pakistan sees new opportunities for itself in the new situation developing in Afghanistan post the withdrawal of US and NATO troops. While instability in Afghanistan will harm it also, yet, it will try and extract the maximum advantage from the USA. The conversations between Gen Bajwa and US Defence Secretary Lloyd Austin and NSA Moeed Yousuf's meeting with his US counterpart point to that. Speculations were rife that the USA was seeking a military base in Pakistan to keep an eye on Afghan terror groups after the US troop withdrawal from Afghanistan. USA-Pakistan relations are likely to enter into a new phase. Pakistan is seeking greater cooperation with the USA going beyond security and encompassing economics and technology.

Russia: Pakistan in recent years has made strong efforts to develop a relationship with Russia. Russia and Pakistan have signed an intergovernmental agreement to build a gas pipeline from Karachi to Kasur. Dubbed the Pakistan Stream, the 1,100-km long pipeline would cost over USD 2 billion to build and carry 12 billion cubic metres of gas annually. It is not clear where the funding would come from. Construction is scheduled to begin soon. Pakistan hopes to drive a wedge between India and Russia by striking an independent relationship with Russia. Russian Foreign Minister Lavrov visited India and Pakistan in the same trip in 2021. The growing Russia-Pakistan relationship is a manifestation of the transformation of the geopolitical environment in the region. Russia regards Pakistan as an important country in the Muslim world and a valuable partner in the resolution of the Afghan problem. Yet, Russia has to keep in mind its old relationship with India, built over several decades and India has to take care not to overreact to Russian-Pakistani rapprochement.

India: The Directors-General of Military Operations (DGMOs) of India and Pakistan issued a joint statement on 25 February 2021 reiterating their commitment to "fully implement" the 2003 cease-fire agreement on maintaining the ceasefire along the Line of Control (LOC) and the International Border (IB) and addressing "each other's core issues and concerns which have the propensity to lead to violence."[39] This was an unexpected development that took analysts and observers by surprise. Such a move would not have come about all of a sudden. There were also reports of secret meetings between the Indian and Pakistani security establishments. Yet, the chances of normalisation of India-Pakistan relations appear dim as the basic positions on both sides remain unchanged. The centrality of Kashmir in Pakistan's stance and the centrality of ending support to cross-border terrorism in the Indian position.

The DGMO-level agreement is reported to have been the result of back-channel contacts between India and Pakistan. The existence of a back channel has not been confirmed by the Indian side but rumours are rife in Pakistan. Some other developments—Gen Bajwa's speech at the Islamabad security dialogue, the decision to import sugar from India, later withdrawn, and exchange of letters between Modi and Imran Khan, gave rise to the expectations of an impending thaw in bilateral relations. It is rumoured that the Pakistan military establishment is in favour of such a thaw. But soon, the civilian government hardened its position on Kashmir. Not only was the decision for relaxation of trade reversed, but the Pakistani prime minister also said that there could be no talks with India unless the latter reversed its August 2019 action on Kashmir. Pakistan also sought to link the Palestine question with Kashmir. The hopes of a thaw in bilateral relations have receded.

The joint statement created the hopes of normalisation of India-Pakistan relations. Pakistan army chief spoke about moving forward. The flip-flop on Pakistan's India policy has exposed the fissures between the civilian government on the one hand and the military on the other. These flip-flops have given rise to the speculation that the military establishment and the civilian government are not on the same page on India policy.

Islamic World: Pakistan's foreign policy ideology is informed by pan-Islamism. It regards itself as the leader in the Muslim world or the Ummah. This is because it is the only Muslim country to possess a nuclear weapon and a large military. It provides troops to Saudi Arabia for its defence. In the OIC, Pakistan heads the contact group on Kashmir, which was set up in 1994. Over the years, it has forced the OIC to adopt resolutions on Kashmir.

Pakistan has had a special relationship with Saudi Arabia. The latter has bailed out Pakistan on several occasions with loans and gifts. Prime Minister Imran Khan has visited Saudi Arabia several times. His last visit was in May 2021. Crown Prince Mohammed Bin Salman visited Pakistan in 2019. During that visit, Saudi Arabia promised investment to the tune of US$ 20 billion in Pakistan, including in an oil refinery in Gwadar. To bail out Pakistan from a difficult economic situation, Saudi Arabia also extended the facility of US$ 6 billion that included a loan of US$ 1 billion and a delayed payment facility for the import of Saudi oil.

Just at a time when Pakistan's relationship with Saudi Arabia seemed to be coasting along, Pakistan's ambition to see itself as a leader of the Muslim world surfaced. The Pakistan Foreign Minister criticised the OIC for not convening a special session to condemn India on Kashmir. Pakistan also flirted with Malaysia and Turkey who have their own ambitions of leadership in the Muslim world. This miffed Saudi Arabia and created palpable tensions between the two countries. Imran Khan was all set to visit Kuala Lumpur to attend an Islamic summit convened by Malaysia. However, under Saudi pressure, he withdrew from the meeting at the last moment. Yet, a miffed Saudi Arabia showed its displeasure by asking Pakistan to return the US$ 1 billion loan that it had given. Pakistan had to borrow the money from China to return the loan. Pakistan has been concerned about the treatment meted out to the Pakistani labour force in Saudi Arabia. Eventually, in 2021, the relationship began to show signs of a thaw. Imran Khan, eating humble pie, visited Saudi Arabia to placate the leadership, as did the army chief Gen Bajwa. The episode showed that all is not well between Saudi Arabia and Pakistan.

Pakistan is also unhappy with the UAE since the latter invited the Indian Foreign Minister, the Late Sushma Swaraj, to a meeting of the OIC foreign ministers as an observer. Pakistan refused to attend the meeting. The steady improvement of India's relations with the Gulf countries has been a matter of concern for Pakistan.

Pakistan has a hot and cold relationship with Iran, its neighbour on the west. The relationship is subject to the dynamics of Saudi-Iran rivalry, Shia-Sunni sectarian tensions, Pakistan's closeness to the Taliban, incessant instability in Afghanistan and a host of border management related issues. Following the withdrawal of US and NATO troops from Afghanistan in August 2021, the chances of violence in Afghanistan will increase. This will create problems in the Iran-Pakistan relationship if the Taliban come back to power.

West Asia is undergoing a transformation. After the Arab Spring, the Arab regimes feel insecure. Several Arab countries have normalised their relations with Israel. China's footprint in West Asia is growing. India is following a proactive policy in the region. Pakistan feels threatened and insecure for these reasons.

Conclusion

Imran Khan's dream of transforming Pakistan into a *Naya Pakistan* and realising the *Riyasat-e-Medina* is far from being fulfilled. In the last few years, Pakistan's problems have multiplied. Politics remains as murky as ever, ridden with scandals, political bickering and infighting. Major institutions of state power seem to be working at cross purposes. Lack of sufficient resources makes it difficult for the government to spend on socio-economic development. Pakistan's Islamic identity comes in conflict with the model of a democratic, moderate, inclusive state in which every citizen has equal rights. The minorities feel discriminated against and live under the constant shadow of blasphemy laws. The tension between the open media and the state have sharpened under Imran Khan's tenure.

For Pakistan to become a normal country, the role of the military, direct or indirect, needs to be diminished. The attempt of the security establishment to recast its security paradigm and making Pakistan a hub of geo-economics rather than geopolitics will require fundamental changes in the Pakistani mindset which is highly security oriented and thrives on creating an enemy image of India. Kashmir comes in handy. No politician in Pakistan dares to recognise that Pakistan's woes are rooted in its policies of making India a perpetual enemy.

Bad politics has led to bad economics too. Pakistan at one point in time consistently registered higher growth rates than India. Now the story is very different. Although the government claims it has stabilised the economy, a closer look reveals that the structural problems remain unresolved. Pakistan has to borrow every year to stay afloat. The economy remains fragile.

While incidents of terrorism may have come down, the spectre of terrorism still hangs. The threat of radicalisation has gone up. Numerous terror groups exist in Pakistan unchecked. The government follows a policy of appeasement towards groups like the TLP.

The growing instability in Afghanistan will also have a debilitating impact on Pakistan. With elections due in 2023, the focus of political parties will shift to maximise their gains. Imran Khan's policy of using state instruments to go down on and browbeat the opposition is likely to continue. A lot changes in Pakistan in a short period and yet nothing seems to change.

As far as India is concerned, the bilateral relationship continues to remain troubled. Pakistan has hardened its stance on Kashmir. It has left no stone unturned to raise Kashmir at international fora. It has used Chinese good offices to have closed-door discussions on Kashmir organised at the UN Security Council.

Cross-border support for terrorism continues. Pakistani leaders and media routinely denigrate Prime Minister Modi and the ruling dispensation.

ENDNOTES

1. https://www.dawn.com/news/1524724, accessed on 2 June 2021.
2. https://acenews.pk/26-point-charter-of-demand-issued-by-opposition-apc/
3. Ibid.
4. Najam Sethi, "Naming Names", *The Friday Times*, 4 June 2021, https://www.thefridaytimes.com/naming-names/
5. "Stakeholders reject Pakistan Media Development Authority Ordinance", https://www.thenews.com.pk/print/843433-stakeholders-reject-pakistan-media-development-authority-ordinance
6. *Dawn*, 2 June 2021, https://www.dawn.com/news/1627027/draconian-media-law
7. "Pakistani media faced unique challenges in 2020", https://ifex.org/pakistani-media-faced-unique-challenges-in-2020/
8. Ashok Bhan, "Pakistan's dangerous turn: Shift from Jinnahist to jihadist ideology", 27 February 2021, https://www.sundayguardianlive.com/legally-speaking/pakistans-dangerous-turn-shift-jinnahist-jihadist-ideology,
9. Quratulain Fatima, "Forced conversions of Pakistani Hindu girls", 17 September 2021, https://dailytimes.com.pk/116289/forced-conversions-of-pakistani-hindu-girls/
10. Farahnaz Ispahani, "Slow genocide of minorities in Pakistan", https://www.livemint.com/Politics/F4r3Tmf51k8Sm6DGjPRaEN/Slow-genocide-of-minorities-in-Pakistan-Farahnaz-Ispahani.html, 19.12016
11. Ashok Bhan, "Pakistan's dangerous turn: Shift from Jinnahist to jihadist ideology", 27 February 2021, https://www.sundayguardianlive.com/legally-speaking/pakistans-dangerous-turn-shift-jinnahist-jihadist-ideology
12. Finance ministry's press release.
13. Sushant Sareen, https://www.orfonline.org/research/covid19-and-pakistan-the-economic-fallout-67296/
14. Ibid.
15. Quoted in Sushant Sareen above.
16. https://www.dawn.com/news/1589984#:~:text=Earlierper cent2Cper cent20aper cent20Worldper cent20Bankper cent20report,byper cent20handper cent20underper cent20travelper cent20restrictions
17. The figures have been taken from https://www.business-standard.com/article/international/pakistan-govt-unveils-rs-8-5-tn-fy-budget-defence-gets-rs-1-370-bn-121061200084_1.html; https://www.dawn.com/news/1628803); https://www.brecorder.com/news/amp/40099198
18. "Power sector circular debt rises to Rs 2.26 tr", 3 November 2021, The article says, "Payables to independent power producers (IPPs), which were Rs 718 bn in December 2018, jumped to Rs 1,042 bn, according to the statistics presented to the PAC. Likewise, the power holding companies' outstanding, which was Rs 607 bn two years ago, rose to Rs 1,003 bn. Also, the amount payable by Gencos (generation companies) to fuel suppliers increased from Rs 89 bn to Rs 105 bn." The power sector has been reeling under the impact of what is called 'circular debt' since 2007-2008. https://www.dawn.com/news/1588319
19. http://www.apgml.org/documents/Default.aspx?pcPage=8
20. *Dawn*.com 15 May 2021.

21. https://nation.com.pk/11-Nov-2020/comparing-the-pak-india-covid-fights
22. https://www.worldbank.org/en/country/pakistan/overview
23. Critical Analysis of the Problems of Education in Pakistan: Possible Solutions, Iqbal Ahmad1, Kahil-ur-Rehman, Asghar Ali, Itbar Khan, and Fazal Akber Khan, *International Journal of Evaluation and Research in Education* (IJERE) vol. 3, no. 2, June 2014, pp. 79-84, https://files.eric.ed.gov/fulltext/EJ1091681.pdf
24. https://www.worldbank.org/en/country/pakistan/overview
25. Ibid.
26. The Global Human Capital Report 2017 says, "From South Asia, Sri Lanka (70) is the top performer, while Nepal (98), India (103), Bangladesh (111), and Pakistan (125) lag behind. With the exception of Sri Lanka, the rest have yet to reach the 60 per cent threshold with regard to developing their human capital." http://www3.weforum.org/docs/WEF_Global_Human_Capital_Report_2017.pdf.
27. "Problems of Education in Pakistan & Solution", https://blueskyconsultancy.com.pk/problems-of-education-in-pakistan-solution/
28. Robert Hunter, *World Education Services—Education in Pakistan*, 25 February 2020, https://wenr.wes.org/2020/02/education-in-pakistan
29. Ibid.
30. Ibid.
31. Ibid.
32. Ibid.
33. Ibid.
34. Govt removes Tariq Banuri as HEC Chairman, *Express Tribune*, 27 March 2021, https://tribune.com.pk/story/2291711/govt-removes-tariq-banuri-as-hec-chairman
35. Ibid.
36. Ibid.
37. Zahaid Rehman, "Recalibrating Priorities", 8 May 2021, https://jinnah-institute.org/publication/recalibrating-priorities/
38. https://tribune.com.pk/story/2302799/gwadar-to-generate-10b-economic-activity-annually-asim-bajwa
39. https://www.moneycontrol.com/news/politics/india-pakistan-loc-joint-statement-imran-khan-sri-lanka-dgmo-dgsmo-new-delhi-islamabad-mea-mofa-6572141.html, 25 February 2021, https://www.moneycontrol.com/news/politics/india-pakistan-loc-joint-statement-imran-khan-sri-lanka-dgmo-dgsmo-new-delhi-islamabad-mea-mofa-6572141.html

1

Pakistan: Governance and Politics: 2021-2022

Rana Banerji

Three years into its tenure, the Pakistan Tehrik-e-Insaf (PTI)'s civilian government led by Prime Minister Imran Khan continues to drift, seemingly rudderless and ill prepared, failing to tackle simple and complex issues of governance, despite frequent hand holding or bail-outs by the Military Establishment. This was a 'familiar' scenario generating *'déjà vu'*, of 'a volatile mixture of political unrest, stalled governance, and a powerful military continuing to exert significant influence over national security and politics.'[1]

Khan disappointed people of the country who had high expectations, because most of his idealistic hyperbole about setting up 'an enlightened new Medina dreamt of by the Prophet (PBUH)', was not based on any systematic planning and failed miserably in implementation. He did not share any comprehensive, strategically-made plans to get the people of Pakistan out of poverty, hunger, or under-development. Rather, he just seemed to have memorized 'vague definitions of governance without understanding basic concepts.'[2] Instead of 'politically empowering the ordinary people of Pakistan', the PTI's vision 'could not think being beyond the receiving end of charity.'[3]

A key factor that hounded the government was the issue of legitimacy as well as the process that led to its formation, a thinly-veiled reference to the 'hybrid' support extended by the military.[4] Gaining traction, especially after 2014, the PTI tried to sell to the electorate, dreams about performance and delivery becoming key harbingers of change. These buzz words became central tenets of the PTI's soaring rhetoric on addressing corruption of the well-ensconced, suppression of violence or addressing socio-economic inequalities.

Disillusionment ensued rapidly, 'symbols of grassroots democratization set us apart from the rest, as the PTI's main weapon', but 'fast forward to 2021, the chickens have come home to roost.'[5] Observers hostile to the PTI alleged that most 'Pakistanis were quite livid,' as 'unemployment had risen by 20 million', 'double digit inflation, especially of food, had eroded real wages and incomes of the lower classes, the by-elections had sounded the death knell of the PTI, the PML (N) was surging ahead.'[6] 'The many failures of the PTI government' were now being 'linked by many to the establishment'[7] and 'criticism of the 'Miltablishment' (term commonly used in Pakistan, for 'Military Establishment') had increased, for hoisting and propping up of an incapable Imran Khan.'[8] By the end of 2021, this support or 'same page' trust seemed frayed at the edges.

One-sided Accountability

One of the most important priorities of the PTI was its promise to cleanse the system of endemic corruption. Yet the only panacea offered in this context was one-sided pursuit of accountability against chosen Opposition politicians, through the National Accountability Bureau (NAB), an institution that seemed determined to bend over backwards to please its masters, throwing to the wind basic norms of the rule of law.[9] 'Both premier anti-corruption institutions, the FIA and NAB, worked on overlapping legal mandates', an experienced police officer claimed. 'Unfortunately, they have been often misused for political purposes at the behest of the ruling elite and security establishment.'[10]

In time, Imran's oft-repeated bravado 'about not giving NROs (national reconciliation ordinances) to anyone' (read Zardari/Sharifs), became a stratagem to cock a snook at the military, whenever reports surfaced about the military's quest for alternatives.

Economic Dilemmas

Economically, the government remained bogged down in a quagmire. The situation was not comfortable from the outset. The COVID-19 pandemic caused further strains even as half-hearted remedial measures were implemented. GDP growth 'fell from 5.5 per cent in 2017-18 to 1.1 per cent in 2020; real wages of the working classes declined by nearly 6 per cent in the least three years compared to growth of 3 per cent in the previous regime.'[11]

An extended fund facility was ultimately re-negotiated with the International Monetary Fund (IMF) after dumping first choice Finance Minister, Asad Omar midway. Thereafter, Hafiz Sheikh had to quit after losing the elections to enter the Senate (March, 2021). As the second IMF tranche of $ 500 million was released, the government appointed a fourth new Finance Minister, Shaukat Tareen (shifting a hapless Hammad Azhar, who had come in only a few days earlier, to Energy). Tareen declared that Pakistan would not be in a position to implement new IMF directives to increase tariffs and taxes at present.

The Circular Debt Trap

As the IMF noted in December, 2020, power distribution companies in Pakistan lose between 20 per cent and 40 per cent of the energy supplied to them. This loss makes them critical contributors to the circular debt. Controlling its continuous growth is a critical part of stabilizing the fiscal framework. If the losses are not brought down, then accumulated costs are passed on to paying consumers. This is what the IMF called 'full cost recovery.' Something substantially similar could be happening in the gas sector.[12]

CPEC Projects Hit

Under the China-Pakistan Economic Corridor (CPEC) Energy Framework Agreement (EFA), China was to set up 12 power plants. These projects were hit by the circular debt issue. Pakistan was supposed to set up a CPEC Revolving Fund equal to 22 per cent of monthly invoices, backed by the sovereign guarantees provided by the Ministry of Finance, to pay back the dues of Chinese firms. The government has not been able to clear Rs. 188 billion, due as payments, in breach of the EFA.[13]

In its audit report for 2018-19, the Auditor-General of Pakistan (AGP) criticized the purchase of 'sukuk' (bonds) worth Rs. 200 billion, to deal with the power sector debt and payment of liabilities to independent power producers (IPPs). About 70 properties of power companies were sold and leased back from Meezan Bank Ltd. (head of a consortium of banks). The auditor noted that though Pakistan now has at its disposal excess energy capacity, significantly more than the current or short-term expected demand, "power sector government properties could face a risk of *en masse* sale/transfer out to private bodies on account of default in any principal re-payments."[14]

The Budget (2021-2022)

In May 2021, the National Accounts Committee (NAC) released estimates claiming 3.94 per cent GDP growth for FY21. Though these 'rosier' figures were questioned by Opposition parties, the State Bank of Pakistan (SBP) supported the findings.[15] The data helped generate an impression about the economy being on an upswing, enabling PTI loyalists to crow about its performance.[16]

The Economic Survey presented by new Finance Minister Shaukat Tareen (June 10, 2021) assessed growth at almost 4 per cent and estimated further improvement in GDP to touch 5 per cent next year. Better performance in industries and services sectors and high remittances were claimed.[17]

A Rs. 8.48 trillion budget was presented for fiscal year 2021-2022 on June 11. Rs. 1,370 billion was earmarked for Defence (6.2 % increase). The fiscal deficit would be Rs. 3,420 billion, which is around 6.3 per cent of the GDP. A 45 per cent increase has been planned for public sector development (Rs.900 billion) and minimum wages were fixed at Rs. 20,000. The GDP has been estimated to rise by 4.8 per cent. Inflation would be sought to be kept down to 8.2 per cent. The tax collection target has been set at Rs. 5,829 billion. Several tax exemptions were announced to boost industry. It was not immediately clear how the tax targets asked for by the IMF would be achieved.[18]

The IMF delayed release of its second aid tranche. Negotiations stalled on their perception of inadequate taxation and autonomy of the State Bank of Pakistan, forcing the PTI government to ultimately frame a bill for this purpose, despite the combined Opposition raising a chorus of protest on the 'sovereignty of the nation being bartered.'[19] A mini-budget too had to be introduced to raise more revenue.

Administrative Mismanagement

Some administrative schemes were announced with great fanfare during the pandemic. Ehsaas Emergency Cash programme launched by the Prime Minister on April 1, 2020 sought to alleviate the economic hardship being experienced by vulnerable sections of the population. Financial assistance of Rs. 12,000 per family was earmarked, with a total budget allocation of Rs. 203 billion. Claiming to cover more than 15 million families, its impact may not have been very different from the Benazir Income Support Scheme (BISP). A tree plantation drive was launched in August, 2020 to benefit PTI's 'Tiger Force' (youth volunteers). In February 2021, another innovative loan scheme was introduced to give tractors to youth under the so-called 'Kamyab Kisan' programme. Designed more as sops for party cadres, none of these schemes seems to have impacted positively, either to generate employment or to reduce the burden of increasing prices on the food and essential commodities front. Atta and sugar prices remained high. Electricity and water tax payments also hit the common man badly.

Education Policy Changes

The PTI government's attempt to introduce a Single National Curriculum (SNC) attracted adverse criticism. An internationally respected Pakistani academic claimed it would actually grossly damage whatever was good in the existing system, flooding young minds with a bulk of religious fanatical material they would be unprepared to handle. Ordinary schools will henceforth impose more rote learning than the two major existing madrassa systems—Tanzeemul Madaris and Rabtaul Madaris. Normal schoolteachers being under-equipped religiously, the SNC would involve summoning an army of madrassa-educated holy men—hafiz and qaris—as paid teachers in schools. This could adversely affect the general ambiance and safety of students. 'Be prepared, Pakistan! Imran Khan's government is poised to inflict damage upon this country's education system in a manner never seen before.'[20]

Frequent Cabinet Re-shuffles

Frequent reshuffles were undertaken in Federal and Provincial cabinets, not only in the key ministry of Finance, keeping both elected politicians as well as a nominated retinue of Imran Khan's sycophants perpetually insecure.

The erstwhile Military Establishment favourite, Brig (retd) Ejaz Shah was eased out from the Interior Ministry to Narcotics Control. Though the Military leadership may have preferred to shift Defence Minister and former Khyber Pakhtunkhwa (KP) Chief Minister, Pervez Khattak to the Interior portfolio, he seemed to have forfeited the Prime Minister's trust. Instead, the 'man for all seasons,' Sheikh Rashid, was appointed there, discounting previous criticism by Imran, when in the Opposition, as also his lacklustre performance in the Railways. These changes proved hard for PTI loyalists to swallow.[21]

Every new reshuffle was preceded by feverish jockeying for seats at the high table. Federal Information Minister Fawad Chaudhry was first shifted to Science & Technology, bringing in former People's Party heavyweight, Firdaus Ashiq Awan, before dumping her. Shibli Faraz, son of the famous poet, Ahmed Faraz, was inducted as Information Minister, only to exchange places again with Fawad Chaudhry. Firdaus, meanwhile, was restored to glory in the Punjab Provincial Cabinet of Chief Minister Usman Buzdar. Omar Ayub Khan, grandson of the former dictator and frequent party hopper, was moved from Energy to Economic Affairs.

Indulgences of non-elected special assistants in the Imran Cabinet like Shahbaz Gill, Zulfi Bokhari and Shahzad Akbar continued to cause a lot of heartburn among defected 'electables' from South Punjab, who had joined the Imran bandwagon in 2018 due to Army nudging. They now faced uncomfortable thoughts about their dimming re-election prospects in 2023.[22]

In a surprise development, Shahzad Akbar had to resign from his post in January 2022 as he had failed, in PM Imran Khan's perception, to deliver on accountability against Shehbaz Sharif.

Bureaucratic 'Musical Chairs'

Similar games extended to the bureaucracy, both in assignments of the Federal and Provincial governments. In November 2019, almost the entire top bureaucracy in Punjab was reshuffled by CM Usman Buzdar, including 31 secretaries (Home and Additional Chief Secretary among them), eight out of nine commissioners and 31 deputy commissioners. Principal Secretaries to the Governor and the CM were also changed. Federal government Finance Secretary, Dr. Kamran Afzal, was shifted just two weeks before presentation of the next budget (May, 2021). A similar fate befell police officers, especially those assigned to Lahore.

Nine senior officials were changed in Khyber Pakhtunkhwa (KP) in July, 2020. In Balochistan, a move by the Federal government in March, 2021 to earmark a greater number of bureaucratic posts for Federal pool bureaucrats saw a revolt by the association of provincial bureaucrats, which vowed to challenge the decision in the high courts.[23] Amanullah Khan Yasinzai, Governor, Balochistan, had not resigned even after a month of receiving PM Imran Khan's letter, informing that he would be replaced by Zahoor Agha.[24]

Muhd Azam Khan, Principal Secretary to PM, attracted ire from his peer group of senior bureaucrats for enjoying disproportionate and indiscriminate clout in effecting many of these changes.

The brass (military) had long advised PM Imran Khan to invest in competent, go-getting chief ministers so that the PTI could deliver good governance, especially to the hapless people of the two provinces, Punjab and KP. Instead, 'after relentless rounds of musical chairs' for senior bureaucrats, 'the situation is so dire in Punjab now that a 'forward bloc' of dozens of MPAs 'banded around the outcast, Jehangir Tareen, to blackmail Usman Buzdar.'[25]

Foreign Service

The Prime Minister criticized Pakistani diplomats for 'callousness' in public dealings and holding on to 'a colonial mindset', timing his remarks just before his visit to Saudi Arabia in May, 2021. A career diplomat there was recently replaced as Ambassador by a retired Army General.[26] Expectedly, Foreign Service officers expressed their angst against these remarks,[27] whereupon, on return from Saudi Arabia, Imran sheepishly retracted from his comments.[28] Subsequently, reports surfaced in the media about the premature recall of the retired General from Riyadh, contributing further to deteriorating civil- military ties.

Changes in FIA

Disclosures in media by a highly respected police officer, Bashir Memon, who served as Director-General, Federal Investigation Authority (Aug. 2017-Aug. 2019), brought considerable egg on the face of the PM. Memon alleged pressure by the PM to implicate prominent politicians in terrorism cases and independent judges like Qazi Faiz Isa, in unwarranted references.[29] Another erstwhile Army favourite, Wajid Zia, who rendered stellar service to discredit the Sharifs, was suddenly replaced as DG, FIA in June, 2021, ostensibly due to overlap and undue interference by Shahzad Akbar, the PM's Special Assistant on Accountability.[30] These accusations by the former FIA director gained serious traction in the public's imagination, greatly disappointing PTI loyalists about the party's reputation—and that of the PM's with it.[31]

PIA Plane Impounded in Kuala Lumpur

The PTI government's embarrassment was writ large when a Pakistan International Airlines Boeing 777 aircraft was impounded by Malaysia at Kuala Lumpur airport on January 15, 2021, apparently on the orders of a local court over non-payment in a 14-million-dollar lease dispute. The plane would eventually be flown home via Dubai and Doha two days later, after the government decided to settle the matter out of court in the UK, with the PIA paying seven million dollars to a private company, Peregrine Aviation Charlie Limited.[32]

The Broadsheet Payments & Enquiry by a Retired Judge

In another case which surfaced in December, 2020 the London High Court ordered that $28.7 million, inclusive of interest, be debited from the accounts of the High Commission of Pakistan in London, to pay service fees to a private arbitration company, Broadsheet, owned by a London-based Iranian, Kaveh Mousavi. He was employed to recover allegedly illegally acquired assets from former PM Nawaz Sharif. Meanwhile, payments had already been made to one Jerry James of the USA, who owned a similarly named company, through intermediation of some Pakistani middlemen, including a prominent lawyer,

Ahmer Bilal Soofi. Some payments were also made to Kaveh Mousavi pursuant to orders of the court.

In January 2021, the Federal Government appointed a one-man inquiry commission headed by former Supreme Court judge Azmat Saeed Sheikh to probe into the Broadsheet scandal. The Opposition objected to this judge's appointment, as he had earlier been involved in persecuting Nawaz Sharif in the Panama Papers case. The commission completed its investigation in March 2021 rather inconclusively finding that the payment records of $1.5 million (Rs. 234 mn) to the fake Broadsheet Company in the USA was missing. These records had disappeared from the ministries of Finance and Law, the office of the Attorney-General as well as the High Commission, in London![33]

Persisting Poor Railway Infrastructure

The Ghotki train disaster (June 7, 2021) in northern Sindh, killing over 60 persons, emphasised the poor state of track maintenance, dilapidated wagon stock and financial crunch facing the Pakistan Railways. The Government looked on helplessly. Much store is set on the upgrade of the Karachi–Peshawar main line (ML–1), dependent on investment of USD 6.8 billion by China.

Continuing Media Repression

The International Federation of Journalists ranked Pakistan as the fifth most dangerous place for the practice of journalism, with 138 media persons having lost their lives in the line of duty from 1990 till 2020. In recent years, the military's intelligence agencies were involved in forcible disappearances of Baloch, Pashtun, and Sindhi nationalists, human rights defenders, journalists and professors. Official statistics indicated that since 2009, the authorities recovered 4,557 corpses of suspected victims of extra-judicial killings.

Media professionals all across the country are often targeted with impunity by militants, criminal elements, government actors, and security agencies. Threats, beatings, trumped up criminal charges, even murders are common. Every time such incidents occurred, state agencies suspected to be involved were quick and profuse in denial, yet they failed to nab the suspects.

In April 2020, Sajid Hussain, a Pakistani journalist who reported for *Balochistan Times* and was living in exile in Sweden as a political refugee, was found dead in suspicious circumstances, leading to adverse criticism by Reporters Sans Frontiers.[34] In July 2020, intelligence personnel dressed as police officers abducted ex-Army officer Matiullah Jan, now a prominent journalist/TV channel owner, known for his vocal criticism of the military, from a busy street in the centre of the capital, Islamabad. His captors had to release him within hours as the abduction was captured on CCTV and sparked outrage on social media.[35] Others were less fortunate. Col (retd) Inamur Rahim, who worked in the Judge Advocate General's office was mysteriously picked up from Islamabad in December 2019 and had to undergo a long 37-day incarceration before being released.[36]

'Whistleblower' in Asim Bajwa Case Nabbed

In September 2020, Sajid Gondal, Additional Joint Director in the Securities and Exchange Commission of Pakistan (SECP) was abducted from the outskirts of Islamabad[37] after it was suspected he may have been behind leaks connected to the story broken by a journalist, Ahmed Noorani, now living abroad, on the disproportionate assets of Lt Gen (retd) Asim Saleem Bajwa's family, who had prospered running a chain of pizza stores in the USA.[38] Bajwa, who was then Special Assistant, Media, to the PM, resigned from that post but stuck on brazenly to his other hat, as Chief Executive of the CPEC Authority. Gondal returned home after five days without a satisfactory explanation of his absence.[39]

Gulalai Ismail, woman's rights activist (Aware Girls NGO) and supporter of the Pashtun Tahafuz Movement (PTM), managed to escape to a Western country but her father, Muhd Ismail and another elderly associate, Idris Khattak were picked up by suspected security personnel in Peshawar. Khattak disappeared on November 19, 2019, and remains 'missing.' Gulalai's father was released on bail in April 2021.[40]

On March 17, 2021 in Saleh Pat, Sukkur district of Sindh province, Ajay Lalwani, a journalist, died from gunshot injuries while getting a shave in a barber shop.[41] In yet another attack on April 20, 2021, Absar Alam, a well-known journalist, was injured by gunshots outside his home in Islamabad but luckily, he survived.[42] On the night of May 25, Asad Ali Toor, a producer who worked for some TV channel programmes lately critical of the military establishment, was beaten up by three assailants who broke into his house in Islamabad. Reporting to someone on phone, they claimed to be from Inter Services Intelligence (ISI) and bragged that they had roughed up Toor ('*ghus ke maara*').[43] Observers tweeted in concern about Toor awaiting treatment in hospital, 'upright but bloodied and shaken.'[44]

On May 28, 2021, Matiullah Jan's TV channel covered a protest rally of prominent journalists, including Hamid Mir of Geo TV, who reiterated their determination not to be intimidated by the Army. Mir was uncharacteristically bold in threatening exposure of alleged misdemeanors of Generals![45] Geo TV had to promptly take him off air from his Capital Talk show.[46]

Though a bill was recently drafted on disappearance cases, it is yet to become law and Imran Khan's civilian government has looked on passively, as others before it. In fact, efforts were fast culminating, to push through a draconian 'Media Development Authority' ordinance, 2021, to further centralize media oversight.[47]

Senate Elections

Since winning the 2018 elections, the PTI government had been eager to hold Senate elections early and through an open vote. The 1973 Constitution provides only for secret ballots. The ruling party claimed that open ballots would promote transparency. The Opposition was sternly opposed and termed it an attempt by the government to prevent its lawmakers from switching loyalties. Subsequently, the government presented a bill seeking to amend the Constitution for an open vote in the Senate elections. Though it was passed by the standing committee concerned, the National Assembly (NA) witnessed noisy scenes when the government presented the 26th Constitutional Amendment Bill in the NA. On February 6, 2021, sensing strong resistance in the NA, President Dr. Arif Alvi signed off an Election Amendment Ordinance, 2021, under which upcoming Senate elections could be held through open ballot.[48] A presidential reference was also sent to the Supreme Court, pending a decision.

Surprisingly enough, the Election Commission of Pakistan (ECP) took an independent stand on both issues, that of open ballot and advancing of elections. It clarified that according to Article 224(3) of the Constitution, elections cannot be held before the 30-day period after the expiry of the term of Senate members. It also opposed Attorney General, Pakistan, Khalid Jawed Khan's plea to amend the Election Act, 2017. Ultimately (01.03.2021), a five-judge bench of the Supreme Court, headed by Chief Justice of Pakistan (CJP) Gulzar Ahmed ruled to continue the *status quo* of secret ballots.[49]

The Senate elections, held on March 3, 2021 threw up a major political surprise with former People's Party Prime Minister, Yousuf Raza Gilani, defeating Finance Minister, Hafiz Sheikh from the Islamabad Capital Area seat, in a 169 to 164 vote.[50] This forced the Prime Minister to send an SOS to the Army Chief and the DG, Inter Services Intelligence (ISI), who met him on March 4. Messages were sent out to PTI's loyalists to rally against Gilani for the election to the Senate Chairman's post on March 12, where the tide was reversed, with 48 votes to Gilani's 42 in the 99-member Senate.[51] The President appointed arbiter, former Sindh Chief Minister Syed Muzaffar Hussain Shah, ruled seven votes on the ballot invalid, to shepherd home the PTI Government nominee, Sadiq Sanjrani as Senate Chairman for the second time. Though challenged by the Opposition, the Islamabad High Court declined to interfere with Shah's verdict.[52]

Former President Asif Zardari of the Pakistan People's Party (PPP) played a mercurial role in first foisting Gilani as the 'joint Opposition candidate' in the Senate and later, making deals with the Military Establishment and PTI leaders to get Sanjrani re-elected as Chairman. In the process, the PPP emerged as the largest Opposition party there with 21 seats, compared to the Pakistan Muslim League's (Nawaz) 18. The ruling PTI retained 25 seats while the Balochistan Awami Party (BAP) supporting it, returned with 13 seats. Maulana Fazlur Rehman's Jamiat Ulema-e-Islam (JuI-F) could get 5 seats while MQM (3), ANP (2), National Party (2), Pakhtunkhwa Milli Awami Party (2) and Independents (5) completed a motley group of the 'Others' of 19 in the 99-member Senate. Majority support would remain elusive in the Senate in the foreseeable future.[53]

Subsequently, Yousuf Raza Gilani was chosen Leader of the Opposition, sowing seeds of discord in the Pakistan Democratic Movement (PDM) between the PPP and the PML (N), who claimed that an earlier understanding with the PPP to back their own nominee, Azam Tarar, had been ignored.[54]

In late December 2021, Shaukat Tareen, the PM's Finance Adviser, was finally co-opted as a Senator through a by-election for a general seat from Khyber Pakhtunkhwa, courtesy the resignation of the PTI's Ayub Afridi, and formally sworn in as Finance Minister thereafter.[55]

On February 1, 2022, the Senate passed, with the casting vote of the Chairman, the controversial bill providing autonomy for the State Bank of Pakistan under IMF pressure to do so. Gilani who was absent during the vote, offered to resign as Leader of the Opposition, sending his resignation to PPP Chairman Asif Zardari who declined to accept it.

Election Reforms

In early May 2021, the Government pushed through, by a Presidential Ordinance, an ambitious plan for electoral reforms, which proposed the introduction of electronic voting machines, right to vote for overseas Pakistanis, registration of political parties, open ballot for Senate elections, possibility of complaining against, and changing polling officers, preparation and use of electoral rolls based on National Data Registration Authority (NADRA) data.[56] The PML (N) challenged this move in the Islamabad High Court.[57]

In February 2022, the Election Commission (EC) disqualified PTI Senator Faisal Vawda, a close associate of PM Imran Khan, on grounds of concealing his dual nationality. Another adverse verdict by the EC seemed to be on the anvil against the PTI in the foreign funding case.

Pakistan Democratic Movement (PDM)

Eleven Opposition parties got together in the middle of 2020 to constitute the Pakistan Democratic Movement (PDM), with a professed agenda of 'respecting the vote', protesting against alleged rigging in the 2018 elections by the military establishment, and holding a series of big rallies, which were to culminate in a 'Long March' and *en masse* resignations of elected legislators to National and Provincial assemblies.[58] The lead in organising this front was taken by Maulana Fazlur Rehman of the Jamiat Ulema-e-Pakistan (JuI-F). A 26-point resolution was issued, demanding Imran Khan's resignation and fresh elections. A series of impressive rallies were held in Gujranwala, Karachi, Quetta (October 2020), Peshawar, Multan (November, 2020) and Lahore (December, 2020). Despite COVID raging in the country, considerable momentum was generated through these rallies in expectation of an imminent change.

Nawaz Sharif's Direct Attack on Army Leadership

Though speaking from exile in London, PML(N) leader and three times former Prime Minister Nawaz Sharif stole the thunder at the PDM's inaugural All Parties Conference in Islamabad on September 20, 2020, with a frontal attack on Pakistan's Military establishment. "Today, our struggle is against those who installed Imran Khan and who manipulated elections to bring an incapable man like him into power and thus destroyed the country." Referring to an earlier statement[59] of former PM, Yousuf Raza Gilani about the Army and the ISI acting as 'a state within a state', Nawaz went further to note, "It is saddening that the situation has escalated to a state above the state." He added, "This parallel government illness is the root-cause of our problems."[60]

Nawaz Sharif followed up this speech by directly naming Army Chief Gen Qamar Javed Bajwa and the DG, ISI, Lt Gen Faiz Hamid at the PDM's Gujranwala rally (October 16, 2020). 'This challenge to the military leadership was certainly novel', an astute observer, himself troubled by the military, observed, as 'an opposition politician from Punjab, that too someone of Sharif's stature' was directly naming Generals.[61] Some explained Nawaz Sharif's outburst as a "suicidal" gesture born of rage and frustration, progressively brought upon by three successive dismissals from power (1993, 1999, 2017). Others insisted that he had been 'egged on by disgruntled elements within the Miltablishment, who had serious issues with the way in which their institutional interests were being compromised. One service extension (Bajwa's) had robbed a clutch of colleagues of the most coveted post.'[62]

Capt (retd) Safdar's Arrest and Sindh IGP 'Kidnap' Incident

Meanwhile, an embarrassing impasse developed during the PDM's Karachi rally, three days later (October 19, 2020) when the Karachi IGP, Mushtaq Meher, was forced by some junior security personnel, at an unearthly hour of dawn (October 20, 2020), to raid the Karachi hotel room of Maryam Nawaz and arrest her husband, Capt (retd) Safdar, for allegedly having insulted Quaid-e-Azam Mohd Ali Jinnah at his mausoleum the previous day.

This forced the IGP and a set of his subordinate officers to announce they were proceeding on leave, in protest. The situation had to be defused after PPP leader, Bilawal Bhutto's telephone conversation with Army Chief Bajwa, wherein the latter indicated he was asking the Karachi Corps Commander, Lt Gen Humayun Aziz to undertake an enquiry into the entire incident. Though its report never saw the light of day, it forced the Army to eat humble pie and assuage the injured sentiments of the Sindh Police.[63] PM Imran Khan down played the imbroglio as 'a comedy' or 'non-issue'. However, the incident appalled most political observers and responsible media analysts in Pakistan described the unprecedented police revolt as something 'that could have far-reaching impact', signifying 'intra-institutional conflict, and political consequences.'[64]

Not unexpectedly and not only due to long interruptions in its agenda of rallies, the PDM's agitation lost impetus after differences emerged on the issue of the election to the Leader of Opposition's post in the Senate. The timing of *en masse* resignations also became contentious. The PPP made it clear it was not prepared to lose control of the Sindh Provincial government. The JuI (F) and PML (N) continued to favour the option of going ahead with the Long March and *en masse* resignations of elected legislators, at a later moment of their choosing.

Punjab and Karachi By-elections

Despite the PTI government being in power, their candidates lost in ten out of eleven by-elections. In the postponed by-election to the NA 75 Daska seat on April 10, the PML (N)'s Nosheen Iftikhar defeated the PTI's Ali Asjad Majhi by over 16,000 votes. On May 6 in Khushab, the Provincial Assembly PP-84 seat was won by the PML (N)'s Moazzem Sher Kallu, defeating the PTI's Ali Hussain Baloch by over 10,000 votes. In the NA-249 by-election in Karachi on May 9, the PPP's Abdul Qadir Mandokhel narrowly defeated former PML (N) Finance Minister Miftah Ismail by about 900 votes. The PTI candidate, Amjad Afridi, came in a poor fifth, behind candidates of the Tehrik-e-Labbaik and the Pakistan Sarzameen Party. In December 2021, the PML(N)'s Shaista Pervaiz Malik comfortably retained the NA 133 seat from Lahore, with the PTI pushed to third place due to a rather surprising resurgence of the PPP.

Mishandling of the TLP Agitation

In mid-April, 2021, cadres of the Tehreek-e-Labbaik Pakistan (TLP), a religion-inspired party, descended in 'tens of thousands' on the streets of Pakistani towns demanding expulsion of the French Ambassador in Pakistan, Marc Barety, for disrespect shown to Islam in France. The PTI government had concluded an interim agreement with the TLP in February 2021 to defer this issue to end-April 2021. Attempts to control the agitation by the Punjab police left over a dozen demonstrators dead, and scores injured including policemen. Rumours of martial law surfaced in Islamabad. Hundreds of TLP supporters were arrested, including its leader, Saad Rizvi, son of recently deceased (November 19, 2020) founder of the movement, Khadim Hussain Rizvi.[65]

The authorities hurriedly used Anti-Terrorist laws to impose a ban on the TLP and stop it from marching to Islamabad. In the event, another "dialogue" ensued between leaders of the TLP and representatives of the state. It was decided to defuse the situation by shunting the matter to the National Assembly for a resolution at a later date. It seemed as if the government had contrived another hollow pledge it could not keep. Nearly 669 TLP supporters were set free straight away. Saad Rizvi was released a little later, on April 19, 2021. A plea by the TLP to remove the ban on it was filed before the Interior Ministry.

The next time the TLP decides to flex its muscle to challenge the writ of the state or society, it may well demand much more and behave in a more empowered and aggressive manner.[66] Much would depend on how the Army leadership deals with its plan of mainstreaming the TLP, which seems to have gone awry at present.

Simmering Pashtun Discontent

The Pashtun Tahafuz Movement (PTM) continued to face State repression despite remaining largely peaceful. Manzoor Pashteen was arrested in Kohat on June 4, 2021 while on his way to Janikhel, Bannu, to join the protest being staged there against killing of some of their local leaders by unknown miscreants.[67] He was apparently set free eight hours later, after the PM's intervention![68]

Khyber Pakhtunkhwa (KP) Local Body Elections

In the first phase of the much delayed KP local body elections, the ruling PTI government in the province suffered serious reverses, with the Jamiat Ulema-e-Islam (JuI Fazlur Rehman) winning decisively (21 seats) in major cities and the Awami National Party also faring much better (8 seats won). The PTI lost the Peshawar Mayor's seat to the JuI (F).

Islamabad Security Dialogue (ISD)

On March 18, 2021, the Army Chief, Gen Bajwa, addressed the Islamabad Security Dialogue, organised by the Strategic Affairs Adviser to the PM, Moeed Yusuf, on the pattern of the Raisina dialogue in India. Significantly, Bajwa observed, 'the contemporary concept of national security' is not only about protecting a country from internal and external threats but 'also providing a conducive environment, in which aspirations of human security, national progress and development could be realized.' Clarifying, he added, 'It (national security) is not solely a function of armed forces anymore.' 'A nation at peace and a region in harmony are essential prerequisites for attainment of national security in the true spirit.' Whether it be 'human security, extremism, human rights, environmental hazards, economic security or pandemics, responding in silos is no longer an option, Bajwa acknowledged, ' we end up spending a lot of money on our defence, which naturally comes at the expense of human development.' He stressed a 'desire to change the narrative of geo-political contestation into geo-economic integration,' which, in the context of 'stable Indo-Pak relations' would have to take cognizance of the 'Kashmir dispute (which) is obviously at the head of this problem', adding that 'without (its) resolution through peaceful means', the process of sub-continental rapprochement 'will always remain susceptible to derailment due to politically motivated bellicosity.' However, Bajwa observed, 'it is time to bury the past and move forward.'[69]

It was not immediately evident if Bajwa was speaking for the entire senior military leadership. Discordant voices of hard-line former diplomats evinced at a seminar later (Islamabad, May 3, 2021) seemed to belie such a conclusion.[70] PM Imran Khan also kept repeating *ad nauseum* that no dialogue with India was possible till India's August 19, 2019 changes in Jammu & Kashmir were reversed. 'The pall bearers of Pakistan's foreign policy—the GHQ as represented by General Qamar Javed Bajwa, Prime Minister's Office as represented by Imran Khan and the Foreign Office as represented by Shah Mahmood Qureshi' seemed to be 'on different pages.'[71]

Moeed Yusuf Appointed NSA

On May 18, 2021, the PMO announced that the National Security Adviser's (NSA) office was being revived and Moeed Yusuf, Special Assistant, was being re-designated as the NSA in the rank of a Cabinet Minister. This decision seemed to have the nod of the military establishment.

It may be recalled that in Moeed's earlier incarnation at the United States Institute of Peace (USIP), his academic work, '*Brokering Peace in Nuclear Environment: US crisis management in South Asia* (Stanford, 2018)' received considerable scholarly acclaim. In it, he develops an interesting theory of 'three-way brokered bargaining', describing 'how regional rivals and a third party intermediary seek to influence each other to behave in line with their crisis objectives.'[72]

Moeed's long stint with USIP (2010-2019) may stand him in good stead in Pakistan's interactions with the new Biden Administration in the USA. Unusually, even as the PM and Foreign Minister Quereshi were abroad, Moeed took a special flight to Geneva on May 23, 2021, to meet his American counterpart, Jake Sullivan, where matters of future mutual co-operation were discussed.[73] Despite strenuous denials, speculation persisted about the USA wanting base facilities in Pakistan after their withdrawal from Afghanistan. Reports of a secret visit to Islamabad by CIA Chief William Burns during this period (mid-May–early June 2021) and his calls on the Army Chief and DG, ISI were not denied.[74]

In the foreseeable future, Moeed would be the civilian face of this hybrid dispensation, as also perhaps, in any track II interaction with India.[75] However, in the context of persisting instability on Pakistan's domestic front, an observer claimed, Moeed 'has been told to fasten his seat belt, if he is to stay on, and prepare for a rocky ride.'[76]

National Security Policy (NSP)

In December 2021, Moeed Yusuf dutifully came up with a 'National Security Policy' which was passed with much fanfare by Imran Khan's Cabinet, without making public its contents. The public was sanctimoniously told a sanitised version thereof would be revealed shortly. It was not immediately clear to what extent the Army was on board its contours and contents.

Intended to improve Pakistan's international image, of a security state in transition towards economic security and human development, it contained several pious hopes and clichéd security jargon which promised progress in the right direction without providing adequate substance on how to reach these goals.

Opposition politicians like former Senate Chairman Raza Rabbani tellingly pointed out that the National Assembly and Senate were bypassed before its formulation. There was no consultation or discussion on the floor of either legislature.

Though wishing to improve relations with India, the NSP talks of 'India's hegemonistic designs', 'the rise of Hindutva-driven politics' and 'political exploitation of a policy of belligerence towards Pakistan by India's leadership', which 'has led to the threat of military adventurism and non-contact warfare.' This is not just Moeed Yusuf wanting to prove more loyal than the King but a reiteration of unchanged, age-old mindsets of animosity that have characterized policy making in Pakistan.[77]

Bajwa's '*Iftari*' Inter-action with Journalists

On April 23, 2021, Gen Bajwa met about twenty Pakistani journalists in an 'off the record' *iftari* (daily fast breaking event during the Muslim holy month of Ramzan) briefing, where he spoke about various contemporary topics, including the recent India-Pakistan Track II initiative which led to the reiteration of the Line of Control (LoC)/International Border (IB) ceasefire agreement in February 2021. He also repeated his 'new security thinking' prioritizing 'geo-economics', outlined in the Islamabad Security Dialogue (ISD).[78] The discussion took place at the Inter Services Public Relations (ISPR) premises. Interestingly enough, the DG, ISI, Lt. Gen Faiz Hamid, was not present during this inter-action though other senior Army officers, including the DG Military Intelligence (DGMI), Maj Gen Azhar Waqas, who belongs to Bajwa's own Baloch Regiment, were.

The intention of this long 'pow-wow' with journalists could be two-fold. Some journalists gathered the impression that the Army Chief was trying to disarm them in the context of the general disenchantment that persisted about the Imran government's functioning and the apparent failure of the Army's 'Hybrid model' experiment, to foist him on the nation.[79] Others believed he was pushing for support on the new policy line indicated on India.[80] In his outburst during the Asad Toor protest (May 28, 2021), Hamid Mir had hinted at 'the apparent absence of a consensus in Pakistani civil society, and perhaps even within the Army', on Bajwa's efforts to craft a 'paradigm shift' on India's policy.[81]

Army Postings, Transfers

On the postings/transfers front, Gen Bajwa appeared in control over his flock of senior Generals. Only one Lieutenant General retired in April, 2021. Retirements of three Lieutenant Generals were due in October, 2021. An impending change in the ISI did not fructify.[82]

After Hamid Mir's insinuations during the Asad Toor protest, about a General's wife having shot at him, fingers were pointed against DG (ISI), Lt Gen Faiz Hamid. His controversial visit to Justice (retd) Shaukat Siddiqui's home, came up in the latter's written deposition before the Supreme Court (June 08, 2021). In consequence, Faiz Hamid's chances of making it to the top slot in November 2022 may have dimmed.[83] One view was that Gen Bajwa had made his own job more difficult, as public controversies about senior officers erupted, making it more complicated to post or promote them.[84]

DG ISI Transfer

Serious differences of opinion emerged between PM Imran Khan and Army Chief Gen Bajwa in October, 2021 on the appointment of a new ISI chief. On October 6, the ISPR notified that Lt Gen Faiz Hamid would be going as XI Corps Commander to Peshawar while Lt Gen Nadeem Ahmed Anjum, V Corps Commander, Karachi, would be coming in as the new DG, ISI.[85] The Prime Minister's Office refrained, however, from formally notifying this change. This impasse persisted over three weeks and led to intense speculation about civil-military relations entering a new phase of confrontation in the days to come.[86]

The takeover by Lt Gen Nadeem Ahmed Anjum as Director-General, Inter Services Intelligence (ISI), occurred eventually on November 20, apparently bringing to a close the unseemly spat that occurred between Army Chief Gen Qamar Javed Bajwa and Prime Minister Imran Khan over the held-up October 6 chain of Lieutenant General transfers. Farewell calls of Lt Gen Faiz Hameed on the President, Prime Minister and Foreign Minister were unusually played up in the media before his departure to the XI Corps assignment in Peshawar. In sharp contrast, there was complete silence on Anjum's advent.

All manner of speculation surfaced in the interim, about the rupture in civil-military relations and options for change being considered at either end. The name of Lt Gen Muhd Abdul Aziz, IV Corps commander, Lahore, senior-most among Lieutenant Generals, floated briefly for Army Chief, in case Imran took the drastic step of sacking Bajwa prematurely. This rumour did not gather much traction, no doubt, because the collegiate group of senior Generals remained steadfast in support of the incumbent Chief.

Predictably, questions came up about a new 'patch up' deal to restore the 'same page' between the Army and its 'hybrid' protégé, through another extension to Gen Bajwa in November 2022.

Under the amended Army Act, the Army Chief can continue till he is 64 years old. Though Bajwa would get two more years, such an extension would be very unpopular within the Army, as 16 more Lieutenant Generals would retire before a new Chief came in. If Imran Khan continues as Prime Minister till the end of his term as PM in July, 2023, Lt Gen Faiz Hameed would be the front runner to become COAS, after he completes one year at the Peshawar Corps command. However, his closeness to the PM may rankle with senior Generals, who dislike excessive military kowtowing to civilians.

Subsequent months have witnessed an undercurrent of persisting sullenness and tension in relations between Army Chief Gen Bajwa and Prime Minister Imran Khan.

Judiciary–Establishment Relations

In November 2021, the Higher Judiciary suddenly flexed its muscle, urging the Prime Minister to appear in the Supreme Court while petitions of aggrieved parents of the Army Public School, Peshawar, calamity of December 2014 were being heard. Angry judges asked why no FIRs were filed against those at the helm, including the Army Chief, Gen Raheel Sharif and DG, ISI, Lt Gen Zaheer-ul-Islam. The PM's appearance proved to be more of a distraction.

Supreme Court Review of Qazi Isa Reference

In a significant development, on April 26, 2021, a 10-member Supreme Court bench accepted Justice Qazi Faiz Isa's review petition against the Presidential reference on his wife's assets abroad, which were referred for enquiry to the Federal Board of Revenue (FBR) in an earlier Supreme Court decision in June 2020.[87] This would not be required now. The Supreme Court Bar Council and other Provincial Bars added supportive petitions in Qazi Isa's case and the judgement this time was split 6 to 4, with the senior-most Judge and next Chief Justice-designate, Umar Atta Bandial, ruling in the minority. In a move smacking of the government's desperation,[88] a review petition was sought to be filed against this judgement, which was not accepted.[89]

Despite the well-known dislike of Qazi Faiz Isa within the senior Army leadership, they 'have not been able to get rid of him' so far. In December 2021, Justice Isa's wife, Sarina complained again about military and civilian intelligence officials harassing her and family members in Karachi with some enquiries. 'The last thing they would want is to have the next general elections during the Qazi's watch, which begins in September 2023, just a month after the dissolution of the National Assembly and the beginning of the election cycle is due.'[90]

Shaukat Siddiqui Case

Hearings in the Supreme Court during the appeal of dismissed Islamabad High Court Judge, Shaukat Siddiqui, saw allegations re-surfacing, of visits by senior intelligence personnel to homes of judges, apparently to influence verdicts. This brought into the open once again the problems that the Judiciary continues to face in its relationship with the Army.[91]

Doubts on Saqib Nisar's Bias

Former Gilgit Baltistan Judge, Rana Shamim's affidavit, signed curiously enough before a public notary in London, alleged that former Chief Justice Saqib Nisar had suggested harsher judgments against former PM Nawaz Sharif and his daughter, Maryam. An audio clip to that effect was leaked though its authenticity has been denied. Much to media consternation, Justice Minallah at the Islamabad High Court deemed this to be a contempt matter against journalists who raked up the issue.

Fiery speeches by lawyers at the Asma Jehangir memorial conference in Lahore (November 20) berated the Army's repeated interruptions of democracy in Pakistan, leading an upset Chief Justice Gulzar Ahmed to remonstrate that judicial independence remained unfettered! A speech by exiled former PM Nawaz Sharif was delivered virtually at its concluding session, despite abortive Internet disruptions.

Release of Hamza and Shehbaz Sharif on Bail

In February 2021, Hamza Shehbaz, son of former Punjab Chief Minister, Shehbaz Sharif was released on bail by the Lahore High Court after spending 20 months in Kot Lakhpat jail, Lahore, under arrest by the National Accountability Bureau (NAB) in a money laundering investigation.[92]

This was followed, on April 14, 2021 by another bail order releasing Shehbaz Sharif, which was initially kept in abeyance as one of the judges refrained from signing it. A larger bench had to be constituted to confirm Shehbaz's bail nine days later![93]

The Lahore High Court (LHC) granted Shehbaz Sharif conditional permission to travel abroad for medical treatment from May 8 to July 3, 2021, and directed that his name be removed from the Exit Control List (ECL) forthwith. However, when he tried to take a flight from Lahore to Doha, Qatar, on May 8, he was prevented from boarding, as his name had not been removed from the ECL.

Hudaibiya Scam Enquiry to Re-open?

In a step aimed to keep the Sharifs under pressure, Prime Minister Imran Khan ordered a re-opening of investigations in the Hudaibiya Paper Mills money laundering case.[94] It may be recalled that after Musharraf's coup in October 1999, Sharif's relative, Finance Minister Ishaq Dar, had confessed to massive siphoning of funds abroad from loans taken by the PML (N) government for this project in 1992. Dar later reneged from this confession, holding before courts that they had been obtained under duress. Later, in October, 2018, a three-judge bench of the Supreme Court deemed the case time barred.[95] One legal view was that the case could be reopened only if new information connected to the substance of allegations in the case is now brought before the Judiciary.[96]

Miltablishment's Search for Other Viable 'Hybrid' Alternatives and PDM Revival

Even as 'the indiscreet charm of Imran Khan seemed to be wearing thin' where 'he was looking more like a modern-day Don Quixote, with his team of punters tilting at the windmills,'[97] Shehbaz Sharif's release on bail set rumour mills churning, indicating a possible search by the Military establishment for alternatives under the 'Hybrid model.' Mainstream political parties sought to make adjustments to their political strategies in the space which seemed to have emerged due to these developments.

Despite persisting tension between the PPP and the PML (N), efforts were revived to get the Opposition to coalesce again under the PDM umbrella. Shehbaz Sharif held a dinner reception (Islamabad, May 24) to forge Opposition consensus on strategies during the ensuing Budget.[98] On May 29, 2021, Maulana Fazlur Rehman, JuI-F leader, announced that the PDM would start a fresh phase of anti-government protests from July 4, with a demonstration in Swat (KP).[99]

PTI

Having sensed the possibilities of an early election, PTI Planning Minister Asad Umar threatened that Imran Khan would rather "dissolve" the assemblies and call for fresh elections rather than be kicked out in this manner. He was not ready to "take dictation" or abandon his quest to root out corruption by giving an NRO to the `corrupt' PPP and PML-N leaders.[100]

Jehangir Tareen's 'Like-minded Group' in PTI

In what was seen as a serious setback to PTI's stability, a like-minded group of supporters of Jehangir Tareen, an erstwhile close associate of PM Imran Khan, was formed within the party. The question was, would the government last if 6-7 of its members from the National Assembly pulled away support?

Between 31 to 40 PTI MNAs and MPAs from Punjab met in Lahore (May 18, 2021).[101] Saeed Akbar Nawani, MPA, would lead it in the Punjab Assembly. At the national level, one of its main protagonists, Raja Riaz, claimed, grievances of the group were still being addressed. Their main grouse was against the PM's Special Assistant on Accountability, Shahzad Akbar.[102] Examining the veracity of these complaints, Senator Ali Zafar told PM Imran Khan he could not find much substance to prosecute Jehangir Tareen for any claimed irregularities.[103]

Meanwhile, 'I am with Imran' tweets surfaced from handles of National Assembly Speaker Asad Qaiser and another Imran loyalist, Planning Minister Asad Omar.

On May 21, the Nawani group of MPAs met Punjab CM, Usman Buzdar in Lahore to present their grievances, which were apparently discussed in a cordial atmosphere. This led some media analysts to suggest that the 'storm in a tea cup'[104] had ended and the PTI factional rift 'had lost steam.'[105] Other observers were less sanguine, however, and felt that the fault-lines within the PTI in Punjab had only deepened, 'because the wounds that caused the original rupture' were 'still bleeding.'[106]

PPP

The PPP won a by-election in Karachi and seemed poised to hold on to their rural Sindh bastion, whenever elections are held next. If they could then win back a small presence in the Seraiki areas of Punjab, they could be back in contention as an alternative under the Army's new 'hybrid model' quest. To achieve 'these very well defined objectives,' the PPP realises, 'they will require some facilitation from the elephant in the room (read Miltablishment).'[107] Reports surfaced in the media, about Zardari's parleys with the military establishment, suggesting the Bilawal Bhutto Zardari option as interim PM, if the Army decided to dump Imran. Zardari camped in Lahore to ensure a strong PPP showing in the NA 133 Lahore by-election.

PML (N)

PML (N) cadres seemed to be faced with a more complex choice. Despite their Karachi by-election loss, the morale of PML (N) supporters remained buoyant. Nawaz Sharif's narrative of 'vote ko izzat do' (respect the mandate) continued to draw huge support, especially in the Punjab. Most party supporters realised this would be the key factor, whenever elections are held next. Yet, neither Maryam nor Nawaz seemed acceptable to the Army at present.

With Shehbaz Sharif's return to the domestic political firmament a 'softening of the party leadership's position' regarding interaction with the military establishment became apparent.[108] 'Clear signs of a thaw in the extremely cool relations between the PML (N) and the military establishment', could be seen, '(though) without any confirmed reports of direct, behind the scenes contact between Nawaz Sharif and key figures representing the institutions.'[109] Several leaders, including former Prime Minister, Shahid Khaqan Abbasi and Maryam Nawaz's spokesperson, Mohammad Zubair, acknowledged that 'relations had improved.'[110] Shehbaz Sharif seemed to be emerging finally, 'as the man in charge, on the ground.' Confronted by talk of burgeoning differences between Maryam and Shehbaz Sharif, a well-regarded political analyst claimed, 'in some strange way, both the narratives work well with the party, when they prepare to go for elections.'[111]

Chaudhry Nisar Ali Returns to Punjab Politics

Though no longer formally a PML (N) member now and with his personal equations frayed with Nawaz Sharif,[112] former Interior Minister Chaudhry Nisar Ali decided, after almost three years, to return to the Punjab Provincial Assembly and take oath as MPA in the vacant PP 10 Rawalpindi seat. He had figured several times in the past as a bridge between the PML (N) and the Army though it seemed unlikely that he could emerge again as a major political player in the present scenario, or even as an independent option in Punjab politics.

As time passed without the military establishment pulling the rug from beneath Imran Khan's feet, the inevitability of his survival for a full electoral term, lasting till July 2023, started to stare more realistically in the face of most political opponents.[113]

After two bills could not be passed in the National Assembly and a planned joint session of Parliament had to be deferred on November 11, for lack of support from the ruling Pakistan Tehrik-e-Insaf (PTI)'s allies, Opposition parties appeared buoyant about the Military establishment's new found impartiality in domestic politics. The Chaudhries of Gujrat, Pervez Elahi and Shujaat Hussain, criticised the PTI for ill-treating their Pakistan Muslim League (Quaid-e-Azam) (PML-Q) workers in Punjab. Governor Mohd Sarwar joined the chorus of criticism.

The Opposition's Pakistan Democratic Movement (PDM) announced a revised schedule of public rallies in Karachi, Quetta, Peshawar and Lahore, culminating in a 'Long March' to Islamabad to protest against high inflation and continued mismanagement of the economy by the Imran Khan administration. Before tabling a possible vote of no-confidence against the PTI government, they toyed with the idea of a 'get Sanjrani' operation, to remove the Senate Chairman or Speaker in the National Assembly, Asad Qaiser, first.

However, this optimism proved short-lived as the joint session was held on November 17, 2021, comfortably passing 33 bills including controversial ones introducing electronic voting machines and empowering overseas Pakistanis to vote. Legislators ruefully acknowledged having 'been brought' to the joint session, familiarly receiving telephone calls from the ISI urging them to attend.

Gwadar Fishermen's Agitation

Through the last six months, a sit-in agitation by Gwadar's fishermen, supported also by their womenfolk, simmered in Balochistan. Cudgels for the Gwadar fishermen were taken up by Maulana Hidayat-ur-Rehman, a resident of Surbandar, an outlying village near the old city He is a Jamaat-e-Islami cleric, known through his 'Gwadar ko Huqooq do' (Give rights to Gwadar) rally.

They were protesting against 'illegal fishing activity' by trawlers, believed to be Chinese, equipped with latest fishing techniques, which left them hungry, poor and weak against the powerful trawlers. For months they failed to find fish to sell, posing a grave threat to their livelihood. Though China has officially denied their presence, these trawlers still remain on the high seas.

Securitisation of the city precincts is another problem. Sporadic attacks against Chinese personnel by Baloch insurgents belonging to the Baloch Republican Army (BRA) and Baloch Liberation Army (BLA) have taken place from 2003 onwards, intensifying in later years. A large number of checkposts have sprung up, which subject locals to harassment. Removal of these has been one of the demands voiced by the agitating fishermen.

On December 10, 2021, the situation escalated after the police arrested veteran Baloch politician, Mir Yousaf Masti Khan, for an allegedly inflammatory 'anti-State' speech at the Gwadar sit-in. Belatedly, Prime Minister Imran Khan extended an assurance to stop fishing by foreign trawlers. The agitators dispersed thereafter.

Symptomatic of a larger malaise, where top-down development is forced down the throats of a hapless people, in utter disregard of age-old economic practices, employment patterns and cultural habits, the agitation reflected six years of disappointment with Chinese investments expected to benefit the area. Nothing has changed for the locals, who continue to struggle with endemic water shortages, massive unemployment and spreading destitution. Inadequate planning by the State to cope with infrastructural shortfalls and haste to consolidate geo-strategic gains, if only to oblige a domineering China, have led to administrative bungling and slowing down of projects under the CPEC.

Whither 'Hybrid Model'?

Several academics and quasi-liberal intelligentsia have of late expressed concern, bemoaning the imperfect democratic experiment underway in Pakistan.

In a classic denouement, Advocate Babbar Sattar wrote, 'The Military's role in politics is a matter of governance design.' It 'impacts the Constitution and rule of law in this country, to democracy, to separation of powers, sustainable institutional evolution, and to the military.' Sattar exasperatedly asked, `Do we wish to entrench and legitimize this hybrid model as our *de jure* system of governance? Or are we still justifying the hybrid model on grounds of necessity?'[114]

Identifying three types of the so-called 'hybrid model', Sattar enumerated 'the back-to-barracks mode', which never happened, 'the pulling-strings-from-behind-the-curtain mode', where the Army controlled only key decisions and left day-to-day governance to an elected civilian regime, and 'the selector or umpire mode', where the Army is called upon to act as an arbiter in overseeing distribution of power between political actors or resolve conflicts between institutions. In the current dispensation, Sattar felt, the military has become 'an active partner in day-to-day governance.'[115]

Another Pakistani scholar based abroad suggested 'the military has tried to sustain this carefully curated halfway house between democracy and dictatorship by curbing every avenue of dissent and opposition.' It has 'used its rivalry with India to legitimize its political and economic power and place itself above reproach', and now they 'run the country from behind the thinnest façade of civilian rule Pakistan has ever seen.'[116]

Castigating the Army leadership in no uncertain terms, outspoken Pakistani Police officer Tariq Khosa observed, 'Frequent military rule has resulted in erosion of democratic institutions', leading to 'constant tension and an undercurrent of mistrust between the military and civilian leadership.' While the military projects itself 'as defender of national interests, leaders of political parties, feudal barons and business tycoons are perceived (only) as defenders of special interests.' Criticizing the extension given to Gen Bajwa, Khosa added, 'If they (the political leadership) think that by giving extension in service to army chiefs, they can attain stability of tenure and promote the mantra of civilian and military on the same page, they are sadly mistaken.'[117]

Academic and former civil servant Ayesha Siddiqa saw two sets of relationships emerging: '(a) between military governments and the civil bureaucracy; and (b) between political regimes and the civil bureaucracy, which suffered from a 'trust deficit at both ends.' She claimed, 'Pakistan's political class never built a partnership with the civil bureaucracy to push back interference from the military.'[118]

The nature of this crisis seemed 'fundamentally different from apparently similar ones in the past when political parties used to vie with, even conspire against, one another for favours of the Miltablishment.'[119] The process now presaged 'a historic role reversal', where the Army's failures in imposing different hybrid models were being questioned by discerning critics in civil society. These developments were 'riven with deep contradictions and conflicts', that are spawning a 'new round of instability and uncertainty.'[120]

Pakistan's economy continues to cause serious concern. Inflation has hit the common man badly as essential commodity prices remain high. The rupee continues to slide downwards against the dollar (currently, @ Rs. 175 or lower to $ 1). An increase in electricity tariffs is imminent. Pakistan Muslim League's (Nawaz) former Finance Minister, Miftah Ismail, criticised the State Bank's latest decision to raise benchmark interest rates to 8.75 per cent as 'catastrophic.' None of the government's managers seems to have cogent remedies for a bail out.

Army-Civilian 'Same Page' Rupture

Lack of trust and sullenness persist in civil-military ties. The terror attacks on Frontier Corps outposts in Panjgur and Nushki by Baloch National Army rebels in early February, 2022, added to pressure on the Army leadership. Unusually, Gen Bajwa had to brief the President and PM on the same day (February 14).[121] How much of a long rope the Army leadership gives to the Imran Khan government may depend on a variety of complex factors—whether Imran Khan is determined to foist Lt Gen Faiz Hamid as the new Army Chief on an unhappy group of Generals in November 2022 or even earlier, or whether he buys peace by offering Gen Bajwa another extension, which may be equally unpopular;

whether the collegiate leadership of Army Generals realises it has had enough of the opprobrium that devolves on them, for failed 'hybrid' constructs of a democratic façade in Pakistan, and instead, lets normal politics revive and allows free and fair elections.

PDM Decides to Move No-confidence Motion against PM

After a flurry of meetings in Lahore between PML (N) leader, Shehbaz Sharif, the PPP's Asif and Bilawal Bhutto Zardari, and Maulana Fazlur Rehman of the JuI (F), on February 11, 2022, the PDM announced its decision to introduce a vote of no-confidence in the National Assembly against the incumbent PTI government soon.[122] Two separate 'Long March' dates were announced by the PPP on February 27 and by the PDM, on March 23. There seemed to be some uncertainty still, about the numbers of MNAs needed in this regard, as conventional wisdom reported the Government's numbers to be 182 and the combined Opposition's 162 currently, but with a varying number of about 20-30 MNAs waiting and ready to switch support on signals from the 'right quarters.'

The question that looms before Pakistan's civil society is how long it will remain prepared to cynically bear with current standards and practices of governance under such 'hybrid' constructs? All portends are that we may not get an early answer. 'The Ides of March (2022)' seem to have arrived, though it is still not clear for whom 'the bell tolls', or when.

ENDNOTES

1. Cyril Almeida, 'Pakistan politics foiled by familiar triangle-Military, Govt, Opposition', Report for United States Institute of Peace (USIP), 16 December 2020.
2. Irfan Mahar, An Evaluation of the Performance of Imran Khan's Government, *Eurasia Review*, 16 March 2021, www.eurasiareview.com
3. Zirgham Nabi Afridi, 'Saving the PTI (Part II)', *The News*, 8 May 2021; www.thenews.com.pk
4. Fahd Hussain, 'Winds of change', *Dawn*, 12 April 2021; www.dawn.com
5. Zirgham Nabi Afridi, op cit., Saving the PTI (Part I), *The News*, 7 May 2021, www.the news.com.pk
6. Najam Sethi, 'Droning the countdown', *The Friday Times*, 7 May 2021, www.thefriday times.com;
7. Ansar Abbasi, 'Stepping back from the brink', *The News*, 21 May 2021, www.thenews.com.pk
8. Najam Sethi, op cit., 'Droning the countdown', *The Friday Times*, 7 May 2021, www.the fridaytimes.com
9. *Pakistan Today*, op cit., 'One-sided accountability', 25 January 2021, www.pakistantoday.cm.pk
10. Tariq Khosa, 'A reform agenda', *Dawn*, 20 May 2021, www.dawn.com
11. Khurram Hussain, 'The wages of truth', *Dawn*, 20 May 2021, www.dawn.com
12. Khurram Hussain, 'Quagmire', *Dawn*, 13 February 2020, www.dawn.com
13. Shahbaz Rana, 'Circular debt hits CPEC projects', *The Express Tribune*, 9 May 2021,

www.tribune.com.pk
14. Khaleeq Kiani, 'Problems in Power sector', *Dawn*, 15 July 2020, www.dawn.com
15. Shahid Iqbal, 'SBP fully backs 3.94% growth estimate', *Dawn*, 25 May 2021, www.dawn.com
16. Fahd Hussain, 'Waging the data war', *Dawn*, 5 July 2021, www.dawn.com
17. *Express Tribune*, 11 June 2021, www.tribune.com.pk
18. Khurram Hussain, 'Something for everybody in budget—except IMF', *Dawn*, 12 June 2021, www.dawn.com
19. Amir Wasim, 'Opposition blasts govt in NA over bill...', *Dawn*, 30 December 2021, www.dawn.com
20. Pervez Hoodbuoy, What Imran Khan is doing to Pakistani school textbooks even Zia-ul-Haq didn't, *Dawn*, 18 July 2020, www.dawn.com
21. Zirgham Nabi Afridi, op cit., Saving the PTI (Part I), *The News*, 07 May 2021, www.thenews.com.pk
22. Fahd Hussain, op cit., *Dawn*, www.dawn.com
23. Malik Asad, 'Provincial bureaucrats up in arms against centre's move', *Dawn*, 16 March 2021, www.dawn.com
24. Saqib Virk, *Express Tribune*, 3 June 2021, www.tribune.com.pk
25. Najam Sethi, 'Droning the Countdown', *The Friday Times*, 7 May 2021, www.the fridaytimes.com
26. Article by Author: Rediff.com, 21 January 2021, www.rediff.com/news/column/rana-banerji-pakistan-tries-to-cement-ties-with-saudi-arabia/20210121.htm
27. *Dawn* Editorial, 'Foreign Service Officers miffed at Imran jab', 9 May 2021, www.dawn.com
28. Baqir Sajjad Syed, 'Imran retracts...', *Dawn*, 12 May 2021, www.dawn.com
29. Bashir Memon, Interview on Matiullah Jan TV Channel, 6 October 2020, dawn.com, www.dawn.com
30. Ansar Abbasi, 'Wajid Zia's removal routine affair or result of administrative mess', *The News*, 10 June 2021, www.thenews.com.pk
31. Zirgham Nabi Afridi, op cit., *The News*, www.thenews.com.pk
32. Tahir Imran Miah, 'PIA's plane truths', *Dawn*, 7 February 2021, www.dawn.com
33. Wikipedia, Broadsheet case, accessed on 8 May 2021.
34. RSF-Dokument #2029300: Ecoi.net-Umfrage2021
35. Aqil Shah, 'Will Pakistan's Military Lose Its Grip on Power?', *Foreign Affairs*, 22 December 2020.
36. Article by Author, 'Why a Pakistani Colonel was kidnapped', Rediff, 28 August 2020, www.rediff.com
37. *Express Tribune*, SECP official goes missing, 5 September 2020, www.tribune.com.pk
38. Ahmed Noorani, Fact Focus:'Bajwafamily business empire grew in four countries in sync with Asim Bajwa's rise in Military', 27 August 2020, https:/factfocus.com/politics/1756
39. Malik Asad, 'Missing SECP official returns home after 5 days', *Dawn*, 8 September 2020, www.dawn.com
40. Amnesty International, 'Where is Idris Khattak', Petition for release: November, 2020, www.amnesty international.org
41. Naziha Syed Ali, Target on their backs: Media in chains—the cost of speaking truth to power, *Dawn*, 3 May 2021, www.dawn.com
42. Akram Shaheedi, 'Value dissent, not silence', *The News*, 28 April 2020, www.thenews.com.pk
43. *Express Tribune*, News desk, 26 May 2021, www.tribune.com.pk
44. Cyril Almeida tweet, @cyalm, 26 May 2021.
45. MJ TV, 28 May 2021, mjtvnewslive @youtube.com

46. *Dawn*, 1 June 2021, www.dawn.com
47. Huma Yusuf, 'Attempt to gag', *Dawn*, 31 May 2021, www.dawn.com
48. Rizwan Shamshad, 'Upper House polls—PTI may dominate,but not control Senate polls', *Express Tribune*, 10 February 2021, www.tribune.com.pk
49. *Pakistan Today*, 'SC upholds secret ballot for Senate elections', 1 March 2021, www.pakistantoday.com.pk
50. *The News*, Web desk, 3 March 2021, www.thenews.com.pk
51. *Dawn*, 'COAS, ISI Chief call on PM, Imran Khan', *Dawn*, 5 March 2021, www.dawn.com
52. Tahir Naseer, 'IHC dismisses Gilani's petition', *Dawn*, 24 March 2021, www.dawn.com
53. *Dawn*, 'PTI makes major gains but suffers setback in Islamabad', 11 March 2021, www.dawn.com
54. Amir Wasim, 'PML-N, PPP spar over Senate Opposition leader slot', *Dawn*, 22 March 2021, www.dawn.com
55. *Dawn*, 27 December 2021, www.dawn.com
56. Geo TV, Election reforms in Pakistan, 4 May 2021, www.geotv.com
57. *Express Tribune*, 4 June 2021, www.tribune.com.pk
58. Wikipedia, accessed on 9 May 2021.
59. Salman Masood, 'Pakistani PM warns of plotting by Military', *New York Times*, 22 December 2011, https://www.nytimes.com/2011/12/23/world/asia/pakistani-premier-yousaf-raza-gilani-lashes-out-at-his-military.html
60. *Dawn*, 'Struggle not against Imran Khan...', 20 September 2020, www.dawn.com
61. Cyril Almeida, op cit., 'Pakistan politics foiled by familiar triangle—Military, Govt, Opposition', Report for USIP, Dec. 2020.
62. Najam Sethi, 'Good boys, bad boys', *The Friday Times*, 30 October 2020, www.thefridaytimes.com
63. *The Daily Guardian*, 'Crisis in Pakistan as Sindh Police rise in revolt against Army', 22 October 2020, www.thedailyguardian.com
64. Mazhar Abbas, 'Political significance of Sindh IGP incident', *The News*, 27 October 2020, www.thenews.com.pk
65. Najam Sethi, 'Labaik, labaik, labaik', *The Friday Times*, 23 April 2021, www.thefriday times.com
66. Najam Sethi, op. cit.
67. Afrasiab Khattak Twitter, 4 June 2021, "#ReleaseManzoorPashteen", @twitter
68. Sirajuddin, 'PTM's Manzoor Pashteen released nearly 8 hours after being detained', *Dawn*, 5 June 2021, www.dawn.com
69. *Express Tribune*, 19 March 2021, www.tribune.com.pk
70. *Dawn*, 'Experts air concern over backchannel engagements with India', 4 May 2021, www.dawn.com
71. Najam Sethi, 'A wink or a nod', *The Friday Times*, 14 May 2021, www.thefridaytimes.com
72. P. Sahadevan, 'Book review', 22 December 2019, https://journals.sagepub.com/doi/10.1177/0020881719885527
73. Sanaullah Khan, 'In first meeting, Pakistan and US NSAs discuss bilateral issues, ways to advance cooperation', *Dawn*, 24 May 2021: www.dawn.com
74. Mark Mazetti & Julian Barnes, 'CIA scrambles for new approach in Afghanistan', *New York Times*, 6 June 2021, www.nytimes.com
75. *Express Tribune*, Kamran Yousuf, 'NSA Office revived amid Pak-India rapprochement push', 19 May 2021, www.tribune.com.pk
76. *The Friday Times*, 'Such Gup' column', 'Pack to fly', May 2021, www.thefridaytimes.com

77. Article by author: Pakistan's National Security Policy: Why this will be just another eyewash and not make any reversal of policy direction, https://www.firstpost.com/world/*First Post*, 28 January 2022.
78. Nirupama Subramanian, 'In build up to ceasefire, NSA Doval met ISI chief in UAE, *Indian Express*, 28 April 2021: www.indianexpress.com
79. Mohd Ziauddin : Comments to Naya Daur TV channel, 'Bajwa's Iftar Dinner was a Grand PR Exercise to Influence Media', 26 April 2021, https://nayadaur.tv:www.unewstv.com
80. Hamid Mir, Remarks made at Asad Toor protest, op cit., *MJ TV*, 28 May 2021, mjtvnewslive @youtube.com
81. Nirupama Subramanian, 'In Pakistan turmoil over journalist's beating, a curious subtext', https://indianexpress.com/article/explained/Pakistan-journalists-military-establishment-hamid-mir-asad-ali-toor-general-bajwa-7338965/
82. Article by author, 'When will ISI get a new boss?', 5 April 2021, https://www.rediff.com/news/column/rana-banerji-when-will-isi-boss-be-elevated/20210405.htm
83. Nirupama Subramanian, op cit., 'In Pakistan turmoil over journalist's beating, a curious subtext', https://indianexpress.com/article/explained/Pakistan-journalists-military-establishment-hamid-mir-asad-ali-toor-general-bajwa-7338965/
84. Pakistani Defence Historian, based abroad, Private communication with author, 6 June 2021.
85. ISPR, https:/ispr.gov.pk: No. IR-166.2021-06.10.2021
86. Fahd Hussain, 'Is the party over?', *Dawn*, 16 October 2021, www.dawn.com; Najam Sethi, Downhill, *The Friday Times*, 15 October 2021, www.thefridaytimes.com
87. Haseeb Bhatti, 'SC accepts review petitions in Justice Isa presidential reference verdict', *Dawn*, 26 April 2021, www.dawn.com
88. *Dawn*, Editorial; 'A time to move on', 28 May 2021, www.dawn.com
89. Hasnaat Malik, 'Top court Registrar returns govt's review petition', *The Express Tribune*, May 27, www.tribune.com.pk
90. *The Friday Times*, 'Such Gup' column, 'Fresh Options', 7 May 2021, www.thefridaytimes.com
91. Haseeb Bhatti, 'Ex-judge denies maintaining ties with Army officers', *Dawn*, 8 June 2021, www.dawn.com
92. *The News*, 'Hamza Shehbaz released on bail', www.thenews.com.pk
93. *The News*, 'PML-N President Shahbaz Sharif released on bail', www.thenews.com.pk
94. *The News*, 'Govt to re-probe Hudaibiya case', 11 May 2021, www.thenews.com.pk
95. Hasnat Malik, 'Top Court throws out Hudaibiya Paper Mills case', *The Express Tribune*, 30 October 2018, www.tribune.com.pk
96. Aitzaz Ahsan to Kashif Abbasi, *ARY* News TV channel, 10 May 2021.
97. *The Friday Times*, 'Such Gup' column, 'Fresh Options', 7 May 2021, www.thefridaytimes.com
98. *Pakistan Today*, 'Is the ice breaking', 25 May 2021, www.pakistantoday.com.pk
99. *Express Tribune*, 30 May 2021, www.tribune.com.pk
100. *GeoTV*, May 1, www.GeoTV.com & *The Friday Times*, 'Such Gup' column, 'Sher Aya, sher aya', www.thefridaytimes.com
101. *Express Tribune*, 19 May 2021, www.tribune.com.pk
102. Capital Talk, Hamid Mir show on *Geo TV*, 19 May 2021, www.unewstv.com
103. Umar Cheema, 'Ali Zafar has concluded what the government didn't hope for', *The News*, 26 May 2021, www.thenews.com.pk
104. Naseem Zehra, 'Storm in a Tea cup', *The News*, 21 May 2021, www.thenews.com.pk
105. Mansoor Malik, 'Tareen group loses steam after Buzdar meeting', *Dawn*, 22 May 2021, www.dawn.com
106. Fahd Hussain, 'The Punjab problem, again', *Dawn*, 24 May 2021, www.dawn.com

107. Fahd Hussain, 'Elephant in the room', *Dawn*, 29 May 2021, www.dawn.com
108. Nasim Zehra, op cit., 'Storm in a Tea cup', *The News*, 21 May 2021, www.thenews.com.pk
109. Ansar Abbasi, op cit., 'Stepping back from the brink', *The News*, 21 May 2021, www.thenews.com.pk
110. Ansar Abbasi, op cit., 'Stepping back from the brink', *The News*, 21 May 2021, www.thenews.com.pk
111. Zahid Hussain, 'The PML(N)'s change of tack', *Dawn*, 26 May 2021, www.dawn.com
112. 'Such Gup' column, 'Forgive & forget?', *The Friday Times*, 28 May 2021, www.fridaytimes.com
113. Nasim Zehra, op cit., 'Storm in a Tea cup', *The News*, 21 May 2021, www.thenews.com.pk
114. Babbar Sattar, 'How to un-hybrid', *The Friday Times*, 2 October 2020, www.fridaytimes.com
115. Ibid.
116. Aqil Shah, 'Will Pakistan's Military Lose Its Grip on Power?', *Foreign Affairs*, Dec. 2020, www.foreignaffairs.com
117. Tariq Khosa, 'A reform agenda', *Dawn*, 20 May 2021, www.dawn.com
118. Ayesha Siddiqa, op. cit., 'The politician versus the bureaucracy', *The News*, 10 May 2021, www.thenews.com.pk;
119. Najam Sethi, 'Trojan horses', *The Friday Times*, 28 May 2021, www.fridaytimes.com
120. Najam Sethi, 'Trojan horses', op cit., www.thefridaytimes.com
121. *Dawn*, 15 February 2022, www.dawn.com
122. *The News*, 12 February 2022, www.thenws.com.pk

2

Pakistan's Ethnic Fault-lines[1]

Tilak Devasher

Pakistan is a cauldron of fault-lines: from political to economic, from religious to social, from ethnic to developmental, there is a full menu to choose from. Among all these fault-lines, perhaps the most critical for Pakistan is the ethnic one. Pakistan lost half the country when the then East Pakistan broke away in 1971 and became Bangladesh, largely due to unresolved ethnic issues. This chapter assesses how Pakistan fares in keeping its other nationalities together.

The main general issue triggering ethnic resentment in Pakistan is of identity. Simply stated, into the seventh decade of its creation, there continues to be a debate over the meaning of a 'Pakistan identity.' Khalid Muhammad, a columnist, wrote in *The Nation*: '*The world may like to call us Pakistanis, but there are few within the borders of this country that identify themselves by that moniker. No, many of our citizens are ashamed to call themselves Pakistani and that is where the problems of this nation start and end. Pakistan is a divided nation to say the least. We are divided on ethnic, linguistic, political, religious, education and provincial lines. We gather together under different political flags. We pray in masjids that are 100 feet from each other because of slight differences in the way we practice Islam.*'[2]

Defining a Pakistani identity was a critical issue in 1947 and it continues to be today for at least two reasons. First, the geographical areas that came to constitute Pakistan in the East and the West of the Indian sub-continent had never before existed as a single country. At its creation, Pakistan inherited four provinces in the West (Balochistan, NWFP, Punjab and Sindh), and one in the east. East Pakistan was the most homogeneous province, ethnically and linguistically. In the west, however, there was considerable ethnic and linguistic diversity. As Selig Harrison noted aptly: '*There is no precedent in the history of South Asia for a state consisting of the five ethno-linguistic regions that made up Pakistan as originally constituted in 1947, or even for the truncated Pakistan consisting of the four regions that remained after Bangladesh seceded in 1971. The ideologues of Pakistani nationalism exalt the historical memory of [Mughal emperors] Akbar and Aurangzeb as the symbols of a lost Islamic grandeur in South Asia. By contrast, for the Balochis, Sindhis and Pashtuns, the Mughals are remembered primarily as the symbols of past oppression.*'[3]

In fact, even before the creation of Pakistan, there were significant warnings. For example, in 1944, the president of the Bengal Muslim League, Abdul Mansur Ahmed, declared in his presidential address: '*Religion and culture are not the same thing. Religion transgresses the geographical boundary but tamaddum [culture] cannot go beyond the geographical boundary. ...Here only lies the difference between 'Purba' [Eastern] Pakistan and Pakistan. For this reason, the people of Purba Pakistan are a different nation from the people of the other provinces of India and from the 'religious brothers' of Pakistan.*[4] These prophetic words became a reality with the creation of Bangladesh in 1971.

In the west, not only was there considerable ethnic and linguistic diversity but each province did not contain a single ethno-linguistic group. Thus, Balochistan had the Baloch, but also a significant number of Pashtuns in the north; NWFP had Pashtuns but also significant numbers of Hindko-speakers; Punjab, dominated by the Punjabis, had a significant Seraiki population; Sindh had Sindhis but, post-Partition, saw a massive influx of Mohajirs from India who settled in the urban areas. The challenge for the new state was to weld these different identities into one Pakistani identity.

Second, the identity had to be different and distinct from India since Pakistan had been carved out of India. India was a historical entity but Pakistan as a newly-created country with an unfamiliar name had to be acknowledged by the world as such. In a fundamental sense, as Aparna Pande notes, creating a Pakistani identity amounted to erasing any traces of 'Indian-ness' within Pakistan; '*Denying the "Indian-ness" of Pakistan's identity meant emphasizing the "Hinduness" of India and reinforcing the "Islamic" nature of Pakistan.*'[5] This why in many conversations and on TV debates, the stress is always to portray India as Hindu as opposed to a Muslim Pakistan.

To complicate matters, the new state perceived itself to be the successor of the Muslim empires in India, especially the Mughals, who had ruled India prior to the coming of the British. Unfortunately, Pakistani leaders had to face the uncomfortable reality that these Muslim empires were centred in India while Pakistan had been pushed to the periphery of those empires, to areas that did not have even a shared history. The symbols of Islamic splendour like the Taj Mahal (Agra), Red Fort (Delhi), Char Minar (Hyderabad), were in India, leaving the new state with very little to show for the proclaimed grandeur of its past. This made the task of developing a national identity even more difficult.

Reflecting the preoccupation with a definition for Pakistani identity, as late as 2000, the newspaper *Dawn* stated: '*Since its inception Pakistan has faced the monumental task to spell out an identity different from the Indian identity. Born from the division of the old civilization of India, Pakistan has struggled for constructing its own, a culture which will not only be different from the Indian culture but that the whole world would acknowledge.*'[6]

This need for distinctiveness led to the emphasis of an identity that was Islamic, taking its cue from the two-nation theory that was the philosophy behind Pakistan's creation. The two-nation theory claimed that the Muslims of the Indian subcontinent constituted a separate 'nation' which bore a distinct and potentially sovereign political identity and that religion could bind diverse ethno-linguistic identities. Continuing with the two-nation theory after Pakistan's creation generated problems of its own, the need for 'Hindu' India constantly as an essential reference point for its *raison d'être* ensured that Pakistan could not succeed in evolving a separate and positive national identity. Its national identity would continue to be a negative, anti-India narrative.[7]

While an Islamic identity was a continuation of the two-nation theory, Pak leaders felt that it would have an added advantage of potentially papering over the multiple identities of the geographical area that became Pakistan. Pakistani identity thus became based on Islam. Prof. Waheeduz-Zaman graphically enumerated Pakistan's identity dilemma in these words: '*...the wish to see the kingdom of God established in a Muslim territory was the moving idea behind the demand for Pakistan. If we let go the ideology of Islam, we cannot hold together as a nation by any other means. If the Arabs, the Turks, or the Iranians give up Islam, the Arabs yet remain Arabs, the Turks remain Turks, the Iranians remain Iranians, but what do we remain if we give up Islam*?'[8] A rhetorical answer was given in 1980: '*If we are not Muslims, what are we? Second-rate Indians*?'[9]

The problem with the emphasis of an Islamic identity was that the opportunistic use of Islam was effective in creating a country by whipping up hysteria and communal passions but was not effective as a glue to keep the country together. This was because in the area that came to constitute Pakistan, there were historical states with significant linguistic, cultural, and ethnic diversities. Here people instinctively thought of themselves as Bengalis, Baloch, Pashtuns, Seraikis, and Sindhis, rather than as Pakistanis. As noted above, even the geographical regions in the west had never before been strung together as one country. Additionally, these provinces were not even in the forefront of the Pakistan movement and had no shared history. Wali Khan, the Pashtun leader, perhaps best exemplified the identity dilemma when he said in the National Assembly, '*I have been a Pashtun for thousands of years, a Muslim for 1300 and a Pakistani for just over forty.*'[10] Clearly, for him and millions of others, the specific ethnic identity was far more important than a Pakistani identity.

Not surprisingly, the attempt of the Pakistani state to force an Islamic identity on its diverse population has come a cropper. In fact, Maulana Azad had warned Jinnah that his thesis was contrary to what Islam preached. In an interview, he said: '*It [Pakistan] is being demanded in the name of Islam.... Division of territories on the basis of religion is a contraption devised by Muslim League. They can pursue it as their political agenda, but it finds no sanction in Islam or Quran...' Strictly speaking, Muslims in India are not one community; they are divided among many well-entrenched sects. You can unite them by arousing their anti-Hindu sentiment but you cannot unite them in the name of Islam. To them Islam means undiluted loyalty to their own sect.*'[11]

In a sense, Maulana Azad foresaw that the overt use of Islam would ultimately lead to sectarianism and strife. Even otherwise, the concept of '*qaum*' (nation) in the Quran is composite. The believers and the unbelievers, according to the Quran, do not constitute separate *qaums.* They belong to one nation, one group only.[12]

Ethnic identities have also been reinforced by the simple fact that after the creation of Pakistan, the fear of a Hindu majority suppressing a minority Muslim population was taken out of the equation. Muslims were faced with the prospect of competing with other Muslims for jobs and loaves of office, and not with the Hindus. Such competition was on the basis of quotas—of language and ethnicity. Thus, once Pakistan was created, an overarching Islamic identity that had been useful against the 'Hindu' was no longer valid in a situation where a Muslim had to compete against another Muslim.

As such, into the seventh decade of its creation, Pakistan has not yet been able to establish an overarching 'Pakistani identity.' Islam was not able to supplant the linguistic, cultural and historic bonds of its diverse population leading to the alienation of different ethnic groups, despite being Muslims. Such alienation has continued to be a persistent phenomenon in Pakistan. East Pakistan broke away to become Bangladesh because for the Bengalis, language was a more important part of their identity than Islam. After East Pakistan broke away, the fear of secession by other provinces has come to haunt Pakistan's rulers. A fifth insurgency is happening in Balochistan while there is unrest among the Pashtuns and the Sindhis, despite all of them being Muslims.

Apart from religion, another instrument used by the state to forge a common identity was through centralisation, suppressing provincial aspirations and denial of provincial rights.

One of the key points of difference that Jinnah had with the Congress was his opposition to the centralised state system based on the Government of India Act of 1935. He termed it a 'dangerous scheme' and that 'it must go once and for all' because it would impose a highly centralised federal government with no room for regional autonomy.[13] Even earlier, the first point in Jinnah's fourteen points of 1929 was: 'The form of the future Constitution should be federal with the residuary powers vested in the provinces.' For Jinnah, the issue of provincial autonomy was central to keep the Muslim-majority provinces interested in the idea of Pakistan. Thus, on 8 November 1945, in an interview he gave to Associated Press of America Jinnah said: '*The component states or provinces of Pakistan would have autonomy.'... Pakistan's theory, he said, guaranteed that federated units of the national government would 'have all the autonomy that you will find in the constitutions of the USA, Canada and Australia. But certain vital powers will remain vested in the central government, such as the monetary system, national defence and other federal responsibilities.*[14]

In retrospect, this was clearly a tactic. Centralisation of power began immediately after the creation of Pakistan with Jinnah concentrating powers in himself. He was the Governor-General, President of the Constituent Assembly, president of the Muslim League and even a minister in the cabinet of his own prime minister, Liaquat Ali Khan, with the portfolio of States and Frontier Regions.[15] All pre-Partition talk of provincial autonomy was given a hasty burial. He dismissed provincial governments of the NWFP on 22 August 1947, within a week of Pakistan's creation and Sindh on 26 April 1948. In fact, he extended the 1935 Act that he had so opposed. He proclaimed: '*What we want is not talk about Bengali, Punjabi, Sindhi, Baluchi, Pathan and so on. There are of course units. But I ask you: have you forgotten the lessons that were taught us thirteen hundred years ago. You have carved out a territory, a vast territory. It is all yours: it does not belong to a Punjabi, or a Sindhi or a Pathan or a Bengali. It is all yours. You have got your central government where several units are represented. Therefore, if you want to build yourself up into a nation, for God's sake give up provincialism.*'[16]

Unfortunately for Pakistan's leaders, such attempts at centralisation had the reverse effect and were to give encouragement to provincial discontent. For example, the one-unit scheme adopted in 1955 was a crude effort of the West Pakistan elite to join all the provinces in West Pakistan in order to neutralise the electoral influence of the Bengali majority in East Pakistan. While the Bengali majority could not be neutralised, the smaller provinces of West Pakistan chafed at being denied autonomy. One consequence of centralisation was that the ruling elite did not feel the need to evolve a consensus over crucial political and economic issues like provincial autonomy, distribution of resources, etc. Policies were rammed down the throats of the smaller provinces, which only had the effect of bringing out in greater relief the multiple identities constituting Pakistan.

Jinnah's legacy of centralisation was to be followed by his successors, to the detriment of Pakistan's unity. Both Ayub Khan and Yahya Khan, being soldiers, were in any case intolerant of any dissent. They were concerned that an emphasis on the provinces would weaken central authority, undermine the concept of an Islamic Pakistan and would lead to the break-up of the country. The state machinery encouraged the imposition of cultural uniformity based on Islam. Bhutto was authoritarian by nature. His dismissal of the elected Baloch government was to lead to an uprising that lasted four years. Zia, like his uniformed predecessors, was aghast at the possibility of autonomy. According to Selig Harrison, '*...on the critical autonomy issue, Zia made it clear that he had little sympathy for the concept of a "multinational" Pakistan in which Baluch, Pushtun, Sindhis and Punjabis are entitled to self-rule.*' Zia said, '*I simply cannot understand this type of thinking. We want to build a strong country, a unified country. Why should we talk in these small-minded terms? We should talk in terms of Pakistan, one united Pakistan.*'[17] The democratic governments of Benazir Bhutto and Nawaz Sharif in the 1990s were too busy fighting with each other and ensuring their own survival to have rectified the situation.

After he overthrew Nawaz Sharif in October 1999, Musharraf started by big announcements on provincial autonomy. He promised to 'strengthen the federation, remove inter-provincial disharmony and restore national cohesion' as one of the seven-point agenda he laid out before the country.[18] However, like most of his other ideas, this too fell by the wayside. Thus, provincial autonomy was to remain a major issue in Pakistan.

A big step to resolve the issue of provincial autonomy and to restore the balance in the Constitution was taken by the eighteenth amendment to the Constitution that was adopted under the PPP government in April 2010. The amendment sought to remove the distortions in the Constitution introduced by military dictators like Zia and Musharraf that had converted Pakistan's parliamentary system into a semi-presidential one. Thus, the amendment did away with the sweeping powers of the presidency and gave a large measure of provincial autonomy, restoring the balance between the Centre and the provinces.

Even though the issue of provincial rights has, at times, got intertwined with the political wrangling between Opposition governments in the smaller provinces and the governments at the Centre and Punjab, the fact remains that provincial autonomy is not working as smoothly as it should. The reason for the scepticism is that the implementation of the devolution of power to the provinces has not taken full effect. According to Peter Jacob, 'Operating in an environment of lack of trust and lack of civil society input, the constitutional review process has been marred by bottlenecks and the failure of the government to appoint a body to supervise the devolution of ministries from the federal to the provincial level.'[19] Currently, the relations between the PTI government at the centre and the PPP government in Sindh are fraught with tensions.

At a discussion organised by the HRCP in Islamabad in September 2015, speakers highlighted that 'forces' could be trying to undo the progress made. A reference was made to two specific cases: the presence of the National Curriculum Council as an example of 'federal encroachment' and failure of the Council of Common Interests to meet regularly. According to *Dawn*, there have also been issues with division of resources and funds between Islamabad and the provinces. It has been pointed out that departments with liabilities have been handed over to the provinces, while the Centre is reluctant to let go of profitable institutions.[20] The issue of education and especially the Single National Curriculum, discussed in a later chapter, is just the latest example of the Centre trampling on provincial rights after the passage of the 18th constitutional amendment.

The moot question is why, despite the passage of almost seven decades, Pakistan has not been able to develop an overarching national identity. There is no easy answer but the fact is that the alienation of different ethnic groups is because it was not Islam that kept them united but their linguistic, cultural and historic bonds. Islam could not supersede these bonds in the same manner that it could in the Muslim-minority provinces of British India. In these provinces, especially in north India, due to their minority status, the Islamic identity was very salient. In the Muslim-majority provinces that came to constitute Pakistan, the Islamic way of life was not threatened. Thus, the effort of the post-partition elite, that was predominantly from the minority provinces of India, to transplant Muslim insecurities into the new state was to come a cropper since Islam was not in any danger.

Added to this were the exploitative policies of Punjab that led to a Punjabi–non-Punjabi divide. All this made forging an overarching Pakistani identity problematic. As Pakistan developed, the process of Islamisation, which stressed a religious (non-territorial) rather than a secular national identity, further impeded the idea of a common identity. Islamisation put the people in a dilemma concerning their identity: whether they were first Muslims and then Pakistanis, or first Pakistani and then Muslims. For example, a survey of 2,000 young Pakistanis in the 18–27 age group found that three quarters identified themselves first as Muslims and only secondly as Pakistanis. Just 14 per cent defined themselves as citizens of Pakistan first. 'This result should be no surprise,' writes Pervez Hoodbhoy. 'Pakistani schoolchildren learn to chant in unison: Pakistan ka matlab kya? La ilaha ilallah! (What is the meaning of Pakistan? There is no god but God!)'[21]

An interesting development in the identity debate has been the gradual Arabisation of the *lingua franca*, Urdu. By trying to deny its sub-continental roots, Pakistan has tried to locate them in the deserts of Arabia and the arrival of Muhammad bin Qasim in Sindh in 712. As a spin-off, there is now a linguistic struggle that reflects the identity dilemma of Pakistan. The gradual Arabisation is indicated by the replacements of sub-continental words by their Arab counterparts, like Ramzan by Ramadan, Khuda Hafiz by Allah Hafiz, namaz by Salat and even Pakistan by Al-Bakistan and now Punjab by Bunjab. Of course, the latest trend is to look for identity in Turkey.

Let us now turn to specifics.

The Baloch

Balochistan has been racked by intermittent insurgencies since 1948, with the last one continuing since 2005. The reasons for it have as much to do with its strategic location and demography as with the historical context of its accession to Pakistan, and policies of successive federal governments.

The Baloch are ancient people who had their own history, culture and identity centuries before the creation of Pakistan. Historically and legally, the princely state of Kalat (as most of Balochistan was then called) in 1947 was not really obliged to join either India or Pakistan, as were the other princely states in British

India at the time of Partition of the sub-continent. It is an irony of history that Mohd. Ali Jinnah was the lawyer of the Khan of Kalat who argued the case for Kalat's independence before the Cabinet Mission in 1946. In August 1947, just before the creation of Pakistan, Jinnah even acknowledged this in an agreement with the Khan as a result of which the Khan declared Kalat to be an independent state. However, by October 1947, Jinnah was urging the Khan to accede to Pakistan. Both Houses of the Kalat State Assembly rejected such an idea. In the Lower House, Ghaus Bux Bizenjo made his famous speech: 'We can survive without Pakistan. We can remain without Pakistan. We can prosper outside Pakistan. But the question is what Pakistan would be without us.... If Pakistan wants to treat us as a sovereign people we are ready to extend the hand of friendship and cooperation. If Pakistan does not agree to do so, flying in the face of democratic principles, such an attitude will be totally unacceptable to us, and if we are forced to accept this fate then every Baloch son will sacrifice his life in defence of his national freedom.'[22] Despite the Khan's resistance, the Pakistan army marched into Kalat and forced the Khan to sign the instrument of accession.[23]

The forced manner of the accession of the state of Kalat to Pakistan led to the strengthening of the Baloch identity and its demand for separatism. Martin Axmaan has written probably the best epitaph for Kalat: '*The death of the state was the birth of the nation. The Baloch lost their 'national homeland' and turned into a marginal ethno-linguistic minority of Pakistan. This situational switching moulded the Baloch nation.*'[24]

Second, the treatment meted out to Baloch nationalists after Kalat's accession further accentuated Baloch resentment. Dishonouring solemn pledges made on the Koran of safe passage to Baloch leaders like Abdul Karim and Nauroz Khan (who had risen in rebellion in 1948 and 1958, respectively) and executing their family members, have strengthened the Baloch identity and their distrust of the Pakistani state.

Third, the development of the Gwadar port and the China-Pakistan Economic Corridor (CPEC) provides a classic example of the insensitivity and arrogance of the federal government that has led to the alienation of the ordinary Baloch. Gwadar is the lynchpin of the CPEC, but for the Baloch it is the symbol of how wrongly they have been treated: they have not been consulted about the project; they are not the beneficiaries of the project, which will adversely alter Balochistan's demography due to the influx of non-Baloch to take up prime jobs. In short, the Baloch feel threatened by the project.

Fourth, the Baloch fear that they will become a minority in their own homeland. Balochistan is the largest province in Pakistan with 44 per cent of the land area, but has a population of only 7 per cent of the total, half of which is Pashtun. The scanty population has been an open invitation for 'settlers' raising fears of the Baloch being converted into a minority in Balochistan. Baloch fears were confirmed by advertisements in the national and even international media inviting investment into Gwadar city, which was initially visualized for 2.5 million people but later raised to five million.[25] Given that the entire population of Balochistan is only 6–7 million, Baloch apprehensions of being converted into a minority in their own homeland and their identity being wiped out are clearly justified.

Fifth, the socio-economic indicators in Balochistan are the worst in Pakistan; (i) of the Ten Highest Deprived Districts of Pakistan nine are from Balochistan; (ii) percentage of the population living in a high degree of deprivation stands at 88 per cent in Balochistan, 51 per cent in NWFP, 49 per cent in Sindh and 25 per cent in Punjab; (iii) 13 most underfed districts are from Balochistan; (iv)Rural poverty in Balochistan was 21 per cent (1998-99), which jumped up to 57 per cent (2005-06); (iv) 83.4 per cent children face severe malnourishment. The province had to declare a nutrition emergency in Balochistan in May 2017.[26]

Sixth, the government, especially the military, continues to see the insurgency as being led and instigated by a few tribal sardars for the sake of their vested interests and personal fiefdoms. The army typically is looking for a military solution by using brute force coupled with a media blackout. Apart from 'operations', they have adopted the strategy of 'enforced disappearances' and 'kill and dump'—picking up suspects who then 'disappear' and their dead bodies are found dumped. Amnesty International's report 'Denying the Undeniable' in 2008 exposed the tragic reality of what was happening in Balochistan.[27]

Not surprisingly, the causes, the issues, the demands and the goals of the current insurgency that began in 2005 continue to be the same as the insurgencies in 1948, 1958, 1962 and 1973-77—independence. What is different is the scale of the violence, the geographical spread of the insurgency and, most important, the participation of ordinary middle-class Baloch in it who are seeking an independent and democratic Balochistan rather than a Balochistan dominated by the sardars. The Baloch insurgency that has sustained itself for the last seventeen years is, even in its current low-key phase, likely to continue to be a big thorn in the side of the Pakistan Army.

The Pashtuns

Like the Baloch, the Pashtuns are historical people with their own territory, history and culture that predates the creation of Pakistan.

Allah Nawaz Khan, Speaker of the Frontier Provincial Assembly, articulated the basis for a Pashtun identity when he declared in 1946: '*Pathans and Punjabis are two major nations by any definition or test of a nation and the very thought of grouping the NWFP with the Punjabis is revolting to the Pathan mind....we, the Frontier Pathans, are a body of people with our own distinctive culture, civilization, language, literature...history and traditions and aptitudes and ambitions. In short, we have our own distinctive outlook on life and by all canons of international law, a Pathan is quite separate from a Punjabi.*'[28]

The roots of the Pakistan movement were extremely weak in the NWFP partly due to the strong Pashtun consciousness, institutional weakness of the Muslim League in the province and the presence of the Khudai Khidmatgars led by the larger-than life Khan Abdul Ghaffar Khan, popularly called 'Sarhadi Gandhi' (Frontier Gandhi). He was a Pashtun nationalist, strongly anti-colonialist and a Congressman opposed to the creation of Pakistan.

The League had no presence in the province in the 1937 elections when the Congress formed the government under Dr. Khan Sahib, Ghaffar Khan's brother. Like elsewhere in India, the Congress government resigned in the wake of WWII. Viceroy Lord Linlithgow asked Governor Cunningham to help Jinnah install a Muslim League ministry. This the governor did by making a Muslim League leader, Aurangzeb Khan, as chief minister though he did not last long. This was a task that only the British could have accomplished since not a single Leaguer had been elected in the 1937 elections. Even in the crucial 1946 elections when the British rallied the *maulanas* and the *pirs* in favour of the Muslim League, the Congress won and formed the government again.

Unlike the other provinces that voted on the partition plan, the British devised a special procedure of holding a referendum for the NWFP, bypassing the elected assembly where there was a Congress majority, to determine the wishes of the people. This was done to ensure that a Congress-majority assembly did not vote for accession to India. As early as March 1946, Strafford Cripps, as a member of the Cabinet Mission, had said in a secret memorandum '*...the majority in the legislature (of NWFP) is against Pakistan but as the population is predominantly Muslim; if there is to be a Pakistan, it must fall within the Muslim rather than the Hindu area.*'[29] Lord Ismay, Mountbatten's war-time aide, voiced this concern succinctly when he talked of the 'unnaturalness of the present situation in the

NWFP and that the tribesmen were most unlikely to tolerate it indefinitely', a situation for which Ismay coined the phrase 'bastard situation', where the electorate had returned to power a Congress government in a Muslim-majority province.[30]

Ghaffar Khan and his brother, Dr. Khan Sahib, first opposed the referendum and when it became inevitable, asked for the third option of Pashtunistan. When this was refused, they boycotted the referendum. Even so, the Muslim League and the British mobilised their entire strength to ensure that the people voted for Pakistan, using the Islamic card liberally and dangerously. The results were a foregone conclusion.

Jinnah dismissed Dr. Khan Sahib's ministry within a week of Pakistan's creation and banned the Khudai Khidmatgars. Even though the Khan brothers swore allegiance to Pakistan, Farzana Sheikh notes that Jinnah could not accept a separate Pashtun identity that would have vitiated his whole argument that there were only two nations—Hindus and Muslims—and only two legitimate successors to the British in India—Congress and Muslim League.[31] The call for Pashtunistan was to sow the seeds of doubt in the Pakistan establishment about the loyalty of the Khan brothers and of their progeny towards Pakistan, for decades. The issue itself was seen as the most potent internal threat to the existence of Pakistan. It was also because of such suspicions that it took Pakistan over six decades to change the name of the NWFP to Khyber Pakhtunkhwa (KPK) and that too by adding the name Khyber to distinguish it from the Pashtuns of Afghanistan.

The legacy of the Pashtunistan movement lingers and the key issue even today is of identity—whether the Pashtun identity is nationalist or religious. The over four decades of war in Afghanistan with Pakistan playing the role of a front-line state has had one pivotal impact above all else. This has been to stress the religious content of the Pashtun identity. While such an identity was egged on by the USA for the tactical purpose of defeating the Soviets in the 1980s, for Pakistan it had more than a tactical salience. For Pakistan, preservation of the Durand Line, the British-era demarcation that marked the spheres of influence between Afghanistan and British India, and underplaying the nationalist element in the Pashtun identity has been an existential problem since 1947.

Hence, Pakistan willingly and enthusiastically jumped on the bandwagon of painting the conflict in Afghanistan in religious terms and stressing the religious content of Pashtun identity. But Pakistan was playing with fire in doing so. As Wali Khan put it in the late 1970s, '*This fire you have lit in Afghanistan will one day cross the Attock Bridge and burn Pakistan.*'[32] Given the violence unleashed by the Tehrik-i-Taliban Pakistan (TTP), Wali Khan's words have proved prophetic.

For a while, this fire was masked with the Taliban control of Afghanistan in the late 1990s, and Pakistan was assured that the issue of the Durand Line would not be raised. The mistake that Pakistan made was in turning a blind eye to the steady growth of the al-Qaeda in Afghanistan together with terrorists from other countries who sought shelter there after the Soviet jihad, and to whom the Taliban played host. The second mistake Pakistan made was not to recognise that the traditional structures of Pashtun society had broken down. The Taliban filled the vacuum and were able to get rid of the last vestiges of the old structures, the maliks, and establish their own version of a *sharia*-based system. In the process, it was the Pashtuns and their culture that suffered the most.

Today, while the nationalist threat has diminished, the birth of the TTP has become a serious menace. The real danger to Pakistan, of course, would be if the TTP were to take on the nationalist mantle. While at present the Taliban have subsumed ethnic nationalism under religious fervour, there is no denying that they are a predominantly Pashtun force with a strong sense of Pashtun tribal nationalism. It is this, as much as religion, that motivated the armed resistance against the USA/NATO forces in Afghanistan. For this to happen, they would have to tone down the Islamic agenda of imposing *sharia* in Pakistan and restrict themselves to Pashtun nationalism. Though, at present, this seems a remote possibility since the TTP is challenging the Pakistani state largely on religious terms, i.e., to overthrow the current system and replace it with their version of *sharia*, there are some ominous signs for Pakistan.

The victory of the Taliban in Kabul in August 2021 is likely to impact the situation in Pakistan and especially among the Pashtuns. For example, in an interview to *CNN*, Noor Wali Mahsud, the leader the TTP, said that their objective would be the independence of the tribal areas.[33] This is a change from the earlier pan-Islamic agenda being followed by the group. It, of course, remains to be seen if the TTP would follow through on such a nationalist agenda and what would be its relationship with the Afghan Taliban on such an agenda.

Thus, just as Pashtun nationalism in Pakistan has over the years mutated into a religious form, the idea of Islamism combining with Pashtun nationalism could well be taken to a new level with the rise and spread of the TTP. Thus, as J. Paris cautions, 'explicit Taliban appeals to Pashtun identity, either in Pakistan, or across the border in Afghanistan' would be worth watching out for.[34]

Into this mix, a new Pashtun movement called the Pashtun Tahafuz Movement (PTM) has taken birth. For the moment it is a rights movement seeking constitutional protection and protection of the Pashtuns from violence.

Its greatest success has been to cross the tribal and gender barriers. Its future development will have to be watched carefully.

While it would, therefore, be comforting for the Pakistani state to have blunted the edge of Pashtun nationalism, the jury is still out on the final shape of politics in KPK—Islamist, nationalist or whether the Pashtuns would forsake both ethnic nationalism and religious radicalism in favour of a larger Pakistani identity. A lot would depend on how Pakistan plays its cards in tackling the Islamist insurgency both in Pakistan and in Afghanistan and in dealing with the PTM. A victory of the Taliban in Afghanistan may not be the prize that Pakistan has been looking for all these decades.

The Sindhi and Mohajir

Historically, Sindh is regarded as the Gateway of Islam since it was here that the Arab general, Muhammad bin Qasim, landed in 712 and defeated the Sindh ruler, Raja Dahir. The British took control in 1843 when Sindh became a part of the territories of the East India Company through the conquest of General Charles Napier. Legend has it that he sent the message (in Latin) to Calcutta, *Peccavi* ('I have sinned').[35] Subsequently, Sindh was brought under the administrative control of the Bombay Presidency where it was to remain till 1936.

The Muslim League was to find Sindh a more fertile ground than it did in Punjab or the NWFP. A Sindh Muslim League set up base in 1938 but the growth was slow. Nevertheless, on 3 March 1943, in a motion moved by G.M. Syed, Sindh became the first province in undivided India to support the 1940 Pakistan resolution. Most analysts agree that by supporting the cause of Pakistan, the Sindhis were actually looking for autonomy to rule their province. When G. M. Syed, the father of Sindhi nationalism, realized what Pakistan was all about, he left the Muslim League, termed the Partition on the basis of the so-called two-nation theory 'unnatural, inhuman and unrealistic' and became an ideologue for Sindh nationalism.[36]

Population mix is central to the problem of ethnic resentment in Sindh and, more particularly, Karachi. In 1947, while the majority of the refugees from India settled in Punjab, about one million (18 per cent of the total refugees) settled in Sindh. They were predominantly Urdu-speaking and ethnically and culturally quite distinct from the local Sindhi population. Though they came to Sindh from different regions of British India, they had enough in common culturally and ideologically to enable the development of a sense of common identity and started calling themselves Mohajirs, a moniker that has continued till date.

The large and compact Mohajir settlement in an urban environment allowed the group to develop its own identity. The declaration of Urdu as the national language of Pakistan and the separation of Karachi as the national capital from Sindh in 1948 diminished the possibility that the Urdu speakers in Karachi would merge in the Sindhi milieu. Even their children did not have to learn Sindhi. For the first two decades, the Mohajirs did extremely well. They were the flag-bearers of the centralising policies of the state and positioned themselves as having created Pakistan. They, together with the Punjabis, dominated the civil services and the military. They were allowed to occupy properties and businesses left by fleeing Hindus at the time of partition and a large number benefited from real or bogus property claims. Ayub Khan made the final settlement of the Mohajir property claims, which he found to be correct only to the extent of 7.5 per cent.[37] Yet property deeds were issued to the Mohajirs for thousands of urban residences and for roughly half a million acres of agricultural land in Sindh left behind by Hindu Sindhis who had been forced to migrate to India. The Sindhi peasants in possession of these lands were forced off the land or made to pay rent to the new absentee landlords.

From the early 1970s onwards, however, the Sindhis started getting their due under Z.A. Bhutto. While the Mohajirs felt squeezed by the Sindhis from one side, they were increasingly under pressure on account of migration of Punjabis and Pashtuns into Karachi, on the other. The Punjabis were also replacing them in the bureaucracy once the capital shifted to Islamabad. As a result, a sense of Mohajir alienation and insecurity began to develop. Very much like the insecurity among their ancestors during the decline of Mughal power, the present-day Mohajirs too felt insecure after running out of official patronage in the country they felt they had created through their sacrifices. The insecurity was only to grow. The year 1971 was a major wake-up call. Zulfiqar Ali Bhutto, a Sindhi prime minister, refused to take back the 250,000 East Pakistani Mohajirs who had migrated there at the time of Partition in 1947 but were now trapped in Bangladesh. This set many Mohajirs thinking about their own fate, especially when coupled with the pro-Sindhi measures taken by Bhutto.

This insecurity was to crystallize into the formation of a political party—the Mohajir Qaumi Movement (MQM) in August 1986 led by Altaf Hussain. By giving the Mohajirs a political identity, the MQM won every election since then in the urban areas of Karachi and Hyderabad except the 2018 one. For the first time, people from the lower-middle class tasted power in Pakistan and were able to rub shoulders with the feudals and industrialists in the corridors of power. It was a huge sense of empowerment for the entire community. That was why sitting in London, Altaf Hussain was, till some time ago, able to run the party like a well-oiled machine. Perhaps the most controversial position of the MQM has been its insistence on calling the Mohajirs a nationality. The Mohajirs distanced themselves from Pakistani nationalism; now it was 'Mohajir identification within a Pakistani framework.'[38]

A major consequence of the ethnic mix in the urban areas, especially Karachi, has been in terms of violence. The security forces have periodically cracked down to bring peace. Starting with an 'operation' in 1992, there was another after Nawaz Sharif became prime minister in 2013. All these operations have followed the same pattern—arrests, display of illegal weapons supposedly recovered, activists with multiple crimes arrested, 'confessions', a huge media mobilisation, attempts to split the organisation, etc. In a few months the episode is forgotten, till the next time. What was alarming about the operation was the huge spike in extra-judicial killings. According to the Human Rights Commission of Pakistan's (HRCP) annual report on violence in Karachi, the year 2015, for example, saw fewer targeted killings (387) but a rise in police encounters that led to the deaths of 586 people.[39] It was the extra-judicial killing of Naqibullah Mehsud, a youth from Waziristan, that led to the creation of the Pashtun Tahafuz Movement (PTM). The killer was a policeman who was reported to have killed over 400 Pashtun youths in Karachi in 'encounters.'

The Punjabi

Punjab was the essential element in Jinnah's demand for Pakistan. It formed the heartland of a future Pakistan state—Jinnah called it the 'corner stone' of Pakistan. Even the Punjab Muslim League had declared: '*It has been said often enough that we are the heart, the brain and the sword arm of Pakistan... Without our decisive and critical struggle, Pakistan would not have been realized.*'[40]

Hanif Ramay, a former chief minister of Punjab and Speaker of the Punjab Assembly, succinctly summed up Punjab's dilemma when he said: '*Punjab lost its identity in order to gain a larger Pakistani identity; it began to perceive itself alone as Pakistan, while others started calling Pakistan the greater Punjab.*'[41] The above statement highlights Punjab's predicament to distinguish between a Punjabi provincial identity and a Pakistani identity, so interwoven have they become. Not surprisingly, it is Punjabi nationalism, Punjabi ideas and concepts that have come to define Pakistani nationalism, ideas and concepts.

Though Jinnah was infuriated when Punjab had to be partitioned, calling the residual Pakistan 'moth-eaten', yet the history of the Muslim League in pre-

Partition Punjab was dismal. No Muslim League government held office in Punjab until Partition. This was the legacy of the Muslim League in a province that was considered so vital that Pakistan would not be complete without it.

Post-Partition, Punjab found itself dominating Pakistan due its strong presence in the bureaucracy and, especially, the army. Punjab's domination of the army has continued apace and with the army ruling Pakistan, directly or indirectly, Punjab continues to dominate all aspects of Pakistan. It would have done so in any case given that post-1971 it constituted 56 per cent of the population. In the National Assembly, Punjab with 148 seats out of 272 general seats and 35 out of 60 seats reserved for women has more seats than all the other provinces combined. Thus, a purely Punjab-based party with 172 seats can form the government in Pakistan without needing representatives from the other provinces. In the 2013 elections, Nawaz Sharif's Pakistan Muslim League-Nawaz (PML-N) had 163 seats from Punjab alone, just eight short of a majority. No wonder that Punjab rules the roost and need not care for the development needs of the other provinces. Punjab's domination of the army and the army's domination of Pakistan has been the icing on the cake.

Conventional wisdom is that as the most populous and dominant ethnic group in Pakistan, Punjab does not have an ethnic problem itself but all the other provinces have a problem with it. As Talbot puts it: '*The Punjab can be seen both as the cornerstone of the country and as a major hindrance to national integration because of the use of Punjabi military and paramilitary forces during civil unrest in Balochistan and Sindh.*'[42]

One problem is that not all of Punjab speaks Punjabi. South Punjab speaks Seraiki, a well-developed language in itself. In the 1981 census, Seraiki was counted as a separate language for the first time and it was determined that 9.8 per cent of Pakistan's and 14.9 per cent of Punjab's households spoke it. As a result, Punjabis, for the first time, were shown to be less than the majority of the then Pakistan's population (48.2 per cent). This encouraged the demand for a Seraiki province consisting of either the erstwhile princely state of Bahawalpur or a larger province consisting of south Punjab.

The Seraiki issue is not one of secession but for the creation of a separate province. The importance of this issue is that division of Punjab would lessen the dominance of the province in terms of population, resources and even in the army. Compounding the problem of south Punjab has been the discriminatory development policies being followed by the Punjab government. According to Prof. Nukhbah Taj Langah, president, Pakistan Seraiki Party, such discriminatory policies had resulted in unemployment and illiteracy in the region and the consequent attraction of the madrassa and *jihadi* culture. She warned that it would be impossible to confine the extremist tendencies within one specific region as it may spread and impact the entire Punjab and, eventually, the rest of the country.[43]

Such discriminatory policies were confirmed by the outgoing head of the United Nations Development Programme (UNDP) in Pakistan who told a seminar held in Islamabad on 10 August 2016: '*Investment (of public funds) in Lahore, the most developed district of Punjab, is six times more than the allocations of the Seraiki belt of the province.*' This, according to him, was increasing the inequality between the rich and poor regions of Pakistan. He underlined that the concentration of public spending was politically driven, implying that by depriving the Seraiki belt of funds, the state was deliberately keeping the region underdeveloped. Akmal Hussain, a renowned economist and social activist, revealed that as much as 80 to 85 per cent of total physical expenditures of the province was incurred in Lahore.[44]

Of late, lip service is being paid to the idea of a separate 'south Punjab' province. The idea gets traction just before elections.

The second issue in Punjab is the fact that the greatest amount of radicalization and sectarianism in Punjab is concentrated in south Punjab. Ayesha Siddiqa has argued that '*radicalization is a greater issue in Punjab than militancy, primarily because militants tend to groom people for battles outside the country or the province. Thus, there is violence in the province but those figures are not commensurate with the actual amount of radicalization that takes place in Punjab.*'[45] In Punjab, it is now difficult to find a city or area that has not been touched by some form of radicalism, be it latent or active. It is significant that while Punjab has the highest number of Deobandi madrassas, within Punjab, the highest number can be found in south Punjab.

In fact, Punjab, especially south Punjab, has been the site of sectarian violence since the 1980s between the Deobandi Anjuman Sipha-i-Sahaba (ASS) and the Shia Sipha-i-Mohammadi Pakistan (SMP). The Shia–Sunni conflict in Punjab is actually a Deobandi–Shia tussle. Not surprisingly, at one time, of Pakistan's 1,764 most wanted persons, 729 hailed from southern Punjab. Over 57 banned organisations were spread out in southern Punjab, several among whom had evinced a desire to hoist the flag of the Islamic State in Pakistan. Punjab, in fact, has become the ideological centre and recruitment ground for terrorist organisations, at times operating out of mosques and madrassas.

Thus, there could be severe trouble brewing under the surface in Punjab. If the burgeoning radicalism, the growth of *jihadi* culture and sectarianism is not tackled adequately, Punjab has the potential of going the KPK way in terms of *jihadi* violence.

Finally, it would sound counter-intuitive but there also is a different kind of resentment in Punjab. It is undeniable that it is Punjabi nationalism, Punjabi ideas and concepts that have come to define Pakistani nationalism, ideas and concepts. However, in the process, Punjab has actually lost its identity in order to gain a larger Pakistani identity, as so well put by Hanif Ramay, quoted earlier. This paradoxically has led several Punjabis, especially writers, to complain as suffering from a 'lost' self.[46]

One reason for this is language. Formal literacy in Punjab means literacy in Urdu, because literary and official life in Punjab has taken place in Urdu since the British Raj and in English that had official patronage. Thus, Punjabi was doubly marginalised.

Since the 1980s, and especially since the 1990s, there is a growing Punjabiyat movement. It is not about seeking power, or financial gain and certainly not separatist. The Punjabiyat activists instead want Punjabi to claim its rightful inheritance as one of the great world languages. Its rhetoric is entirely framed in terms of recovering a 'lost' identity.

The movement got a fillip with Mohammad Hanif Ramay's seminal work titled *Panjāb kā Muqaddama* (The Case of Punjab), published in 1985 followed by other tracts like *Panjābī Zabān Nahīn Maregī* (The Punjabi Language Will Never Die); *Panjāb kā Maslā* (The Problem of Punjab); and 1992, *Ao, Panjābī ko Qatl Kareṉ*! (Come, Let's Kill Punjabi!)

In a parallel development in the 1980s, Punjabi cinema rose to a position of market dominance, primarily through the iconic revenge-seeking peasant-warrior 'Maulā Jaṭ' and similar films.

The most surprising aspect of Punjabiyat literature is the extent to which the Punjabi language is characterised as 'lost', lost through the oppression of Urdu. This stance turns upside down the idea of 'Punjabistan' as an oppressor. In this view, the Punjab of Punjabiyat is itself a kindred spirit to the other ethnic victims of the Pakistani state, making common cause with Bengal and Bengali in particular.

Two examples in recent writings will explain the position.

According to one writer: '*Having given up their identity, and though Punjab built a tradition of living as a Pakistani, in this way, they became intellectually developed but their emotional development remained halfway, and they became the prey of several such dreams, on account of which not just they but Pakistan as well was harmed...Punjab's new generations are not proud of Punjabi, but are excluded from it; in a bid to walk like a swan, the crow forgot its own gait.*'[47]

According to another: *When I started to put a tape of Punjabi songs on in the car, my four-year-old son said 'Please turn it off.' I asked 'Why?' He said 'Only dogs speak this language.*'[48]

These narratives also illustrate how Punjabi-speakers fare poorly in status consciousness. A survey carried out asked various groups of students (Punjabis in both Urdu- and English-medium schools) to rate their 'native language' on aspects such as 'social grace', 'culture' and 'modernity.' The survey found that as opposed to the Punjabistan narrative, Punjabi students consistently rated themselves lower in these aspects than they rated their Urdu-speaking peers.[49]

Conclusion

To conclude, the issue of ethnic fault-lines is a serious one in Pakistan. In its origins, it harks back to the Pakistan movement when religion was believed to be a bond strong enough to weld together the diverse nationalities that came to constitute Pakistan. Two other issues aggravated the problem: the failure of the early leadership to follow through on promises of provincial autonomy made during the Pakistan movement and the centralising response of successive leaders to such demands. The result was the breakaway of East Pakistan to become Bangladesh and bruising insurgencies in Balochistan, the fifth of which is continuing today. The situation in KPK, Sindh and in Punjab itself is festering and could explode for differing reasons.

Whether or not Pakistan's separatist movements and provincial discontent repeat the Bangladesh example is a matter of conjecture. However, what is undeniable is that they do pose a significant challenge to the state of Pakistan. If nationalist movements morph with growing Islamist sentiment as they potentially can in KPK, or if the growing radicalisation and sectarianism in Punjab explodes, or if the ethnic cauldron in Sindh, especially Karachi, gets out of hand and if the insurgency in Balochistan gathers momentum, the challenge to the Pakistani state apparatus would be severely enhanced. It is an irony that Islam and the slogan of provincial autonomy, which were seen as the binding forces during the Pakistan movement, today pose serious threats to the existence of the Pakistani state and have become among the key drivers for ethnic resentment in Pakistan.

In this context, the comparison with Afghanistan is instructive. Afghanistan has been described as a strong nation but a weak state, while Pakistan is a strong state but not a strong nation. Afghanistan's weakness as a state is counter-balanced by a strong sense of national unity that has developed among its people. Despite the repeated collapse of central authority and the rise of ethnically based militias in the 1990s, during the Afghan civil war, and the possibility of this happening again, the country has not faced the threat or prospect of partition. The reason is that none of the ethnic groups saw partition as a useful outcome; instead each wanted a stronger position and a larger share within the Afghan polity, rather than independence from the Afghan state or even amalgamation with co-ethnics in neighbouring states. This was because the Afghans' sense of national unity was rooted less in ethnicity than in the will to persist together, united by common experience. Even at the height of political instability, Afghans have not feared the disintegration of their country.[50]

Pakistan, on the other hand, has been unable to develop an over-arching national identity. Since its creation, it has been obsessed with fears of internal disintegration. Apart from East Pakistan that seceded, other nationalities have made their dissatisfaction with Pakistan quite clear and in the case of the Baloch their desire to separate evident. Consequently, Pakistan has had to be held together with force rather than the consent of its people and its serious issues of identity and ethnic fault-lines will continue to be a source of internal tension.[51]

ENDNOTES

1. Parts of this chapter have been excerpted from the Author's book '*Pakistan: Courting the Abyss*,' Harper Collins India, 2016
2. Khalid Muhammad, 'Whither Pakistan?' *The Nation*, 18 January 2015.
3. Selig Harrison, 'Ethnic Conflict and the Future of Pakistan', in Wilson John (ed.) *Pakistan: The Struggle Within*, Delhi: Pearson Education, 2009, p. 18.
4. Cited in Ian Talbot, *Pakistan: A Modern History*, London: Hurst, 1999, p. 90.
5. Aparna Pande, *Explaining Pakistan's Foreign Policy: Escaping India,* London: Routledge, 2011, Indian Reprint 2014, p. 44.
6. Mubarak Ali, 'In Search of Identity', *Dawn*, 7 May 2000, cited in Christophe Jaffrelot (ed.), *Nationalism Without A Nation: Pakistan Searching For Its Identity*, New Delhi: Manohar Publishers, 2002, p. 7.
7. Syed Jaffar Ahmed, Foreword in Mubarak Ali, *Pakistan In Search of Identity*, Delhi: Aakar Books, 2011, p. 8.
8. Cited in M. J. Akbar, *Tinderbox: The Past and Future of Pakistan*, New Delhi: Harper Collins India, 2011, pp. 251–52.
9. Michael T. Kaufman, 'Pakistan's Islamic Revival Affects All Aspects of Life', *The New York Times*, 13 October 1980, cited in Husain Haqqani, *Pakistan: Between Mosque and Military*, Lahore: Vanguard Books, 2005, p. 136.

10. Akbar S. Ahmed, 'Tribes, Regional Pressures and Nationhood', in Victoria Schofield (ed.), *Old Roads and New Highways: Fifty Years of Pakistan*, Karachi: OUP, 1997, p. 14. Wali Khan has also been quoted as saying that he had been a Pakhtun for 6,000 years, a Muslim for 1,300 years, and a Pakistani for twenty-five. See Isabel Hilton, 'The Pashtun Code', *The New Yorker*, 3 December 2001, p. 59.
11. Maulana Abul Kalam Azad's interview to Shorish Kashmiri for a Lahore-based Urdu magazine, *Chattan*, in April 1946. Reproduced in http://www.newageislam.com/books-and-documents/maulanaabul-kalam-azad--the-man-who-knew-the-future-of-pakistanbefore-its-creation/d/2139 (accessed on 20 June 2016).
12. Asghar Ali Engineer, 'Islam & Polity: Contradictions in the State Building of Pakistan', in Pandav Nayak (ed.), *Pakistan Society & Politics*, Jaipur: South Asia Studies Centre, University of Jaipur, 1984, p .3.
13. Adeel Khan, *Politics of Identity: Ethnic Nationalism and the State in Pakistan*, New Delhi: Sage Publications, 2005, p. 62
14. *The Times of India*, Bombay, 9 November 1945, cited in Syed Sharifuddin Pirzada, *Foundations of Pakistan, AIML Documents*, vol. II, 1924–47, New Delhi: Metropolitan Book Co., Indian edition 1982, pp. xxxi–xxxii.
15. Khalid B. Sayeed, *Pakistan: The Formative Phase 1857-1948*, London: OUP, 1968 second edition, p. 239.
16. Adeel Khan, op. cit., pp. 62–63.
17. Selig Harrison, op. cit., p. 151.
18. Pervez Musharraf, *In the Line of Fire: A Memoir*, New York: Free Press, 2006, p. 149.
19. Peter Jacob, 'A serial transformation', *The Friday Times*, 28 February 2014.
20. Devolution "rollback", editorial in *Dawn*, 17 December 2014.
21. Pervez Hoodbhoy, 'Zia Mian, Pakistan, the Army and the Conflict Within', 12 July 2011, Middle East Research and Information Project, http://www.merip.org/mero071211
22. Mir Ghous Bux Bizenjo, addressing the Dar-ul-Awan of Kalat state on 12 December 1947 at Dhadhar, cited in Martin Axmaan, *Back to the Future: The Khanate of Kalat & the Genesis of Baloch Nationalism 1915-1955*, Karachi: OUP, 2008, p. 230.
23. For the historical context see, Inayatullah Baloch, *The Problem of Greater Balochistan: A Study of Baluch Nationalism*, Stuttgart: Steiner Verlag Wiesbaden Gmbh, 1987; Selig Harrison, *In Afghanistan's Shadow: Baluch Nationalism and Soviet Temptations*, Washington, DC: Carnegie Endowment for International Peace, 1981; Martin Axmann, op. cit., Naseer Dashti, *The Baloch and Balochistan,* Bloomington, Indiana, USA: Trafford Publishing, 2012.
24. Martin Axmann, *Back to the Future: The Khanate of Kalat and the Genesis of Baloch Nationalism 1915-1955*; Karachi: OUP, 2008, p. 299.
25. Muhammad Ijaz Laif & Muhammad Amir Hamza, 'Ethnic Nationalism in Pakistan: A Case Study of Baloch Nationalism during Musharraf Regime', *Pakistan Vision,* vol. 10, no. 1, p. 65.
26. Figures taken from Tilak Devasher, *Pakistan: The Balochistan Conundrum*', NOIDA: Harper Collins Publishers, 2019
27. Amnesty International, 'Denying the Undeniable: Enforced Disappearances in Pakistan, 2008.'
28. S.A. Rittenberg, *Ethnicity, Nationalism and Pakhtuns: The Independence Movement in India's North-West Frontier Province, 1901-1947*, Durham, NC: Carolind Academic Press, 1988, p. 337, cited in Ian Talbot, *Pakistan: A Modern History*, New Delhi: OUP, 1998, p. 14.
29. Memorandum by Cripps' (undated), Transfer of Power, vol. VII, Document no. 71, p. 176; Peter Clarke, *The Cripps Version: The Life and Times of Sir Stafford Cripps (1889-1952)*, London: Penguin Books, 2002, p. 417, cited in Yuvraj Krishan, *Partition & Pakistan, Jinnah: The*

Founder, British: The Architects, New Delhi: Mosaic Books, 2013, p. 67.

30. Raghvendra Singh, *India's Lost Frontier: The Story of The North-West Frontier Province of Pakistan*, New Delhi: Rupa Publications, 2019, p. 166.
31. Farzana Sheikh, *Making Sense of Pakistan*, London: C. Hurst & Co., 2009, p. 202.
32. Cited in Sayyed Fawad Shah, 'Countering Pakhtun Nationalism', *The Daily Times*, 23 November 2014.
33. Muhammad Nauman Akhter, 'A Peep into Tehreek-e-Taliban Pakistan's Tricky Relations with Afghan Taliban', *Modern Diplomacy*, 20 October 2021, https://moderndiplomacy.eu/2021/10/20/a-peep-into-tehreek-e-taliban-pakistans-tricky-relations-with-afghan-taliban/2021
34. Jonathan Paris, 'Prospects for Pakistan', Legatum Institute, 2010, p. 38, http://li.com/docs/default-source/publication/2010-publications-prospects-for-pakistan.pdf?sfvrsn=2.
35. Cited in Stephen Cohen, *The Idea of Pakistan*, Delhi: OUP, 2004, p. 211.
36. Adeel Khan, *Politics of Identity: Ethnic Nationalism and the State in Pakistan*, New Delhi: Sage Publications, 2005, p. 15.
37. Ayub Khan, *Friends not Masters*, New York: OUP, 1967, p. 94.
38. Yunus Samad, 'In and out of Power but not down and out: Mohajir identity politics' in Christophe Jaffrelot (ed.), *Pakistan: Nationalism without a Nation*, p. 68.
39. 'Smoking gun: After target killings, encounters come to haunt Karachi', *The Express Tribune*, 16 January 2016.
40. 'The Election Manifesto of the Punjab Muslim League (December 1950)', cited in Kalim Bahadur, 'Problems in the Evolution of a Constitutional Framework for Pakistan' in Pandav Nayak (ed.), *Pakistan Society & Politics*, Jaipur: South Asia Studies Centre, University of Jaipur, 1984, p. 39.
41. Mohammed Hanif Ramay, *Punjab ka Muqadima* (The Case of Punjab), (in Urdu), Lahore: Jang Publications, 1985, pp. 28, 31 and 35, cited in Feroze Ahmed, *Ethnicity & Politics in Pakistan*, Karachi: OUP, 1998, p. xxi.
42. Ian Talbot, 'The Punjabization of Pakistan: Myth or Reality', in Christophe Jaffrelot (ed.) *Nationalism Without a Nation: Pakistan Searching For Its Identity*, New Delhi: Manohar Publishers, 2002, p. 51.
43. Amina Hassan, 'Tackling radicalism', *Daily Times*, 6 August 2016.
44. Shahbaz Rana, 'Allocation and spending is politically driven in Pakistan, says UNDP', *The Express Tribune*, 10 August 2016.
45. Ayesha Siddiqa, 'The New Frontiers: Militancy & Radicalism in Punjab', Haslum, Norway: Centre for International and Strategic Analysis, SISA, 2013, pp. 4, 20.
46. Anshu Malhotra, Farina Mir (ed.) *Punjab Reconsidered: History, Culture and Practice*, New Delhi, OUP, 2012.
47. Ibid.
48. Ibid.
49. Ibid.
50. Thomas J. Barfield, 'The Durand Line: History, Consequences, and Future', Report of a Conference Organised in July 2007 by the American Institute of Afghanistan Studies and the Hollings Centre in Istanbul, Turkey.
51. Ibid.

3

Extremism Trends in Pakistan

Dr. Shalini Chawla

Pakistan's former Prime Minister Imran Khan, after assuming office in 2018, repeatedly claimed that Pakistan paid a heavy price for its role in the USA-led war on terror post 9/11. At the domestic and international levels, Pakistan's messaging has been threefold: Pakistan has sacrificed thousands of lives in the last two decades; the nation has suffered heavy financial losses and is facing the blowback in terms of terrorism on its own soil for being a US ally in the war on terror. Pakistan's inability to reflect back on its strategic choices is not new and the state fails to accept the root cause behind rising extremism (and terrorism) in society—its belief in radical Islamic ideology and adoption of terrorism as a potent foreign policy tool. Currently, we see a rise in religious intolerance within Pakistan, the state's sanction of legitimacy to the Taliban's radical ideology in Afghanistan, an indifferent attitude towards the complete breach of civil rights and liberties of the Afghans, strengthening of the religious political groups and Imran Khan's consistent drive for Islamophobia at the global platform.

The last seven decades have witnessed Pakistan's drift into extremism and its inclination to support extremist ideology. Although the intensity of the drift and nation's reliance on extremism has varied under different regimes, the journey has been consistent. Pakistan presents a unique set of contradictions: it shares an ambiguous relationship with Islam; tries to embrace western notions of modernity and at the same time, tries to retain the orthodox Islamic identity; has an over-powering and ambitious military that cautiously guards its strategic and economic interests and controls strategic decision making; struggles to sustain a democratic regime but the democratic leadership, willingly or unwillingly, follows the *red lines* for their sustenance; and the state consistently claims that it wants peace and not a civil war in Afghanistan, but has never failed to destabilise the political leadership in Kabul (in the past) and extend full-fledged support to the Taliban. These inherent contradictions have grown over the years and encouraged the rise of ethnicity and pluralism within Pakistani society. Born as a result of the demand for a separate Muslim homeland, it eventually stood as the saviour of Islam and in the process, the military-led state has adopted policies based on religion that have had severe ideological and security repercussions for the state. *Religion has been used in Pakistan for nation-building, statecraft and strategic security.* Pakistan has shared a varying relationship with Islam under different leaders and presently experiences Islamist extremism, which is alarming.

Background

Pakistan was born as a demand for a separate homeland for Muslims as the All India Muslim League led by Muhammad Ali Jinnah strongly argued that Muslims had a special identity, which would not be able to survive in a Hindu dominated society; thus, a separate homeland for Muslims was the only solution. There was lack of consensus over Pakistan's ideological and territorial contours as Ayesha Jalal rightly pointed out:

> "Jinnah's resort to religion was not on ideology to which he was ever committed or even a device to use against rival communities; it was simply a way of giving a semblance of unity and solidarity to his divided Muslim constituents. Jinnah needed a demand that was specifically ambiguous and imprecise to command general support, something specifically Muslim though unspecific in every other respect."[1]

Jinnah in his famous speech before the Constituent Assembly on August 11, 1947, outlined his vision:

> "You are free; you are free to go to your temples, you are free to go to your mosques or to any other place of worship in this state of Pakistan. You may belong to any religion or caste or creed—that has nothing to do with the business of the state.... We are starting with this fundamental principle that we are all citizens and equal citizens of one state.... In the course of time, Hindus would cease to be Hindus and Muslims would cease to be Muslims, not in the religious sense, because that is the personal faith of each individual, but in the political sense as citizens of the State."[2]

Jinnah's dream was a modern state where Muslim culture and social norms could be promoted freely. Jinnah's vision was shaped by a different set of circumstances where, in the postcolonial movement, he visualised an arrangement for the Indian Muslims who would enjoy freedom in an independent state. The Muslim League was looking for a Muslim homeland and the thought at the time of conceptualisation of Pakistan (if at all considered!) was liberal Islam. For Jinnah, the *two-nation theo*ry was the justification for the creation of Pakistan. However, Pakistan, over the decades, completely drifted away from Jinnah's spirit. Pakistan never inherited a uniformed vision and there were contesting ideas. The birth of the nation itself suffered lack of consensus and clarity on the issue of Islam. In the coming years, Pakistan hardly became a beneficiary of committed and visionary leadership. The state was driven differently by different regimes following different objectives. Jinnah's death on 11 September 1948 was a deadly blow to the spirit of Pakistan, and altered the course of history.

Many of Pakistan's political elites were uncertain about the role of Islam in defining the nation's constitutional foundations.[3] It took the policy makers close to a decade to formalise the constitution of Pakistan, which dissolved Jinnah's spirit of secular Islam. There was clear lack of consensus on the meaning of Islam. Farzana Shaikh puts it very aptly:

> "While Jinnah's political successors, plagued by uncertainty about the public role of religion, were content to acknowledge Islam as a fundamental component of the country's identity, religious parties pressed for Islam to be embodied in an Islamic state, although they were too notoriously vague about what that entailed."[4]

The persistent confusion about the interpretation of Islam had severe political, social, economic, educational and even military ramifications. Lack of consensus on the issue gave the political and military leadership enough space to exploit the factor of religion to serve their own interests. While the state was looking to define its identity, it also struggled with multiple insecurities and threat perceptions. Pakistan did face rebel and separatist voices within from the time of its creation. Internally, Pakistan was fragmented and the two wings, West Pakistan and East Pakistan, which differed ethnically, culturally and economically and were separated by thousands of miles of Indian territory.

East Pakistan was never embraced fully by West Pakistan, which controlled the political and military leadership. In addition to differences with East Pakistan (which were mainly due to the alienation of the Bengalis), Pakistan experienced insurgency in Balochistan starting in the 1940s. The Baloch were resistant to the idea of being part of Pakistan and thus their incorporation into the federal government consistently remained a challenge. The Frontier Province was also opposed to the idea of being a part of the Pakistani state.

On the external front, Pakistan felt threatened and insecure from the eastern and western sides. Geographically, most of west Punjab's prominent cities lie close to J&K's western border. Considering that Punjabi elites dominated Pakistan's decision-making, this factor of vulnerability weighed heavily on their minds. During times of emergency, India would be in a position to damage the most important communication lines in Pakistan. Fear of Indian aggression is reflected in Maj Gen Akbar's writings where he said that in case of war between the two countries, if Pakistanis had to protect Rawalpindi, it would mean distracting themselves from Lahore and this would enable India to threaten Lahore, Sialkot and Gujrat easily.[5] Hasan-Askari Rizvi commented, "Host of security handicaps accentuated Pakistan's insecurity. Pakistan's territory lacks depth and the main railroad link from south to north (Karachi to Peshawar) runs parallel to the India-Pakistan border; at several points, it is within 60 miles of the Indian border or the Line of Control in Kashmir."[6] At least three important Pakistani cities—Lahore, Sialkot and Kasur—are very close to the border. Most Pakistani military airfields (except Quetta) are not more than 150 miles from the Indian border.[7] Pakistan always suspected that India had hegemonic ambitions, and was unfair in allocating Pakistan with its due share of military resources inherited from British India.

On the other side, on the western front, Pakistan faced a constant threat due to the lingering issue of the (disputed) Durand Line. No Afghan regime including the Rabbani government has ever accepted the legitimacy of the border drawn up by the British in 1893. Pakistan faced constant challenges and has remained under pressure due to the demands to incorporate the Pashtun areas east of the Durand Line, into Afghanistan. Insurgency in Pakistan's tribal frontiers bordering Afghanistan added to the worries of the establishment. With the Soviet invasion of Afghanistan in 1979, Pakistan felt deeply threatened with the destabilised Afghanistan and the presence of the Soviet military forces on its western borders. It anticipated that if the Russians succeeded in Afghanistan, their next targets would be Pakistan and Iran.

The Beginning of the Ideological Drift and Pakistan's Wars for Kashmir

The need to control Jammu and Kashmir and incorporate it into Pakistan was felt very strongly in Pakistan since the British declaration of India's partition. Kashmir was considered indispensable for Pakistan and the prime reasons for Pakistan's quest for J&K were economic and strategic factors. The first factor was that Pakistan felt that with J&K state as an integral part of India, Pakistan's security would be jeopardised. The second factor was economic and psychological. Kashmir going to India could seriously impact Pakistan's economy that was based mainly on canal-irrigated agriculture. West Punjab particularly depended for its agriculture upon the rivers flowing from Jammu and Kashmir. Given the security and economic concerns, Kashmir for Pakistan was seen as a necessity! However, this in no way suggests that the issue of religion was not important in shaping the attitude towards Kashmir. Pakistan's demand for Kashmir was also due to the frustration of the political leaders who felt cheated with a "moth-eaten" Pakistan, which came to their share.

Pakistan launched the first war for Kashmir in 1947-48 in the name of a 'tribal revolt.' The Pakistan Army with the consent of the political leadership invoked the tribesmen and retired and serving army officers in the name of *jihad*, to raid and seize Kashmir. Islam was leveraged in the very beginning of the state itself to respond to the Indian threat. The government in Pakistan called on religious scholars to issue supportive *fatwas* (religious decrees).[8] The 1947-48 aggression laid the basic guidelines for the future aggression by Pakistan. Pakistan *used religion* to support the state policies and used *covert tactics* supported and sponsored by the Pakistani leadership.

At the domestic level, Jinnah's dream of a pluralistic society was being challenged and in the early 1950s there were street protests calling for a declaration that the Ahmadis were non-Muslims.[9] The protests were orchestrated to destabilise the ruling polity and the resignation of Pakistan's first foreign minister, Sir Zafarullah Khan, an Ahmadi, was demanded.[10] In 1974, Ahmadis were officially declared non-Muslims through a constitutional amendment. In 1965, during the first indirect presidential elections, the opposition was raised against Fatima Jinnah, sister of Mohammad Ali Jinnah, from contesting for power and a *fatwa* was issued that Islam does not allow a female head of state.[11] Religion became an important factor for the political groups to lead the power struggle and unequal rights on the basis of sects, gender became prevalent.

Externally, the Pakistan army's covert activities vis-a-vis India, expanded in Jammu and Kashmir after the 1962 India-China War. A close study of the covert activities indicates that the factor of religion started to gain momentum in the 1960s. Pakistan's covert activities in Kashmir were now gradually moving towards using religion as a driving force to gain support for the disintegration of India. Another critical development in the late 1950s and 1960s was Pakistan's alliance with the USA. Pakistan entered into military agreements with the USA-led

SEATO and CENTO and started to receive much desired military assistance in the form of aid and equipment. The inflow of Western military equipment further boosted Pakistan's military capability and confidence and it now wanted to intensify its aggression to acquire Kashmir.

In the 1950s, Pakistan's covert operations in the Kashmir Valley were not effective and failed to yield the desired impact. In 1964, Pakistan developed a strategy that came to be known as *Operations Gibraltar* and *Grand Slam* vis-à-vis India and Pakistan initiated its second war for Kashmir in 1965. Operation Gibraltar was a covert operation conducted by Pakistan, which achieved limited success. Pakistan's defeat in the 1965 war aggravated Pakistan's reliance on religion to carry out its objectives in Kashmir. In the late 1960s, a new set of *jihadis* emerged, deriving their inspiration from left-wing anti-imperialist struggles. The Pakistan military and political leadership were increasingly convinced about the indispensability of covert warfare in their religiously-driven strategies towards the Valley.

1971: Dismemberment of Pakistan

In the late 1950s and early 1960s, Pakistan witnessed the growing stature of the military in the eyes of the people. General Ayub's' period marked the beginning of military control in the political and civil system of Pakistan. Ayub's successor, General Yahya Khan, talked about the Islamic identity of Pakistan and kept defence at the top of its agenda. He utilised the intelligence network to motivate the Islamic parties to work against the two major political parties—the Awami League and the Pakistan's People's Party, which were seen as un-Islamic. The military regime shared close ties with the Jamaat-e-Islami and encouraged the mushrooming of other Islamic groups.[12]

In the 1960s, the military's role expanded and, political and ethnic tensions increased. East and West Pakistan were quite different from each other and the central leadership failed to leverage religion as a unifying factor of Pakistan. Increasing alienation towards the eastern wing of Pakistan eventually led to an insurgency in East Pakistan and Pakistan's third war against India, resulting in the division of the country and creation of Bangladesh in 1971. It is interesting to note that shortly after partition, Mountbatten predicted that East Pakistan would break away from Pakistan within a quarter of a century.[13]

Like the previous wars in 1947-48 and 1965, religion was used as the factor of motivation during the 1971 war. During the war Lt.-Gen. Tikka Khan, drawing from Sir Mohammed Iqbal, recited to the troops:

> "Allah exalts the *mujahid* whether he lives or dies. He is a *ghazi* (crusader) if he lives, and a *shaheed* (martyr) if he dies. The *mujahid* seeks Allah's grace. He does not covet wealth and property."[14]

Yahya Khan, the Commander-in-Chief and President of Pakistan, boosted the soldiers by saying that they (Pakistan Army) were fighting the anti-Islamic "Kaffir" army and were upholding the highest traditions of *mujahideen*—soldiers of Islam.[15]

What was most critical was the evolution of Pakistan's grand strategy after the 1971 war. The grand strategy incorporated two important objectives that decided the future course of action for the Pakistani leadership:

> First, to expand territory eastward (take Kashmir). This implied a rise in covert activities in J&K and added emphasis on radical Islam in the name of *jihad*. Thus, terrorism to be adopted as a foreign policy tool.
>
> Second, to expand control westward (to gain leverage in Kabul). This implied creating strategic depth in Afghanistan and also facilitating a Pakistan-friendly government.

Ideological Shift Post 1971

The loss of East Pakistan not only altered the political and ethnic scenario in Pakistan but also ideological dynamics. More than the Indian or the American response to the 1971 crisis, what shocked the nation was the betrayal of Pakistan by East Pakistan itself. Pakistan justified the division by saying that the East Pakistanis, the Bengalis, were not true Pakistanis and, thus, *not truly Islamic*. This division of Pakistan created a fear of further segmentation, and the ruling elites increasingly believed that religious ideology would be the best option—*to unite people* and motivate the nation for an aggressive anti-India posture (in the name of religion). Also, in the early 1970s, the disturbances in Balochistan created tremendous unrest and kept the leadership in Pakistan engaged. The Balochistan insurgency provided the military and the intelligence agencies in Pakistan an opportunity to project Afghanistan as an additional threat and to support the growing military expenditure and maintain Pakistan's image as a garrison state. The developments in Pakistan coincided with the global rise of Islamic ideology, which facilitated Pakistan's journey into radical ideology, pronounced by Zulfiqar Ali Bhutto and taken forward by General Zia-ul-Haq.

Global Rise of Islamic Ideology

The 1970s and 1980s witnessed the re-emergence of Islam as a potent global force, starting with the spread of Saudi Wahabi ideology. It was the Iranian revolution that shattered the secular basis of nationalist thinking and expectations of the modernisation and development theories. The revolution drew attention towards the significant changes that were taking place in many Muslim countries across the globe in the 1970s. Ironically, the revival of Islamic ideology was most prominent in the societies that were modern or in the process of modernisation, and having a well-trained, Western oriented, secular elite, for example, countries like Egypt, Lebanon, Tunisia, Turkey and Algeria.

In Egypt and Malaysia, the resurgence of Islam was manifested in the people's lives, the conventional religious beliefs and also state politics. Religion came much more into practice and was reflected in the form of daily prayers, fasting and the way the people dressed. Muslim rulers emphasised on an Islamic identity to gain legitimacy, and Islamic organisations and symbols assumed paramount importance for the state. Bhutto's turning towards Islam has to be studied taking into account the ideological developments worldwide.

Bhutto's Islamic Socialism

Bhutto took forward the idea of *Islamic Socialism* and thus, enforced Islam as a major factor in statecraft. Stephen Cohen rightly pointed out:

> "If the Pakistan movement and the first twenty-five years of the history of Pakistan can be characterised as a struggle to turn Indian Muslims into Pakistanis, the years since 1972 have been an extension of the process; a struggle to turn Pakistanis into good Muslims."[16]

Bhutto's Islamic Socialism was considered insincere and it was seen more to establish the non-Indian identity of Pakistan.[17] General Zia put the state at the services of Islam and took steps to inculcate Islamic practices within the state by banning alcohol and gambling, and declaring Friday as a non-working day (which was later revised by Nawaz Sharif).

General Zia-ul-Haq and Islamisation of the Pakistan Army

General Zia systematically reinforced the *Islamisation of Pakistan*, which was propagated by his predecessor, Zulfikar Ali Bhutto. Zia's vision was candidly pronounced in his own words:

> "Pakistan, which was created in the name of Islam, will continue to survive only if it sticks to Islam. That is why I consider the introduction of the Islamic system as an essential prerequisite for the country."[18]

Zia systematically reinforced the Islamisation of Pakistan, which was propagated by his predecessor. The General introduced mandatory 'Islamic Reforms' impacting the economy and Pakistani society. A number of banking and commercial practices based on Islam were introduced, a dress code in accordance with Islamic norms was stressed, new women's universities were proposed and strict regulations were laid on the sale and consumption of alcoholic beverages.[19] The Pakistan Army in this period developed close links with the various Islamist groups and religion was now used deeply in the strategic thinking. Zia, in the process of Islamisation of Pakistan and introducing Islamic reforms, allowed the Tablighi Jama'at (an Islamic missionary society) to operate freely within the Army. Zia was also the first army chief and the first politician in Pakistan to appear at the Tablighi's annual convention at Raiwind.[20]

It was during Zia's period that "*Jihad*" was included as the motto for the Pakistan Army along with "Iman" and "Taqwa." Zia was entrusted with the task of Islamisation of the Pakistan Army when he took over as the army chief in 1976. Bhutto saw Zia as the most suitable man and trusted that he would assist the military to evolve as the guarantor of an anti-India Islamic ideology.[21] Zia, even as a Corps Commander, had distributed books written by Jamaat-e-Islami founder, Maulana Sayyid Abdul Ala Maududi, as rewards for officers who proved their calibre in various fields in his garrison. Adherence to Islamic practices emerged as a major criteria for selection in the Army. According to Zia, a soldier had to be a true Muslim before he takes the responsibility of defending the Islamic Republic. In the armed forces, the status of the religious teachers was raised to the level of commissioned officers. This became a major attraction for qualified individuals from the universities and religious institutions.

Pakistan, under Zia's regime, started to practice Islamic practices much more as compared to earlier political or military regimes in the country. The state was now being run on the values interpreted on the basis of religion. Perhaps the most critical part of this Islamisation was the impact on the education system of Pakistan, which shaped the young minds of the future generations. During Zia's period, Islam started to feature in the books. Islamic education gained the stature of a well-recognised and acceptable law governing the state structure, judiciary and the military establishment. Very importantly, at the lower and middle levels of the military establishment, there was an emergence of radical military personnel who were *madrassa* graduates and were nurtured on the agenda of protecting Islam.

Islamic training and thought including lectures by Abdul Qayyum was introduced into the curriculum at the Command and Staff College. Qayyum, who resembles Iqbal in his writings, said that a Pakistani must not only be "a professional soldier, engineer, or doctor" but also "Muslim soldiers, Muslim engineers, Muslim doctors, Muslim officers and Muslim men."[22]

Although the students at the Staff College study Western strategy and doctrine, they are instructed to intensify their core Islamic principles and values. Zia, in the process of reinforcing the Islamisation of Pakistan encouraged the Tablighi Jamaat to operate freely within the army. The Islamist parties and especially groups like the Tablighi Jamaat linked to the Deobandi tradition got much more access to military officials. The 'Zia process' altered the culture of the military and Islam became a critical factor in formulating military strategy and doctrine. *The soldiers of the state considered themselves soldiers of Islam.*

It was during this process of *Islamisation* that the major strategic development—*the Afghan War*—started and altered the dynamics of Pakistan's political, military and strategic policies. Looking into history one can say that in the 1980s, mainly two factors propagated the Islamic factor in the military: First, the 1971 war, and the creation of Bangladesh; and, second, the Soviet invasion of Afghanistan, which was viewed as an Islamic war against the communist forces. Zia not only built an army based on ideology but also fully supported the build-up of Pakistan's nuclear weapon capability (initiated by Bhutto!).

The Quranic Concept of War

Post the 1971 war, a strong tide of Islamisation did dominate the strategic thinking of the Pakistani leadership. Zia's active plan for the Islamisation of the Pakistan army derived support from the interpretation of teachings of the Holy Quran. The Holy Quran has been interpreted (to facilitate the strategic objectives) to develop Pakistan's doctrine and strategy of war.

The most comprehensive and precise study on war doctrine and strategy in the context of the Holy Quran has been by Brigadier S.K. Malik in his book, *The Quranic Concept of War*. According to his interpretation, the Holy Quran places war doctrine, its theory, and practice as very different from the Western thinking on the subject. Brigadier Malik interprets, "The Holy Quran has given a comprehensive treatment to its concept of war" and "determines all aspects of the use of 'force' in inter-state relations."[23] Brigadier Malik in his work regards the Quranic philosophy of war as supreme, which provides directions for the initiation, planning and control of war. According to his interpretation, the very "initiation of war is for the Cause of God" and jihad is the "most glorious word in the vocabulary of Islam." General Zia enthusiastically sponsored and supported the Brigadier's work, and in his foreword for the book he suggested:

> "The professional soldier in a Muslim army, pursuing the goals of a Muslim state, CANNOT become 'professional' if in all his activities he does not take on 'the colour of Allah."[24]

Terror, according to the author and the majority of the Pakistani military officers, is central to the war strategy. Use of terror as an instrument to impose your will and decisions on the enemy has been legitimized citing examples from the Holy Quran: "When God wishes to impose His will upon his enemies, He chooses to do so by casting terror in their hearts."[25]

The Islamic concept as derived from the Holy Quran by Brigadier Malik relies on the use of terror in the preparation stages of war itself in order to assure victory and achieve direct results.[26] Thus, terror has been legitimized in the Islamic ideology, which (till today) shapes the military thinking and strategy of Pakistan. Brigadier Malik asserts that the "Terror struck into the hearts of the enemies is not only a means, it is the end in itself."[27] War strategy, according to the Holy Quran, might have different forms depending on various factors but it must be effective and capable of striking terror into the hearts of enemies. It is emphasised that *fear* needs to be an important part of the preparation of war and it determines that "the test of utmost preparation lies in our capability to instil terror into the hearts of the enemies."[28]

The Quranic 'misinterpretation' of conduct of modern war legitimizes *jihad* and use of terror. One of the most effective modes of generating terror is through projection of maintaining a *low nuclear threshold* and *use of covert warfare* (*through terrorism*) and thus, creating physical and mental unrest and fear in enemy territory. Pakistan's strategic thinking and posture does reflect its belief in using terror as an effective instrument of war.

The Afghan War in the 1980s

Following the Soviet invasion of Afghanistan, Pakistan became the USA's front-line state in the fight against communism in the 1980s. General Arif outlined three options available to Pakistan at the time of the Soviet invasion: "Firstly, she could accept the *fait accompli* as she lacked the capacity to challenge the Soviet Union. Secondly, she could provide open and full support to the Afghan freedom struggle, despite the risks involved. And, thirdly, she could give overt political, diplomatic, and humanitarian support to the refugees with covert assistance to the Mujahideen."[29] Pakistan opted for the third option and entered into a second

US alliance. The US alliance was welcomed by the military and General Zia negotiated a substantial aid package, weaponry, including the much-desired F-16s. In addition to the US aid, Pakistan also received enormous funds from Saudi Arabia and Gulf countries to finance the US weaponry, assist Pakistan's nuclear weapon programme and, most importantly, open and sponsor madrassas preaching Wahabi Islam on the Balochistan-Iran border.

Zia's military regime undertook the responsibility of training Mujahideen to carry out covert operations to fight the Soviets. The operations directed by the USA–CIA was one of the largest operations planned by the USA and shaped a relationship between the CIA and the Pakistani intelligence agency, the ISI (Inter Service Intelligence), as the two worked in coordination for about a decade.

The US war in Afghanistan led to structural and organisational development of the factor of *religion in war*. The soldiers for war were being trained to fight in a "holy war" in the name of God. The declaration of "*jihad*" in Afghanistan led to the legitimized structural development of institutions preparing young fighters. It is reported that over 80,000 volunteers were being trained for the Afghan war who came not only from Pakistan and Afghanistan but also from other Muslim countries like Sudan, Bangladesh, Algeria and Turkey. A combination of courage (specifically amongst the Afghan fighters) and strong religious belief made the Mujahideen formidable warriors to defeat.[30] The belief was strengthened that the Mujahideen were fighting a holy war against unbelievers—the Kafirs, and "once the *jihad* was declared by their religious leaders, it was the duty of all men to fight, to save their faith, to defend their honour, to protect their independence and to guard their land and families."[31] The battle cry for the Mujahideen was (and is till date) "Allah o Akbar"—God is Great—which they shout as they are attacking enemy camps, bases or personnel.[32] Thus, the fighting for religion proliferated.

Ever since the creation of Pakistan, the Pashtuns, or the Baloch have been motivated by the creation of an independent state advocated by the Pashtun regimes in Kabul. The Pashtun voices for freedom have always been a matter of concern for the leadership in Pakistan, and the state has been worried about a possibility of an ethnic unrest. The military leadership had agreed to support the guerrilla warfare in Afghanistan against the Soviets with arms, ammunition, money, intelligence, training and operational advice. General Akhtar Abdul Rehman, Director-General of the ISI, suggested to General Zia that Pakistan should offer the border areas of the North West Frontier Province (NWFP) (now Khyber Pakhtunkhwa—KPK) and Balochistan as a sanctuary for both the Afghan refugees and guerrilla fighters. A base was essential for covert forces as without a secure cross-border base, no such campaign could succeed.[33]

Brigadier Mohammad Yousaf and Major Mark Adkin noted in a study, "The border areas of Pakistan had grown into a vast, sprawling administrative base for the *Jihad.* The Mujahideen came there for arms, they came to rest, they came to settle...."[34] Since the US assistance to the Mujahideen started as a covert affair, the ISI Directorate became the channel for not only ensuring the secrecy of the operation but to also provide expert advice and training to the Mujahideen in guerrilla tactics.

In this process, Zia cultivated a venomous strain of Islamic ideology in Pakistan. The ISI in partnership with the right-wing Islamic parties like the Jamaat-e-Islami and Jamiat-e-Ulema-e-Islam, recruited thousands of Afghan refugees in Pakistan and students from the madrassas to join the fight in Afghanistan as holy fighters. In this process, these Islamic parties developed an extensive network in Pakistan and also became much more influential.[35]

Along with this *jihadi* culture, what now found support in Pakistan was *sectarianism* resulting in the killing of hundreds in Pakistan. On the external front, the Islamic revolution in Iran in 1979 played a crucial role and the Khomeini regime started spreading its revolutionary message across the Muslim world. Pakistan became a battle ground for ideological war between Iran and Saudi Arabia, which worked towards restricting the spread of Iranian Shia influence.[36] Balochistan became the hub of hundreds of madrassas that were basically established to limit the Shia influence into Pakistan. On one side were the Iranian-backed Tehrik-e-Nifaz-e-Fiqh-e-Jafaria and, on the other, were Sunni extremist groups within Pakistan like the Sipah-e-Sahaba that demanded that the Shias (who comprised 15-20 per cent of Pakistan's population) be declared non-Muslims like the Ahmadias.[37]

In the 1980s, the US intelligence services followed a strategy of supplying enormous amounts of arms and ammunition to Mujahideen leaders and commanders in the field. The weapons pipeline was under the control of the ISI that was responsible for deciding the recipients and quantity of weapons. The ISI retained the majority of the weapons and equipment (reportedly 60 per cent) for its own covert war against India. The weaponry supplied during the Afghan War remained in the region after the war ended. Reportedly, Washington provided two billion dollars of covert assistance to the Afghan war between 1980 and 1989.[38]

Another important development during this period was the development of the narcotics trade, which flourished with CIA assistance to fund the covert operations. Opium production went up from 200 metric tons in 1980 to 1,200 metric tons in 1989.[39] Initially, in the 1980s, the narcotics trafficking network was used to support the US-Pak strategy of arming and supplying the Afghan mujahideen. Eventually, the military in Pakistan developed significant financial interests in the drug trade and this assisted in the development of the drug economy in Afghanistan and Pakistan. The drug money was also believed to have been used by the military to support Pakistan's active nuclear programme initiated by Bhutto in the early 1970s. The narcotics trade was initially developed to generate funds for the war against the Soviets, and eventually it became one of the most important channels for the Pakistan military to fund the military build-up and covert operations in India (in Kashmir and Punjab).

Rise in Terrorism in the 1980s and 1990s

In the 1980s, religious resurgence coupled with increasing alienation of the youth for diverse reasons, started to grow in Kashmir, and Pakistan's strategy of covert war through terrorism began to concretize. What was happening in Afghanistan and simultaneously in Indian Punjab (with Pakistan's active assistance), had a direct impact in the Kashmir Valley. In the mid 1980s, disturbances in Kashmir were growing with an unusual amount of Jamaat activity, and processions and resentment against the Hindus. The communal divide had started to be a major disturbing factor. Pakistan continued its covert war and the year 1984 witnessed substantive escalation of violent acts in Jammu and Kashmir. In the late 1980s and 1990s, Pakistan became much more active in sponsoring terrorism in J&K. The ISI encouraged young Kashmiris to come to Pakistan for training. The ISI initially trained secular groups in Kashmir and eventually shifted to training of groups linked to Pakistan's own Islamic parties.[40]

The weapons used by the terrorists had undergone a change as Pakistan had acquired modern arms in the 1980s to equip the covert fighters in Afghanistan. On one hand, Pakistan had equipment for the Afghan Mujahideen, which could be easily smuggled into Kashmir. On the other hand, Pakistan also acquired modern weapon systems, including F-16s from the USA during this period and felt psychologically stronger to conduct its covert strategy in Kashmir. However, the most critical factor for the escalation of the covert war in Punjab and Jammu and Kashmir was the acquisition of nuclear weapons by Pakistan, which it perceived as the security guarantee against a robust Indian military response.

Making of Nuclear Weapons: Shield against Terrorism

After its third defeat against India in 1971, the Pakistani leadership was convinced that acquisition of nuclear weapons would potentially neutralise India's conventional military superiority. In the initial years from the early 1950s to 1971, Pakistan's official policy was focused on build-up of the nuclear programme for the development of nuclear energy. Starting from the 1970s under the leadership of Bhutto and subsequently in the coming decades, the development of the nuclear programme was shaped by increasing militarisation of Pakistan's state policies and its strategic alliances.

After the 1971 war, Prime Minister Zulfiqar Ali Bhutto, who had been keen for Pakistan to acquire nuclear weapons even while he was in Ayub's cabinet, made nuclear weapon capability a major public issue in spite of Ayub's antipathy to them. Bhutto was always inclined to have the nuclear capability as a deterrent. Systematic efforts for building the nuclear weapons commenced after the 1971 war. Bhutto called for a secret meeting of top Pakistani scientists in Multan on 20 January 1972 and, curiously, the surreptitious meeting to discuss Pakistan's bomb was held under a *shamiana.* Bhutto (as usual) with his charismatic personality was able to motivate the scientific community to get ready for building the bomb in three years instead of the five that the scientists had asked for. He received an enthusiastic response from the scientists "We can do it...you will have the bomb!"[41]

Appeal for an Islamic Bomb

Soon after the Multan meeting, Bhutto started to seek external support to finance the nuclear weapon programme. He visited the Middle Eastern countries, which included Iran, Saudi Arabia, Libya, Egypt, the United Arab Emirates and Syria. Various reports suggested that the Arab world had been keen to develop a nuclear option. Bhutto's request for assistance received an enthusiastic response. He was looked upon as the champion of the Islamic cause, and was able to convince Saudi Arabia and Libya about the strong possibility of Pakistan being able to build a nuclear bomb as Pakistan's civilian nuclear programme had reached a level of erudition.[42] Bhutto did not have to wait too long for financial support from the Arab world. The prices of oil went up extensively following the international oil crisis in 1973. The moment was appropriate for Bhutto's appeal for financial assistance to support the 'Islamic bomb.' In February 1974, he hosted an Islamic summit in Lahore, which was attended by leaders of 37 Muslim countries. The forum laid the ground for the alliance between the wealthy Muslim nations and poor Islamic countries to fight the Zionists and their Western supporters.[43] According to some unidentified sources, as cited by Steve Weissman and Herbert Krosney (*The Islamic Bomb*), huge sums of money close to a billion dollars were raised for Pakistan. Reportedly, in a few months two couriers from

Libya reached Pakistan, each carrying $ 100 million in cash. The King of Saudi Arabia also offered financial support for the bomb and, in return, expected Pakistan to provide a security umbrella for the kingdom.[44] Libya in return desired complete access to nuclear technology and also wanted the Pakistani scientists to train Libyan technicians in the operation of hot cells, neutronics, and the handling of nuclear waste.[45]

Continued Projection of a Low Nuclear Threshold and Uncertainty

Pakistan acquired the nuclear weapon capability in 1987, although the overt nuclearisation happened much later in 1998. In the pre-nuclear test period, Pakistan's doctrine was that of ambiguity. Although, Pakistan even today does not have an officially announced doctrine, statements made by responsible policy makers in Pakistan outline basic elements of its nuclear doctrine. There is an unofficial code adopted by the Pakistani leadership, based on *Indo-centricity, credible minimum deterrence, strategic restraint* and *first use.* Very interestingly and rather ironically, the code asserts the principles of a peaceful programme revolving more around maintaining a balance against the Indian force build up, but it includes making a first strike in response to not only a conventional attack by India but also a posed threat from India.

Nuclear weapons remain integral to Pakistan's overall strategic positioning against India. While New Delhi's nuclear objectives have been primarily political for deterrence, Islamabad acquired the nuclear weapons for *war prevention* and to conduct the policy of sub-conventional warfare through terrorism without fear of Indian military retaliation. This explicitly explains Pakistan's nuclear positioning which relies on a *first use doctrine* projecting a low nuclear threshold and an element of uncertainty.[46]

1990s: Political Tug of War

After Zia's death, Pakistan struggled with numerous political and ideological challenges. The nation had been under military rule for a long period and, reverting back to a democratic regime was not easy: the economic downslide had started to appear, the *jihadi* culture took firm roots in the country, the US alliance had just ended and Pakistan stood isolated internationally. The democratic regimes between 1988 and 1999 were unstable and changed frequently. The ISI became an important centre of power on account of its role in the Afghan War and its involvement with the Americans. Although the fundamentalists and Islamists appeared to have lost in the elections, their influence continued to grow, especially among the intelligence agencies, military officers and emerging middle class in

Pakistan. The ISI also managed to create and sustain the differences between the political parties.

On the external front, there were important developments during this decade. The leadership in Pakistan intensified its terrorist activities on Indian soil through their proxies and anti-India terrorist organisations became much more active in the Valley and other parts of India. The ISI was now a fully trained and equipped organisation with a ready infrastructure for *jihad* and was diverted towards India to continue Pakistan's strategy of '*Bleeding India Through a Thousand Cuts.*' By 2002, Pakistan became home for more than two dozen militant groups operating in the neighbourhood and pursuing their agenda which was looked at favourably by the state. The largest among them were the Lashkar-e-Taiba (LeT), Jaish-e-Muhammed (JeM), Harkat-ul-Mujahedeen (HuM) and Harkat-ul-Jihad-al-Islami (HJI). The organisations enjoyed state patronage and a flow of funds was never a challenge despite Pakistan's economic struggles. The *jihadi* organisations managed to raise funds from the masses overtly in the name of freedom for Kashmir.

On the western front, Pakistan was keen to create its strategic depth and not have a hostile government. The army and the ISI, along with the political leadership, came together to support a new class of warriors—the *Taliban*. In 1994, Afghanistan saw the outbreak of the Taliban, which was composed of the younger generation of Pakistani-Afghans. Maulana Fazl-ul-Rahman, leader of the Jamait Ulema-e-Islam-F (JUI-F) supported the Taliban, and being a close ally of Benazir Bhutto, played a critical role in facilitating communication between Pakistan and the Taliban.[47] The Pakistani leadership extended full-fledged support to the Taliban and added to their strength from Pakistani madrassas. The Taliban began to take over one province after another in Afghanistan, and finally brought most of Afghanistan under their control in less than five years in 1996.[48]

The US Alliance, War on Terror and Extremism

Post 9/11, Pakistan entered into a third alliance with the USA and once again arrived at a critical strategic crossroads. Ideologically, Pakistan felt the need to position itself as a balanced nation and General Musharraf attempted to project a path of moderation. On 12 January 2002, he publicly said that Pakistani territory will not be used for (*jihadi*) terrorism. In 2004, he announced his plea for *Enlightened Moderation,* which could provide an answer to Pakistan's identity and its relationship with Islam. Defining the enlightened moderation, he said:

"The strategy of enlightened moderation...involves a win-win situation

> for the whole of the world as well as for the Muslim countries. This is a two-pronged strategy. One prong is to be delivered by the Muslim world itself by shunning militancy and extremism and adopting the path of socio-economic uplift to achieve its own emancipation. The other prong is meant to be delivered by the West, and the USA in particular, to determinedly resolve with justice all political disputes in which Muslims are engaged and also assist in the socio-economic betterment of the deprived Muslim world.... The time have come to re-think our position. What we need is a renaissance.... We have to concentrate on human resource development, and the best way for that is through poverty alleviation, greater education, better health and assured social justice.... We have to adopt the path of moderation, a conciliatory approach, a pacific approach, in order to cleanse ourselves of the charge that Islam is a religion of militancy and is averse to modernization, democracy and secularism."[49]

Although Musharraf talked about the moderate, secular path to appease the West, the state strategies remained unaltered contrary to Musharraf's announcement. Musharraf's attempt was to project Pakistan as a moderate Islamic nation focusing on socio-economic development. The projection was intended to attract Western goodwill and aid and assistance for Pakistan.

The military regime came under immense pressure by the Bush Administration to act against terrorist organisations, and Musharraf did issue orders to ban some of the key militant outfits and registration of madrassas. The state got an opportunity to counter and target the militant outfits that had turned against the state, specifically, the domestic sectarian groups, for example, the Sunni Sipah-e-Sahaba and its offshoot, the Lashkar-e-Jhangvi, and the Shia-Tehrik-e-Jafaria and its offshoot, the Sipah-e-Muhammad. These groups have been engaged in massive sectarian violence within Pakistan. Although these groups were initially supported and encouraged by the military, they stood as a major challenge for the military leadership, posing a serious threat to the domestic order. The state leadership was selective in suppressing the organizations and the target groups were the ones whose objectives were out of sync with the military's perception of national interests, and those engaged in the *jihadi* violence within the state.[50]

The top leadership of the Taliban and al-Qaeda was sheltered by the military. A significant number of the Taliban leadership, along with the Pakistani Pashtuns, being the prime targets in the global war on terror, took refuge in FATA. Most of the Taliban's fighters were originally mobilized by the ISI from the Gilzai confederation of Pashtuns who dominated south-eastern Afghanistan and from other Pashtun tribes belonging to FATA, and, thus, their returning to a relatively secure place, their original homeland, was natural after the Pakistan military decided to join the USA in the aggressive military operation against the Taliban.[51] The Taliban made Pakistan's tribal belt the base for training camps and for conducting action plans in Afghanistan and Pakistani territory. The Taliban leadership also reportedly manoeuvred an independent administrative set-up in FATA and the locals were in no position to oppose them. Since 2008, there were reports of the Taliban extending their conservative extremist norms to civilians in the region, controlling even their day-to-day lives.

Anti-India militant groups—the LeT, JeM and Harkat-ul-Mujahideen—continued to garner support from the state. Pakistan's so-called counter-terrorism efforts, which were based on a "selective policy", failed to yield results and insurgency and extremism flourished on Pakistan's frontier borders. Pakistan, for the first time, faced terrorist attacks within its own territory.

The US-led military operations post 9/11 dislocated the Taliban and the al-Qaeda from Afghanistan, and the militants now returned to their original home to coordinate with their support structure to be able to sustain and re-establish themselves. The tribal areas of Pakistan started to flourish with militancy, and the influence of the Taliban ideology was not unpredictable.

The Pakistan Taliban, Rise in Extremism and the Blowback

Towards the end of 2005, there were some signs of collaboration of a group trying to replicate the Taliban ideology. In 2007, the Tehreek-e-Taliban Pakistan (TTP) emerged as an entity in the context of a series of military operations in FATA, as well as the US Unmanned Aerial Vehicle (UAV) strikes in FATA. The TTP started to professionally organize itself when Abdullah Mehsud of the Afghan Taliban returned to Waziristan from the Guantanamo Bay camp. He blew himself up in Pishin, Balochistan, during a siege by Pakistani forces in 2006.[52] After Abdullah Mehsud's death, Baitullah Mehsud, a leading member of the Afghan Taliban, organised all the groups operating in FATA who professed similar ideologies and knit them into one of the most dangerous terrorist/insurgent groups.[53]

The TTP adopted a strictly anti-state and specifically anti-military agenda and has been conveying its message by consistently attacking government/military offices. In other words, the TTP has organised itself as a true insurgency, ideologically as well as organisationally. It shares a symbolic relationship with the al-Qaeda and draws its ideological guidance from it. During the late 2000s, the TTP not only provided safe haven to the al-Qaeda in FATA, but also launched deadly attacks against US, NATO and Pakistani targets. The organisation positions the Pakistani state as an enemy of Islam for siding with the USA. It has claimed responsibility for most of the deadly terrorist attacks, including the assassination of Benazir Bhutto in 2007, the bombing of the Mariott Hotel in 2008, and attack on the Peshawar school in 2014. The organisation has expanded its influence among young and unemployed youth and uses the *Sharia* to promote the political and ideological agenda of the group.

Pakistan witnessed a rising phase of extremism and intolerance in society. More importantly, what was disturbing was the increasing support for intolerance and extremism in society. Perhaps the most glaring incident reflecting the rising extremism in society was on January 4, 2011, when Salman Taseer, the Governor of Punjab, was assassinated by one of his security guards, Mumtaz Qadri. The killer recited *"La Ilaha Allah, Muhammad-ur-Rasool-Allah"* (There is no God but Allah, and Muhammad is his Prophet) before shooting Salman Taseer 27 times. The Governor was supporting Asia Bibi, a Christian woman, who was sentenced to death on charges of blasphemy. The developments post Taseer's assassination were alarming and signalled a serious ideological wave in Pakistan. Not only was Qadri hailed as a hero and *guardian of Islam,* but around 500 Pakistani religious scholars and clerics warned the masses against participating in Taseer's funeral.[54] The Jamaat-e-Ahl-e-Sunnat, a relatively moderate group of Islam in Pakistan, issued a statement, "More than 500 scholars of the Jamaat-e-Ahl-e-Sunnat have advised Muslims not to offer the funeral prayers of Governor Punjab Salman Taseer nor try to lead the prayers."[55] Muhammad Afzal Chishti, the secretary general of the Pakistan People's Party (PPP), Ulema wing, who led the funeral prayers for Taseer received threats and fled the country.[56] Qadri was welcomed with rose petals when he arrived in the court after the killing. Five years later, his execution in 2016, on the orders of the Pakistan Supreme Court, led to massive protests in Pakistan and emotions were strong in Pakistan. Tahir Iqbal Chistie, President of the Sunni Tehreek, Rawalpindi chapter, said during the protests, "At this time, the sentiments of all Muslims have been injured, and our feelings have been badly hurt. For any Muslim believer—no matter what school of thought he belongs to—Ghazi Mumtaz Qadri is a hero of Islam."[57] Qadri's shrine in Bara Kahu, a suburb of Islamabad, is a blooming shrine and hundreds of people visit it every day to pay their respects and show admiration for his bravery and commitment to defend the religion.

In May 2011, Osama bin Laden was killed in an operation carried out by

US Navy SEALs from the US Special Operations Command. Bin Laden was living for over five years in a compound in the garrison town of Abbottabad. Osama's killing led to two critical developments: an alteration in the way the West now looked and treated Pakistan, and secondly, the military's image within the country took a major hit, which was not acceptable to the military and it felt a strong need to rectify and strengthen its position. Externally, there was increasing pressure from the USA on Pakistan to act against the terrorists, and internally, the military wanted to reassert its position as the ultimate guardian and the most important institution. Two important operations were launched by the military—*Zarb-e-Azb* in North Waziristan (2014) and *Radd-ul-Fasaad* (2017)—to support the law enforcement agencies and target the terrorist sleeper cells across Pakistan.

Emerging Trends: Is Pakistan Equipped to Handle?

While it is impossible to track and discuss every incident and development, some trends are critical to understand the state of extremism within Pakistan.

Extremist Parties and Political Space

The 2018 elections in Pakistan provided political space to the candidates representing *jihadi* and extremist groups despite ample controversy and apprehensions raised over the future implications of the development. The USA and the United Nations (UN)-designated global terrorist, Hafiz Saeed's party, the Milli Muslim League (MML), was turned down by the Election Commission of Pakistan (ECP) after a prolonged debate. The Jamaat-ud-Dawa chief collaborated with a little known Allah-o-Akbar Tehreek (AAT) to contest the elections. What was surprising that despite the pressures from the USA and the Financial Action Task Force (FATF), Pakistan did accommodate Saeed's political debut. The AAT party did not manage to win a single seat, but this can be credited to the fact that the party was created a few months before the elections and did not have the time to expand its political presence.

The old religious parties like the MMA, Ulema-e-Islam Nazryati-Pakistan and Jamiat Ulema-e-Pakistan (National) did not perform well as compared to the 2013 elections, but new splinter groups established their presence.[58] The Tehreek-e-Labbaik Pakistan (TLP), a newly formed party and an aggressive face of Barelvi politics, emerged as the fifth largest party which received 2,234,138 votes for the National Assembly.[59] The Tehreek-i-Laibbaik Ya Rasool Allah, started as a protest movement and was registered as a political party by one of the founders, Khadim Hussain Rizvi, in the summer of 2017.[60] The group rose from the protests after Mumtaz Qadri's execution and came to the limelight in 2017, when it blocked Islamabad for several weeks demanding stricter enforcement of blasphemy laws. Imran Khan supported the party and the TLP managed to get a surprising number of votes in the National Assembly and more than 2.38 million provincial votes, which was termed as a "really spectacularly rapid rise."[61]

The TLP managed to gather the maximum number of votes in Lahore. The number of seats that it won were not so significant, but what was relevant was a radical party's entry and performance on the political stage. This indicates the revival of Barelvi sectarian politics in Pakistan, and is likely to have long-term implications for the state. Although lately the leadership has tried to control the TLP's aggressive positioning using punitive means, it will not be totally incorrect to say that Barelvi organisations will continue to try to increase pressure on the government through mass protests/other means. There will be an effort to employ sectarian discourse by these groups which will be a challenge for the state.[62]

Resurgence of the TTP, The Islamic State and Rising Religious Intolerance

After the death of Hakimullah Mehsud, the TTP faced severe challenges in terms of organisational consolidation. There were reports regarding divisions within the TTP due to leadership issues. The counter-terror operations did challenge the operational capability of the TTP but the terror attacks continued with varying intensity. There was a series of attacks in 2017 that were claimed by the TTP and the Islamic State (IS). The attacks drew significant attention and did represent a higher intensity of radicalisation within Pakistan. Perhaps one of the most glaring attacks was on the Lal Shahbaz Qalander dargah in Sehwan, while devotees were in the middle of *Dhamaal* and at least 90 people died. The attack was claimed by the ISIS and victims included women and children, and a 100 were injured. The attack represented intolerance of Sufi Islam in Pakistan. Another attack on liberalism was the assassination of Pakistan's most famous qawwali singer, Amjad Sabri. The TTP claimed responsibility for the attack citing that the assassination was on account of blasphemy.

In 2020, the TTP announced the merger (again!) of its two major splinter groups, the Jamaat-ul-Ahrar and Hizbul Ahrar. The development is important as the militant group has been on the run for some time and found sanctuaries in Afghanistan. The TTP has gained strength and a series of attacks have been conducted over the past two years specifically targeting security personnel. The return of TTP fighters to North Waziristan has seriously complicated the security dynamics in Pakistan. The Pakistan government extended the offer of talks with the group and proposed that the state was ready to grant amnesty to the TTP fighters if the group agreed to give up violence.

The TTP has reunited and gathered its strength. Ever since the Taliban has taken control of Afghanistan (August 2021), the TTP has accelerated the terror attacks specifically targeting the security forces. Surely, the defeat of the democratically elected forces in Afghanistan is seen as a major ideological victory by the group. The TTP was the first organisation to send a congratulatory message to the Taliban in Afghanistan after the group took control of Kabul. Till now (at the time of writing this paper) there have been no confirmed reports regarding formal support from the Afghan Taliban to the TTP. However, a possibility of collaboration between these two groups cannot be ruled out given the fact that the groups share common ideologies and common objectives of establishing a rule based order on *Islamic Sharia law*.

Defeat of Political Forces in Afghanistan: The Taliban Victory

Pakistan has been rejoicing over the Taliban takeover in Kabul and sees it as its strategic victory. At the political level, Prime Minister Imran Khan said that the Taliban has "broken the shackles of slavery."[63] For Pakistan, its long-cherished dream of *seeking strategic depth in Afghanistan* has been finally accomplished. Islamabad always desired a pro-Pakistan regime in Afghanistan to cater to its strategic objectives including managing the rebel Pashtun voices and controlling the Pashtun sentiments in its tribal areas, dealing with the challenges of the disputed Durand Line, using the Afghan soil to train anti-India terror groups and, most importantly, deny India any space in Afghanistan. After the Taliban's victory in Afghanistan, there were Pakistani voices that reflected the sentiment that Islamabad can now use the Afghan Taliban to support its Kashmir agenda.

At the level of religious groups in Pakistan, there is a feeling of victory of the radical ideology. There is a growing rhetoric within Pakistan's religious groups supporting the Taliban victory in Afghanistan. The Jamiat-e-Ulema-e-Islam (S) JUI and Difa-e-Pakistan Council termed the Taliban victory as a glorious victory of the *ideology of Maulana Sami-ul-Haq*. The Jamia Hafsa Seminary in Islamabad celebrated the Taliban victory by chanting slogans, singing a song 'Salam Taliban' and hoisting the Taliban flags on its rooftop.[64] The ideological wave within Pakistan will get strengthened which will have severe fallouts in the longer run for not only Pakistan but also for the region. But certainly, the Generals in Rawalpindi do not feel that way. The Pakistan military and the ISI, in their own minds are closest to achieving their strategic objective of controlling Afghanistan.

Conclusion

Pakistan is facing challenges of increasing extremism and the emerging trends are worrisome. Although one is not sure whether the state essentially feels threatened with rising extremism or seeks to draw support from the extremist narratives and trends. Pakistan's reliance on religion started mainly to assert on its identity which is different from India. Eventually, the widening gap between the two countries and Pakistan's inability to match India's growth trajectory led to intensified use of religion and a narrative of threat perceptions vis-a-vis India. Perceived threat perceptions from India, dominant military lobby and identity crisis have been three critical factors shaping Pakistan's strategic posturing and its policy options domestically and internationally. The dominant Punjabi-Pathan military lobby leveraged the threat perceptions and strategically exaggerated the perceived fears to facilitate a favourable power dynamics. Religion became an essential part of the overall anti-India narrative for Pakistan, and post the 1971 war, critical developments took place using religion in a more structured and organised form: in policy making to deal with Pakistan's implacable enemy (India); developing nuclear weapon capability to conduct covert war (without fear of Indian military retaliation); drawing support from the Muslim world; building up the military capability (despite economic woes); expanding westwards and controlling Afghanistan; and, very importantly, sustaining engagement and interest of the West in Pakistan.

After 75 years of independence, at the national level, there are strong signs of extremist factions gaining ground, increasing intolerance in the name of religion and rise in terror attacks. Violent religious groups have challenged the writ of the state. Freedom of expression stands suffocated with multiple media groups and journalists being frequent targets for giving the military a reality check and pursuing true national security objectives. Peaceful civil rights movement by the Pashtuns—the *Pashtun Tahafuz Movement (PTM)*—has been responded to with brutal tactics by the state. Pakistan was put on the Financial Action Task Force (FATF) grey list in June 2018, and since then, has been struggling to avoid the black list and get out of the grey list. Till now, (at the time of writing this paper) the policy makers in Pakistan have not been able to convince the organisation of its sincerity in recommended actions related to terror financing.

The developments in Afghanistan have found a strong support base within Pakistan. Even though Pakistan has supposedly aspired for modern democratic values and human rights, it is absolutely comfortable with the complete loss of these values in its neighbourhood. The political leadership is hopeful of getting Taliban support in the Kashmir cause.

Jinnah talked about modern values and protection of Muslim culture and rights. The fact is that over the decades Pakistan's insecurity as a state, lack of identity and its inability to decide on the interpretation of Islam, led to a radical interpretation of Islam as a strategic policy option. Pakistan tried to unsuccessfully use religion as a binding force and pursue the *Kashmir cause*. Pakistan's narrative on Kashmir has seen three critical shifts after India decided to revoke Article 370 in 2019:

1. Pakistan took a position that the Indian government is being run on the Nazi ideology. India is a threat to not only Muslims in Pakistan, but Muslims across the globe.
2. Kashmir and Kashmiri Muslims are a global responsibility and the world needs to act on Kashmir against India.
3. *Highlighting Islamophobia* has been Pakistan's focus at international levels.

Extremism has a deep penetration in Pakistan and, according to Hasan Askari Rizvi: "Islamic orthodoxy and radicalism have seeped not only into society at large, but also into the lower echelons of state institutions, including the police and the military. A very large number of people, including those with modern Western-style education, are supportive of variations and aspects of orthodox Islam in national and international issues, viewing everything as a function of religion."[65]

Pakistan has opted for some counter-terror measures including the much discussed National Action Plan (NAP), a 20-point list issued after the gruesome Peshawar Army Public School attack in December 2014. Prior to the NAP, the government approved an elaborate National Internal Security Policy (NISP) 2014-2018 in 2014 which was focused more as security policy. Pakistan has attempted for legal options to control extremism and terrorism but the biggest question here is: Is the state ready to stop its reliance on religion as a foreign policy tool in dealing with India? Is Pakistan ready for the alteration in its strategic calculus? The answer is 'NO.' The thinking and actions of the Pakistani leadership do not show a change in the (decades old) mindset, and conviction in extremism and terrorism as the most potent weapon to deal with India (and Afghanistan), despite the blowback which the state continues to struggle with.

Disclaimer: Some parts of this paper have previously been published in Shalini Chawla, "Growth of Extremism in Pakistan", *Asian Defence Review 2014-2015*, (ed.) Air Marshal Vinod Patney, (Knowledge World, New Delhi, 2015), pp. 37-60.

ENDNOTES

1. Ayesha Jalal, *The State of Martial Rule* (Cambridge, Cambridge University Press, 1990) p. 16.
2. *Quaid-i-Azam Mohammad Ali Jinnah's Speeches as Governor-General of Pakistan 1947-48* (Karachi, Government of Pakistan, 1964).
3. Farzana Shaikh, *Making Sense of Pakistan* (London, Foundation Books, 2009) p. 5.
4. Ibid, p. 5.
5. Maj. General Akbar Khan, *Raiders in Kashmir* (Delhi, Army Publishers, date not available) p. 9.
6. Hasan Askari Rizvi, "Pakistan's Strategic Culture", in (ed.) Michael R. Chambers, *South Asia in 2020: Future Strategic Balances and Alliances*, Strategic Studies Institute, November 2002, at https://www.files.ethz.ch/isn/101060/South_Asia_2020.pdf, p. 311. Accessed on December 20, 2021
7. Ibid.
8. Ziad Haider, "Ideological Adrift", (ed.) Maleeha Lodhi, *Pakistan Beyond the Crisis State* (New Delhi, Rupa Publications, 2011), p. 116.
9. Ahmedis are followers of an alleged nineteenth century messiah called Mirza Ghulam Ahmed.
10. Zaid Haider, n 8, p. 116.
11. Ibid, p. 117.
12. Ibid, p. 118.
13. Larry Collins and Dominique Lapierre, *Freedom at Midnight* (London, Harper Collins, 1997) p. 159.
14. Quoted in unpublished manuscript, p. 217, as cited in Stephen P. Cohen, *The Pakistan Army* 1998 Edition, (Oxford University Press, Karachi, 1998) p. 87.
15. Ibid.
16. Stephen Cohen, n 14, p. 89.
17. See, Stephen Cohen, *The Idea of Pakistan,* (New York, Oxford University Press, 2005) p. 170.
18. "General Zia ul-Haq's Address to the Nation on July 5, 1977", quoted in Hasan Askari Rizvi, *The Military and Politics in Pakistan 1947-1986,* (Lahore, Progressive Publishers, 1986) pp. 289-93.
19. Stephen P. Cohen, n 14, p 91.
20. Stephen P. Cohen, n 17, p. 113.
21. Husain Haqqani, *Pakistan: Between Mosque and Military,* (Lahore, Vanguard Books, 2005), p. 112.
22. *On striving to be a Muslim* (Lahore, Islamic Book Centre, 1978) as cited by Stephen P. Cohen, n 14, pp. 95-96.
23. Brigadier S. K. Malik, *The Quaranic Concept of War,* (New Delhi, Himalayan Books, 1986) p. 1.
24. Ibid, Foreword by Zia-ul-Haq.
25. Ibid, p. 57.
26. Ibid.
27. Ibid, p. 59.
28. Ibid, p. 144.
29. General Khalid Mehmood Arif, *Working with Zia: Pakistan Power Politics 1977-1988* (Karachi, Oxford University Press, 1995) p. 314.
30. Brigadier Mohammad Yousaf and Major Mark Adkin, *The Bear Trap*, (Lahore, Jang Publishers, 1992) p. 32.

31. Ibid, p. 33.
32. Ibid.
33. Ibid, p. 25.
34. Ibid, p. 49.
35. Ziad Haider, n 8, p. 122.
36. Ibid, p. 123.
37. Ibid.
38. Husain Haqqani, n. 21, p. 193.
39. T. Raghavan, "The Narcotics Trade in South West Asia: Geography and Production", *Security Research Review,* at, http://www.bharat-rakshak.com/SRR/Volume14/raghvan.html. Accessed on November 10, 2009.
40. Ahmed Rashid, *Descent into Chaos* (London, Penguin Group, 2008), p. 111.
41. An account of the Multan meeting can be found in Shahid Ur Rehman, *Long Road to Chagai: Untold Story of Pakistan's Nuclear Quest,* Print wise Publication, Islamabad, 1999, pp. 16-19. Also see Zahid Malik, *Dr. A.Q. Khan and The Islamic Bomb,* Hurmat Publication, Islamabad, 1992, p. 128 as cited in Owen Benett Jones, *Pakistan Eye of the Storm,* (New Delhi, Penguin Books, 2001) p. 196.
42. Major Gen D.K. Palit and P.K.S. Namboodiri, *Pakistan's Islamic Bomb,* (Vikas Publishing House, New Delhi, 1979), pp. 6-7.
43. Douglas Frantz and Catherine Collins, *The Man From Pakistan: The True story of the World's Most Dangerous Smuggler,* (New York, Twelve, 2007), p. 22.
44. Ibid, p. 22.
45. Steve Weissman and Herbert Krosney, *The Islamic Bomb* (New York, Times Books, 1981), p. 67.
46. For details, see Shalini Chawla, "Pakistan's Nuclear Brinkmanship", in *Pakistan Insights 2020,* (ed.) Tilak Devasher, (New Delhi, Pentagon, 2021) pp. 103-111.
47. Hassan Abbas, *Pakistan's Drift Into Extremism: Allah, the Army and America's War on Terror,* (New York, M. E. Sharpe, 2005) p. 154.
48. Ibid, p. 155.
49. Speech by General Musharraf, "OIC Challenge and Response: Enlightened Moderation", 1 June 2004, at http://presidentmusharraf.wordpress.com/2005/01/18/musharraf-oic-enlightened-moderation/. Accessed on June 10, 2010
50. Ashley J. Tellis, "Pakistan and the War on Terror: Conflicted Goals, Compromised Performance" (Washington DC, Carnegie Endowment, 2008) p. 4.
51. Ibid, p. 6.
52. Imtiaz Gul, *The Al Qaeda Connection: The Taliban and Terror in Pakistan's Tribal Areas,* (New Delhi, Penguin books, 2009) p. 51.
53. The TTP was the revival of an older organisation of the same name founded in 1998 in Orakzai agency.
54. Michael Georgy, "Pakistan governor buried, clerics warn against grief", *Reuters,* January 5, 2011, https://www.reuters.com/article/idINIndia-53936920110105. Accessed on January 10, 2021
55. Ibid.
56. "Taseer funeral prayer leader forced to flee from Pakistan", *The Express Tribune,* August 19, 2011, https://tribune.com.pk/story/235182/taseer-funeral-prayer-leader-forced-to-flee-the-country. Accessed on 20 April, 2021
57. "Pakistan hangs Mumtaz Qadri for murder of Salmaan Taseer" *Al Jazeera,* February 29, 2016, https://www.aljazeera.com/news/2016/2/29/pakistan-hangs-mumtaz-qadri-for-murder-of-

salman-taseer. Accessed on 16 August, 2021

58. Ramsha Jahangir, "Religious parties clinch over 9 pc share in National Assembly", *Dawn*, May 19, 2018, www.dawn.com/news/1424235. Accessed on January 12, 2019.
59. Ibid.
60. Mossa Kaleem, "The emergence of Tehreek-e-Labbaik Pakistan on Karachi's political map", *Herald*, September 20, 2018, https://herald.dawn.com/news/1398669. Accessed on December 1, 2018.
61. "The rise and rise of Tehreek-e-Labbaik", *Pakistan Today*, July 31, 2018, https://www.pakistantoday.com.pk/2018/07/31/the-rise-and-rise-of-tehreek-e-labbaik/ Accessed on August 31, 2018.
62. For details, see Iqbal Singh Sevea, "The rise of Barelvi Political Activism in Pakistan", *ISAS Insights*, NUS, no. 520, 13 October 2018, https://www.isas.nus.edu.sg/wp-content/uploads/2018/10/ISAS-Insights-No.-520-A-New-Strand-of-Islamic-Politics-in-Pakistan.pdf. Accessed on April 1, 2019.
63. "PM Imran Khan talks about overpowering 'shackles of slavery' at Single National Curriculum Launch", *Dawn*, August 16, 2021, https://www.dawn.com/news/1640988. Accessed on August 17, 2021.
64. Anil Kumar, "Taliban flags hoisted at women's madrasa in Pakistan, children sing 'Salam Taliban'" *India Today*, August 22, 2021, https://www.indiatoday.in/world/story/taliban-flags-hoisted-women-madrasa-pakistan-afghanistan-1843882-2021-08-22. Accessed on August 23, 2021.
65. Hasan Askari Rizvi, "Reversing Pakistan's Drift Towards Radicalism", *JSTOR*, February 23, 2011, https://www.jstor.org/stable/pdf/resrep18868.pdf?refreqid=fastly-default%3A4f66ebc85 f6399dbd9cb0780220471e5&ab_segments=0%2Fbasic_search_gsv2%2Fcontrol& origin =search-results. Accessed on 23 January, 2021.

4

Pakistan: Non-Traditional Security Threats[1]

Tilak Devasher

Traditional analysis of Pakistan's security threats begins with its geographical construct: a flat terrain coupled with several of Pakistan's population centres being close to the border with India. Even before the creation of Pakistan, the Cabinet Mission Plan of 16 May 1946 had stated clearly: '*The two sections of the suggested Pakistan contain the two most vulnerable frontiers in India and for a successful defence in depth the area of Pakistan would be insufficient.*'[2]

Post-creation, Ayub Khan was perhaps the first to articulate the lack of depth of Pakistan. He wrote in his diary on 10 October 1968: 'Unfortunately, we lack depth in our country and besides, some of our centres of population, communication links, head-works and canals lie near the border so we have to be ready to defeat the enemy as soon as he enters our territory. This is what we did last time and we have every hope of success should he aggress again.'[3]

As a consequence, Pakistan has always seen its threats in territorial terms and security primarily in military terms. Analysts have pitched in with articulation of its nuclear arsenal, conventional military capability and its use of non-state actors as force multipliers. Articles in many journals also do a missile for missile, tank for tank, division for division, aircraft for aircraft and ship for ship comparison between India and Pakistan.

Today, there has been a shift away from the exclusive stress on territorial security seen in military terms due to a variety of challenges faced by the nation-states. This has led to the evolution of the concept of 'national security' rather than 'military security' alone. National security essentially involves the capability of the state to overcome the multi-dimensional threats to its people and its survival as a nation-state. This critical element of the power matrix comes under the rubric of Non-Traditional Security Threats (NTST) that encompasses all threats dealing with human security or the wellbeing of the citizens of a country. They include issues like (a) Energy, food and water security; (b) Economic security; (c) Environmental security; and (d) Societal security.

In Pakistan's case, these non-traditional threats actually go to the heart of what is going wrong with it. A comprehension of such threats is crucial to understand where Pakistan is headed and what threats it could pose to itself and to the region in addition to the traditional military and terrorist threats that it poses.

In my book *Pakistan: Courting the Abyss,*[4] I had coined an acronym, WEEP, standing for Water, Education, Economy and Population to elaborate four areas of Pakistan's NTST. Individually, each of these elements has not only a far-reaching impact on every strata of society but is a decisive element in the security of any state. Collectively, they are a fundamental factor in determining the quality of life, health and longevity of the country and its citizens. The degradation in each of these parameters takes a long time to manifest itself just as rectification and reversing the trends take a considerably longer time.

Pakistan today has become a water-scarce country from a water-abundant one in 1947. It is in danger of becoming an absolute water-scarce country by 2025. What this means for an agricultural country with a rapidly expanding population can well be imagined.

Pakistan also faces an education emergency. With twenty-five million children out of primary schools and those who attend school getting an indifferent education, the scale of the problem can well be imagined.

With Pakistan's economy suffering from major structural imbalances, it has not been able to make requisite investments in these crucial sectors for decades thereby compounding the problem. As a result of such imbalances, it is in constant need of external aid. It has, however, squandered the vast amounts of foreign assistance it has received on physical security rather than on the real sinews of power.

An increasing burden on all the resources of Pakistan is the rapidly expanding population. Though Pakistan has the potential of an once-in-a-lifetime 'demographic dividend', it is unlikely to reap the benefits. Instead, it may well be left with a large youthful population that is unemployed and unemployable and will become fodder for terrorist organisations.

Pakistan faced an emergency situation in all these four areas about a decade ago. Today, it should be in the disaster management mode, but there are no signs that it is. These critical issues have been ignored by a succession of leaders, civilian and military, since its creation. Increasingly, these issues could lead to multi-organ complications for Pakistan and continued neglect will haunt the country and be the primary factors impelling it towards the abyss.

Like elsewhere in the world, the COVID-19 pandemic has compounded the problems for the people, pushing millions out of work, and into poverty. Pakistan's economy was severely impacted. With the lifting of lockdown measures, the economy is showing signs of a fragile recovery but other adverse structural factors have prevented any long-term change.

Water

Pakistan is an arid agro-based country where 60 per cent of the population depends on agriculture for their livelihood, especially in the dominant province of Punjab. Agriculture accounts for about 20 per cent of the GDP and over 70 per cent of Pakistan's exports depend on agriculture-based products. Not surprisingly, therefore, up to 95 per cent of all water—surface and groundwater is utilised in irrigation for agriculture.

(i) Water Availability: The total average annual availability of water in Pakistan is estimated at 200 MAF, of which 145 MAF is surface water and 55 MAF is groundwater. However, the per capita availability of water has decreased from 5,650 cubic metres (m^3) per year in 1951 when it was a water-abundant country to 940 m^3/per capita/per annum in 2015[5] to roughly 866 m^3/per capita/year currently. It is estimated that by 2025, water availability would have shrunk to around 500 m^3/per capita/year according to the Pakistan Council for Research in Water Resources (PCRWR) when its population could increase to more than 220m.[6] Incidentally, absolute water scarcity means drought-like conditions in parts of the country. Massive increase of population requiring growth of additional food and thus water utilisation, is one of the main reasons for this state of affairs. But there are other reasons too.

Indus-Pakistan is dependent on just one river system—the Indus and groundwater for its water needs. The Indus river system is the largest contiguous irrigation system in the world. The peculiarity of the Indus is that 75 per cent of its flows occur during four summer months and 25 per cent during the rest of the year. The problem, however, is that the water demand is 60 per cent in summer and 40 per cent in winter. This necessitates sufficient water storage during the short surplus period for use during the longer water stress period.[7]

(ii) Water Storage: Pakistan has built only three major storage facilities—Mangla (1967-Jhelum), Tarbela (1976-Indus) and the Chashma Barrage (Indus). When constructed they had a total live storage of 15.73 MAF. Due to silting, the Tarbela and Mangla dams have been rapidly losing capacity. It is estimated that a storage capacity of around 8.37 MAF will be lost by 2025.[8] As a result, these dams are reaching dead levels earlier. For example, lower than average rainfall has led the Indus River System Authority (IRSA) to believe that neither the Mangla nor the Tarbela dam would be properly filled in 2021, putting the rabi crops at great risk.[9] In mid-March 2022, it was revealed that the water level in the Tarbela reservoir had been stagnant at its dead level of 1,392 feet for the last two weeks, reducing irrigation water supply to the provinces. Therefore, water was being discharged to provinces in line with the amount of inflow in the reservoir, leading to reduction in their supply. Not surprisingly, while at full capacity the Tarbela could generate a total of almost 5,000 MW electricity, but due to reduced water inflow in mid-March 2022, it could generate only 248 MW as only six units out of 17 were operational.[10]

Even otherwise, the major reservoirs can store only 10 per cent of the inflow, against the world average of 40 per cent. This capacity is inadequate to store the surplus water available during the summer months. In fact, Pakistan can store less than 30 days of supply or 121 m^3 per capita per year, that is equal to Ethiopia's capacity. The international standard is 120 days.[11] The USA and China have per capita storage of over 2,000 cubic metres. Even India has per capita storage capacity of over 200 cubic metres.

Without adequate storage, 30 MAF of water in the Indus in the surplus months flows into the sea. To put it in perspective, this is equivalent to more than the entire water of the Chenab river or twice the capacity of the existing storage capacity of Pakistan. In monetary terms, the cost of lack of storage and conservation had been calculated at approximately 21 billion dollars a few years ago and is today estimated at 29 billion dollars.

(iii) Water Utilisation: It is not that Pakistan does not have enough water but its water utilisation is among the worst in the world. For example, (a) its water intensity rate—the amount of water, in cubic metres, used per unit of GDP—is the world's highest, which means that Pakistan's economy is more water intensive and water dependent than any other country in the world.[12] Against the world average of $ 8.6, Pakistan's one cubic metre of water contributes only 34 cents to its GDP;[13] (b) It is also indicative of the inefficiency of water usage because only 36 per cent of the water reaches the fields with 64 per cent being lost in transmission;[14] (c) As noted by the Economic Survey, Pakistan's crop productivity per unit of water is very low at 0.13 kilograms per cubic metre.[15] In the case of wheat, according to the Pakistan Council of Research in Water Resources (PCRWR), Pakistan's water use efficiency (WUE) stands at 0.5 kg/cubic metre compared with 1 kg/cubic metre in India. Similarly, Pakistan gets 2.5 tons/hectares wheat against India's average of 3.5 tons/hectares despite having a similar climate and land characteristics.[16] What this means is that 'Pakistan is using 95 per cent of its allocated water resources to support one of the lowest productivities in the world per unit of water.'[17]

According to a State Bank of Pakistan (SBP) report in July 2019, sugarcane and wheat used around four times the global average of irrigated water, while rice consumed more than six times the world's average. According to the Federal Commission on Agriculture, water-intensive crops like rice and sugarcane were being cultivated over larger areas requiring more water. Thus, in 2021, rice was cultivated on more than 3.3 million hectares. This large scale shifting to rice, even in areas where groundwater resources were already under stress, like district Sanghar in Sindh, has put intense pressure on groundwater reservoirs that are being accordingly depleted at an alarming rate.[18]

(iv) Groundwater Depletion: Groundwater, akin to family gold to be used as a last resort when surface supplies are disrupted, is also depleting very fast. Satellite data shows that the Indus basin aquifer is now among the most stressed in the world.[19] This means that Pakistan does not have much groundwater in reserve that can be used as the river system becomes more stressed. Of the 55 MAF of groundwater, about 45 MAF is being exploited to supplement the surface water through the public sector and private tubewells that have grown from 10,000 in 1947 to 1.2 million currently. This is unsustainable because the gap between withdrawal and recharge is narrowing. Groundwater supplies are depleting at 16–55 centimetres a year, according to a study carried out by the International Waterlogging and Salinity Research Institute (IWASRI), part of the Water and Power Development Authority (WAPDA).[20] The irrigation department of Punjab has stated that while in the 1990s, water could be extracted in the province at a depth of 20–40 feet below the ground, in the 2010s, drilling has to take place at close to 800 feet below the ground. It has been reported that Punjab would have consumed all its underground water in the next 25 years due to injudicious use of this natural resource.[21] Additionally, this indiscriminate pumping and heavy use of pesticides are contaminating the aquifer, where tubewell salinity is increasing. It is estimated that 14 per cent of the groundwater reserves are highly saline, unfit for drinking purposes as well as irrigation, and there is now saline water intrusion into mined aquifers.[22]

(v) The Food and Agriculture Organisation (FAO) measures the pressure on national water resources by calculating water withdrawal as a percentage of total renewable water resources (TRWR). Stresses are considered high if the TRWR value is above 25 per cent. Pakistan's water pressure amounts to a staggering 74 per cent. This pressure is exorbitant even when compared with neighbouring high-pressured countries, including India at 34 per cent and Afghanistan at 31 per cent.[23]

Three other factors need to be noted. First, according to a report of the Pakistan Medical Association released at the end of last year, the poor quality of drinking water was responsible for nearly 30 per cent of diseases and 40 per cent of deaths in the country.[24] In addition, 27,000 children died annually due to water-borne diseases.[25]

Second, the government recently disclosed in the National Assembly that an overwhelming majority of the cities, including the mega cities, in Pakistan did not have safe drinking water for citizens. The underground water was contaminated with arsenic, iron, fluoride and bacteria. Out of the 29 cities where PCRWR tested underground water, there were 20 cities (including Karachi, Multan, Hyderabad, Faisalabad, Peshawar and Quetta) where more than 50 per cent water obtained from various sources was found to be unsafe. Hundred per cent water in three cities—Mirpurkhas, Shaheed Benazirabad (Nawabshah) in Sindh and Gilgit—were unsafe for drinking.[26]

Third, there is also the issue of serious inter-provincial discord, especially between Punjab and Sindh over water distribution as per the 1991 Water Accord. Sindh has alleged that it was now receiving only 50 per cent of its share. Evidence of the cut in Sindh's share is massive sea intrusion, which has devoured some 3.2 million acres of arable land in coastal districts of the province. Such a process could have been prevented if 10 MAF water was allowed to flow into the sea, but this is not available. As a result of sea intrusion, large tracts of land, especially in districts like Thatta, Badin and Sujawal, have turned barren.[27]

The situation is likely to get worse. Why?

(i) **Climate Change:** In May 2021, a report published by the FAO declared that Pakistan was one of the most vulnerable countries due to climate change. The Global Climate Risk Index (GCRI) ranked Pakistan in the top 10 countries adversely affected by climate change.[28] Due to climate change, there has been increased glacial melts causing heavy flooding followed by periods of reduced availability. Already, a reduction in the long-term average availability of water has been noticed. A statistical comparison of surface water availability between the last 30 and 10 years points towards declining water flows. While average flows for the years 1978 to 2008 was equal at 140-145 MAF, the same for 1998–2008 was 128.52 MAF.[29]

Practically speaking, this has resulted in the decline in water availability during the last few years by as much as 30-40 per cent. For example, Pakistan faced 30 to 40 per cent water shortage during the 2021 early kharif season (the sowing phase, 1 April-10 June). The water level in the reservoirs was too low, therefore reliance was on heavy spells of rains or hot weather that would melt the snow and improve the water availability in the dams.[30] Rice, sugarcane, cotton and maize are some of the key crops of the kharif season that lasts from April 1 to November 30. For the rabi 2021-22 season, both Punjab and Sindh faced a shortage of 28 per cent each since, instead of the availability of 38 MAF of water availability, the total water availability was worked out at 26.911 MAF for the entire season.[31]

(ii) Water Demand: Given the estimates of population of 220 million in 2025, water demand is projected to rise to 274 MAF by 2025, while water availability is not likely to change from the current 200 MAF.[32] This gap of about 74 MAF is almost two-thirds of the Indus river's current annual average flow. And this is without India fully utilising its share of the western tributaries of the Indus (3.6 MAF) and Afghanistan not storing the waters of the Kabul river. (4.7 MAF). The International Monetary Fund report, 'Is the Glass Half Empty or Half Full?' takes the figures of water availability at 191 MAF and so projects a water shortage of 83 MAF by 2025.[33]

Where will Pakistan get this additional water/Indus river from? It can be only through one of two ways: The first is massive investment in the water sector: build dams, promote rainwater harvesting, drip irrigation, improve water infrastructure and water efficiency. However, there are very little signs that any of this is happening at the time of writing. The main component of the National Water Policy titled 'Pakistan Water Charter' in 2018 was an increase in the development budget for water resources from 3.7 to 10 per cent by 2019 and eventually to 20 per cent by 2030.[34] However, the actual funds allocated are less than 1 per cent.

The second option that Pakistan has is to blame India for its water woes, accusing it of "water terrorism." Thus, former President Asif Zardari in an article in the *Washington Post* in January 2009 wrote: 'The water crisis in Pakistan is directly linked to relations with India. Failure to resolve the water imbroglio could fuel the fires of discontent that lead to extremism and terrorism.'[35] Such calls will increase, as will calls to either scrap or 'revisit' the Indus Waters Treaty (IWT). For example, the Pakistan Senate passed a resolution on 7 March 2016 asking the government to 'revisit' the Indus Waters Treaty with India, something that *Dawn* called 'bizarre.'[36] The matter was set at rest when the chairman of the IRSA briefed the Senate on 9 July 2015 saying that India was using less that its allocated share under the IWT. He dismissed all media reports about India building dams on Pakistani rivers as 'propaganda.'[37]

In an editorial titled 'The big problem with water' dated 27 September 2017, *The Express Tribune* wrote: 'In reality terrorism and extremism, unpleasant as they are, have never presented a truly existential threat to Pakistan. Neither has come close to bringing down the edifices of state and neither shows that capacity on current form nor is likely to in the foreseeable future. But the water problem just might do what all the forces of darkness have as yet failed to do. Pakistan has a water problem that is across every aspect of supply and demand—from the Himalayan glacier melt, to flooding, to drought, to desertification and loss of arable land to economic and social damage.'[38]

Bottom-Line: The deteriorating water security would be catastrophic for Pakistan where irrigated agriculture plays such a dominant part in the economy, on whom 60 per cent of the population is dependent and any decrease in crop yields will affect both livelihoods and food security. There are no shortcuts here. Pakistan will have to make massive investments in its water infrastructure to stay afloat. At the same time, water scarcity in Pakistan will increasingly have serious implications for Indo-Pak relations and cries of India's 'water terrorism' will increase.

Education Emergency

The greatest threat to Pakistan may be its abysmal education system. Pakistani schools —and not just madrassas—are churning out fiery zealots, fuelled with a passion for jihad *and martyrdom.*[39]—Pervez Hoodbhoy

The Pakistan Education Task Force 2011 described the situation as an 'Education Emergency' primarily because the country's education system was among the least effective in the world.[40] The report estimated that one in 10 of the world's not-in-school children in the primary age group lived in Pakistan (globally placing it the second worst in out-of-school children rankings). It also indicated that nearly 30 per cent of the country's population lived in extreme educational poverty, i.e., less than two years of education in their lifetime. Furthermore, those admitted to schools suffered from massive dropout rates before they reached class five. Pakistan ranked 113th out of 120 countries in UNESCO's Education for All Education Development Index. Its literacy rate (57 per cent) lags well behind the country's neighbours.

In April 2010, Article 25A of the Constitution of Pakistan was amended by the eighteenth amendment to state: 'The State shall provide free and compulsory education to all children of the age of five to sixteen years in such manner as may be determined by law.'[41] Despite the passage of over a decade since the amendment, twenty-five million children within this age bracket, or almost half, are out of school.

Pakistan's education sector is a combination of three parallel streams—public or government-run schools, private schools and madrassas. (The schools run by the military are in a class of their own.) Over 800,000 students were pursuing education in English-medium schools, while over 30 million were studying in public schools and around 2.5 million in seminaries.[42] There are a total of 1.72 million school and college teachers in the country. Each of these three streams has its own curriculum and examination processes. The National Internal Security Policy 2014–18 has summed up the impact of such stratification of education as: 'Serious cleavages have appeared in society as a result of these systems, and continued existence in parallel spheres compounds the possibilities of violence among divided youth.'[43]

According to the NGO, Alif Ailaan, out of 52.91 million school-going children, only 27.89 million attend an educational institute (government or private), leaving 25.02 million children or nearly 50 per cent, out of school. Of these, 5.1 million (other estimates, including that of the Ministry of Education's Education for All is about 6.7 million,) are at the primary level. Furthermore, even those admitted to schools suffer from massive drop-out rates before they reach Class 5—63 per cent boys, 77 per cent girls in 2011.[44] The proportion of out-of-school children increases with the rise in the level of education. Thus, the corresponding figures for middle school (age group of 10–12 years) is 6.6 million or 52.1 per cent; high school (age group of 13–14 years) 5.6 million or 66.7 per cent and higher secondary (age group 15–16 years) 7.5 million or 84.8 per cent.[45] What is unfortunate is that according to official records this figure has remained mostly unchanged since 2005.[46]

While the country needed to spend 4 per cent of GDP on education just to be on track to fulfil international standards and development goals, its budgetary allocations have been abysmally low, hovering between 1.5 per cent and 2.3 per cent during the last 15 years;[47] Nearly 89 per cent of such expenditure is administrative and 25 per cent of the rest remains unutilized.[48] According to the Pakistan Economic Survey 2020-21, the cumulative education expenditure by federal and provincial governments in FY2020 stood at 1.5 per cent of the GDP as compared to 2.3 per cent of the GDP in FY2019. Expenditure on education had been rising gradually until 2018-19 but in 2019-20 education-related expenditure witnessed a decrease of 29.6 per cent, i.e., from Rs. 868.0 billion to Rs. 611.0 billion.[49]

According to the Pakistan Economic Survey 2020-21, the literacy rate of the population (10 years and above) was stagnant at 60 per cent in 2019-20 since 2014-15. The literacy rate was higher in urban areas (74 per cent) than in rural areas (52 per cent). Province-wise, Punjab had the highest literacy rate, with 64 per cent followed by Sindh with 58 per cent, Khyber Pakhtunkhwa (excluding Merged Areas) with 55 per cent, Khyber Pakhtunkhwa (including Merged Areas) with 53 per cent and Balochistan with 46 per cent.[50]

Gender disparity is another major issue. Nationally, in 2015, 15.9 million boys, between the ages of five and 16, were enrolled, compared to just 11.9 million girls. As a result, 13.7 million girls and 11.4 million boys were out of school. Of the total number of girls aged 5–16, 53 per cent are out of school, compared to 42 per cent of boys in the same age group. Of the total number of out-of-school children, the majority are girls, comprising 55 per cent of the total.[51]

Impact: The following chart illustrates the outcome of such an education or the lack of it by showing the educational levels of the labour force:

Labour Force and Education

Year	*Illiterate*	*Primary*	*Middle*	*Matric*	*Inter*	*BA*
1990–91	53.0	22.7	10.9	9.6	3.0	1.7
2001–02	36.7	25.7	15.9	14.6	4.7	2.3
2010–11	35.3	26.0	16.4	13.8	5.3	3.3

In other words, 61 per cent of the labour force was either illiterate or had done just primary and only 3.3 per cent of the labour force were graduates. Moreover, the Senate was informed in September 2021 that 16 per cent of the uneducated population was unemployed, 24 per cent of graduates were jobless, and that nearly 40 per cent of educated women across the country were unemployed.[52]

According to the Annual Status of Education Report (ASER) Pakistan, 2021, 45 per cent students, mostly fifth graders, could not read a sentence in Urdu and their regional languages while 44 per cent could not read sentences in English. Student competencies in learning language and arithmetic had declined as only 55 per cent of children from grade five could read a story in Urdu, Sindhi or Pashto as compared to 59 per cent in 2019. It added that only 55 per cent could do digit division. It pointed out that no serious improvement was noted during the survey and results of the year 2019 and 2021 are almost the same.[53] Interestingly, the Annual Survey of Education Report, 2014, had noted only 46 per cent of class five students could read a class two Urdu/Sindhi/Pashto story while 50 per cent could do so in 2013. Seven years later, this figure had declined to 45 per cent.[54]

According to the United Nations Global Education Monitoring Report, 2016, the cumulative impact of a lack of sustained focus on education had resulted in Pakistan being more than 50 years behind in its primary education targets and 60 years in its secondary education targets.[55]

Given the state of education in Pakistan, especially scientific education, it is hardly surprisingly that Pakistan is among the least innovative countries in the world. According to the Global Innovation Index (GII), 2016, Pakistan ranked 119 out of 128 countries surveyed. The current allocation on research was only 0.29 per cent of the GDP, far below the world average as most developed countries spend between 2 and 4 per cent of their GDP on research.[56]

The most controversial and crucial aspect of education is of course the curriculum or what is actually taught in schools since this provides the road map for future generations. In Pakistan's case, this is all the more so since from the time of Ayub Khan only officially published textbooks are allowed to be used from Class 1 to college level in order to enable the governments to set the curriculum as per their own predilections.

Although much attention has remained focused on the role of madrassas, it is the government educational institutions and academia that have become a key factor in extremism and terrorism. A report titled 'The Subtle Subversion: The State of Curricula and Textbooks in Pakistan', edited by A.H. Nayyar and Ahmad Salim (2004)[57] and published by the Sustainable Development Policy Institute (SDPI), an Islamabad-based think tank, has identified several issues in the curricula and textbooks that included factual inaccuracies and omissions, which distorted the nature and significance of actual events; incitement to militancy and violence that included encouragement of *jihad* and *shahadat*, a glorification of war and the use of force; encouragement of prejudice, bigotry and discrimination towards fellow citizens, especially women and religious minorities, and other nations.

The report revealed that: '*Madrassas are not the only institutions breeding hate, intolerance, a distorted worldview, etc. The educational material in the government-run schools does much more than madrassas. The textbooks tell lies, create hatred, inculcate militancy, and much more...the curriculum encourages ideas that are incompatible with the ideals of Pakistan as a forward-looking modern state committed to equal rights and equitable treatment for its citizens.*'

The situation has not changed much in the last decade-and-a-half. The National Commission for Justice and Peace (NCJP), and the Pakistan Institute of Labour and Research, conducted a seminar in Karachi on 30 March 2016 at which a report on the curricula in all four provinces was discussed. After analysing some 70 textbooks, including Urdu, Islamiyat and optional subjects, the NCJP found that there were still too many examples of content that could be considered divisive and of portions amounting to hate speech. For example, Hindus were portrayed as 'enemies', while Christians were portrayed as 'agents' of the West. The most telling fact, however, was that the report carried only 25 per cent of the NCJP's findings, for, as the project coordinator pointed out, 'sharing the remaining portion may just anger some people so much that they may want to eliminate us.'[58]

The reason for such distortions is clearly the efforts to Islamize education. Zia-ul-Haq laid down the objectives of education in Pakistan. He ordered: '*The highest priority would be given to the revision of the curricula with a view to reorganizing the entire content around Islamic thought and giving education an ideological orientation so that Islamic ideology permeates the thinking of the younger generation and helps them with the necessary conviction and ability to refashion society according to Islamic tenets.*'[59] As a result, political Islam became part and parcel of curriculum up to the university level.

Zia's instructions were operationalised by the University Grants Commission's directive to textbook authors '*... To guide students towards the ultimate goal of Pakistan—the creation of a completely Islamicized State.*'[60] India and Hindus were converted into caricatures with two outstanding features—cowardice and deviousness.

As a result, since Zia's time, '*Islam was used to support the state's own militaristic policies in a way that it appeared to the readers of these textbooks that Pakistan, the*

Pakistan Movement, Pakistan's wars with India and the Kashmir issue were all connected not only with Pakistani nationalism but with Islam itself.'[61]

Single National Curriculum (SNC)

The Pakistan Tehreek-e-Insaf's (PTI's) Education Policy Framework highlighted reforms in four priority areas in education: (1) Putting all the out-of-school children in schools, as required by Article 25A of the Constitution; (2) eliminating apartheid in education by introducing a uniform curriculum; (3) enhancing the quality of education; and (4) emphasising technical and vocational education.[62]

Imran Khan, while launching the first phase of the SNC, described it as a step towards freeing the country from slavery. In other words, a uniform curriculum itself would end existing divisions in Pakistan's education system. In the first phase, the SNC would be implemented in primary classes starting in the current academic year. In the second and third phases it would be extended to the secondary and higher secondary levels. All private, public and religious schools were required to teach the same curriculum and would have to use textbooks prescribed by the government. The Sindh government, however, did not approve of the plan.

Prior to the SNC, there have been at least seven prominent education policies from 1947 to 2017 that also sought to address the problems of the education sector in Pakistan. The focus of these policies was on access and quality of education, the elimination of gender inequalities from education, and the administration of education, science, technology, technical and vocational education. However, all these policies failed to achieve their objectives simply because they could not be fully implemented and remained largely on paper. Evidence of this was the low literacy rates and education standards.[63] Moreover, analysts have pointed out serious problems in the SNC.

According to A.H. Nayyar, first, the government has focussed only on the second priority area by preparing a SNC, but has made no move in the other three priority areas. This reason is obviously because each of the other three priority areas requires a heavy financial commitment, which the meagre national allocation to education cannot fulfil while the introduction of a new curriculum costs nothing. Thus, to put the nearly 25 million out-of-school children into school would be a gigantic task since Pakistan would have to build nearly as many schools as exist today, furnish them and employ as many new teachers as are currently in service. The resources required to do all this can well be imagined. Even today, in the Islamabad Capital Territory (ICT) that is under the federal government, there is a 35 per cent deficiency of teachers in public schools. The posts are not being filled because the government has no money to pay the additional salaries. Some federal government model schools are running at two-thirds of the approved strength of teachers.[64]

Second, the SNC neither reforms the country's decaying education system nor does it bridge the widening gap between various systems of education in the country. On the contrary, as *The News* put it, it is a leap backward than a step forward: Instead of improving standards in public-sector educational institutions and madrassas in order to bring them at par with elite schools, the SNC does the opposite. In effect, the bar has been lowered so as to bridge the gap.[65]

Third, after the 18th Constitutional Amendment, education at all levels and in all aspects, including curriculum development, had become a provincial matter. As such, the Federal government has nothing to do with curriculum development for provinces. It should at best confine itself to the federal education institutions that come under its jurisdiction.[66] By imposing the SNC, the Federal government is treading on provincial rights.

Fourth, the content of the prescribed textbooks of the SNC has come in for criticism. The new curriculum actually reinforces the regressive content of the textbooks. According to media reports, those reviewing the science textbooks objected to a picture of Sir Isaac Newton without a *dupatta* to cover what they perhaps took to be a woman's long hair. A similar attitude was seen when the Punjab Curriculum and Textbook Board confiscated a book that included Malala Yousafzai among Pakistan's heroes. Additionally, the books show women in a restricted role. Even young girls are supposed to be fully covered.[67]

The textbooks issued under the SNC policy have also been objected to for gender stereotyping and 'Islamisation' of the syllabi. More religious material has been included in subjects other than Islamiyat, which is unfair to non-Muslim students.[68] It has also been pointed out that the Islamiyat curriculum in SNC was much heavier than in madrassas. It requires a large amount of memorization in Arabic and, in places, in Urdu translation as well. It requires memorization of ahadith in Arabic and in Urdu. The two madrassa boards' curricula do not require memorization, or even reading, of ahadith. In this sense, the SNC looks like a 'madrassa-isation' of schools.[69]

Moreover, children who have been studying most subjects in English so far will have to re-learn them in Urdu. To disrupt the course of study mid-session would likely hinder progress and cause learning difficulties.[70]

According to Hoodbhoy, 'Imran Khan's government is poised to inflict damage upon this country's education system in a manner never seen before. Its so-called Single National Curriculum (SNC) hides systemic changes going far deeper than the ones conceived and executed by the extremist regime of Gen Zia-ul Haq.' He adds that the huge volume of religious material for Classes I to V beats all curriculums in Pakistan's history. The column-by-column comparison with two major madrassa systems—Tanzeemul Madaris and Rabtaul Madaris—reveals a shocking fact. Ordinary schools will henceforth impose more rote learning than even these madrassas. Normal schoolteachers being under-equipped religiously, the SNC calls for summoning an army of madrassa-educated holy men—hafiz's and qaris—as paid teachers in schools. Moreover, he notes that modern education rests squarely upon critical thinking, and success/failure is determined in relation to problem solving and worldly knowledge. However, madrassa education goals seek a more religiously observant student, a better life after death and where critical thinking is unwelcome.[71] A.H. Nayyar adds, critical thinking is central to modern knowledge, while through the SNC, policy planners seem to be promoting influences that are antithetical to critical thinking. The primary focus is on the sheer quantity of information poured into students' heads.[72]

Interestingly, the SNC ensures providing massive employment opportunities to madrassa graduates. The primary curriculum, for example, requires every school to employ one madrassa-certified qari to teach nazra ["Recitation by sighting", i.e., meaning the *ability to recite the Holy Quran*] in the style that prevails in madrassas. With more of madrassa-style Islamiyat coming in the higher classes, each school will be asked to employ a madrassa-certified *aalim* to teach the extended Islamiyat course. As per the Pakistan Economic Survey 2019-20, there are about 172,500 registered primary schools in the country, and about 260,000 schools of all kinds. Employing two madrassa-certified teachers in each school amounts to providing jobs to 520,000 madrassa-certified persons in public and private schools. This opens an unprecedented floodgate of jobs for madrassa graduates, most of them to be paid out of the public exchequer. In short, under the SNC, the madrassa system has received a huge boost.[73] This could well be a tactic to mainstream madrassa alumni and give them jobs instead of joining *jihadi* organisations.

In a letter dated November 10, 2021, the School Education Department of the Punjab Government has issued a directive that all schools in the province must be rigorously checked for Quranic reading/nazra skills. Each school will be jointly inspected by the head of the district education authority and a district & sessions judge. As a result, magistrates accompanied by rifle-bearing policemen have started visiting schools, interrogating seven- to 12-year-old children with the teachers being ordered out of the classroom or asked to stand silently in the corner. In some cases, school principals have been told to present themselves in person before authorities located in various parts of the province. Punishments have also started being handed out with a sessions judge in Nankana Sahib recommending disciplinary action against three school principals for giving insufficient attention to Quran teaching as a separate subject, a requirement of the SNC. The principals were also accused of allowing students to keep the Holy Quran in their school bags, which was gross negligence.

Overall, despite the PTI government's projection that the SNC will resolve Pakistan's educational woes, the problem is far too complex and, in any case, the SNC does not even address the more important aspects of it. In reality, for the millions of children out of school, the critical first step is access to education. Content comes thereafter.[74] Instead of strengthening the basic objective of any education system of encouraging critical thinking among students and equipping them to meet the modern world's challenges,[75] all that the government has done is to bill the SNC as a way of ending the 'education apartheid' in the country. However, it could well make matters even worse by bringing down standards across the board.

Bottom Line

The current 'educational emergency' in Pakistan is a serious security threat because an uneducated or poorly educated population is a recipe for disaster in an increasingly technological and globalised world. It is the result of decades of neglect of the education sector and it will take decades to be overcome, provided a determined start is made immediately.

In fact, as early as 2001, an analysis had noted that, 'twenty-four percentage points of Pakistan's population [was] illiterate than is normal for a country of its income level.'[76]

In other words, the low level of literacy in Pakistan was indicative of the indifference of the rulers to implement policies that would educate the people. It also indicated the low-level skills required for the country to stay afloat where high and broad-based achievement was not a priority. For Pakistan's leaders to continue to ignore the challenges is suicidal since more than half the population is below 19 years of age and millions of children are entering the education market every year.

The problem, however, is far deeper. In all societies, the primary purpose of education is to educate the young mind to develop a spirit of inquiry and understanding of the world around and to train it for taking up responsibilities in society. In Pakistan, however, education seems to have been hijacked to achieve ideological and political goals in line with the thinking of the elites, especially the military. Such thinking has narrowed down the purpose of education to trying to create a Pakistani identity that has at its core religion, militarism and a hatred of India. These facets have permeated the entire education system and curriculum, and the resultant products are not imbued with a spirit of inquiry but with hatred. Without a basic change in the curricula and textbooks, bigotry, violence and hatred will continue.

The education crisis, like the water crisis, has taken on proportions that would progressively make it extremely difficult for any government to tackle. With the population continuing to grow at an alarming 2.4 per cent and a huge youth bulge, millions of children are entering the education market year after year. The colossal challenge for Pakistan is clearly educating all these millions to reap the 'demographic dividend' before the window of opportunity closes. Without a basic change in the curricula and textbooks, bigotry, violence and hatred will continue. The real fight against terrorism and to reclaim moderate space has to begin here.

Economy

Pakistan's economic growth since the 1950s has been marked by a persistence of periodic crises and bailouts, and by high volatility in growth rates due to a 'stop–go' growth model. The primary reason for this is poor governance that has resulted in Pakistan's economy suffering from structural weaknesses that have not been rectified over the decades and will not be rectified by ad hoc, band-aid type of solutions.

The key among these structural weaknesses are: the high dependence upon external factors like foreign assistance—bilateral or multilateral, exports and workers' remittances instead of internal drivers of growth; high burden of debt repayment; a very high defence burden; revenue shortages, inadequate measures to raise the rate of savings and investment; low investment as a percentage of the GDP in the social sectors such as health, education, etc.

The result of these structural flaws have been: low rates of growth; poor infrastructure; lack of industrialisation; a widening trade gap; high incidence of poverty; low social development indicators; a low literacy rate and an unskilled work force. This was confirmed by the Pakistan Economic Survey 2020-21 according to which 'Pakistan's economy already had a volatile growth pattern over the years, with regular boom-and-bust cycles facing challenges in achieving long-term and inclusive growth. Unsustainable economic growth was caused by unaddressed long-standing structural issues, for example, loss-making State-Owned Enterprises (SOEs), weak external position due to insufficient export capacity and low FDI, under-reformed energy sector, low savings and investment.'[77]

There are several key parameters to judge the health of the economy:

GDP

Even before the COVID-19 pandemic hit the world, Pakistan's economy was on a rapid downslide. In the beginning of 2021, the prognosis was that GDP growth would be around two per cent in the fiscal year ending in June 2021. In April 2021, the International Monetary Fund (IMF) had indicated a growth rate of 1.5 per cent for Pakistan, coupled with a higher rate of inflation and rising unemployment, during the current fiscal year. This was in contrast to the revised 3 per cent GDP growth forecast made by the State Bank of Pakistan. The IMF estimates were in line with those of the World Bank that projected growth at 1.3 per cent for the current year.[78] However, the government came up with a new estimate of four per cent. For the years 2021-22 the estimate is four to five per cent growth.[79] Independent economists have received the government's figures with much scepticism and disbelief.

Employment

According to the Labour Force Survey (LFS) published by the Pakistan Bureau of Statistics (PBS) in September 2021, the unemployment rate jumped from 5.8 per cent in 2017-18 to 6.9 per cent in 2018-19, the first year of the PTI government. In absolute terms, the number of people actively looking for jobs increased by 0.92 million to 4.71 million in FY19 from 3.79 million the previous year as the number of the country's total workforce rose to 68.73 million from 65.5 million during the period under review. It also meant that at least 3.23 million people entered the market seeking employment at a time when the national economy's capacity to create new jobs had just started shrinking and businesses had started laying off their employees owing to the emerging macroeconomic imbalances. Agriculture remained the largest employer absorbing 39.2 per cent of the total workforce compared to 38.5 per cent the previous year despite its less than a fifth share in the economy.[80]

With a growth of around 5 per cent and even less, it was estimated that

Pakistan's economy could generate employment for about a million persons per year. According to the Pakistan Institute of Development Economics (PIDE), the country needed to maintain an average growth rate of over 7 per cent over the next few decades just to absorb the massive youth population (estimated at around 3 million entering the labour market annually), which faces increasing risks of unemployment and underemployment.[81] This does not seem to be happening in the near-to-medium term.

For employment generation on a sustained basis, the country would have to raise the level of investment from the current rate of 15.21 per cent of the GDP to about 25 per cent of the GDP with special attention to human and social development. This level of investment is impossible to achieve without a simultaneous increase in the rate of national savings. The domestic rate of savings would have to be increased from the current 8.3 per cent to about 20 per cent of the GDP on a sustained basis. This will be possible only with policies that encourage savings and discourage consumption.

Poverty

The net impact of Pakistan's economic development over the decades has been the rise in the incidence of poverty from 18 per cent in 1988-89 to about 40 per cent currently. Applying a multi-dimensional poverty index (combination of the levels of education, health and standard of living), the Oxford Department of International Development showed that in 2012–13, 44.2 per cent of Pakistanis were poor, 23.7 per cent were in severe poverty and 15.1 per cent were vulnerable to poverty.[82] The World Bank's Macro Poverty Outlook on Pakistan stated that the incidence of poverty was estimated to have increased in FY20 from 4.4 to 5.4 per cent, with more than two million people falling below this poverty line. Moreover, 40 per cent of households suffered from moderate to severe food insecurity.[83] The World Bank used the lower-middle-income poverty rate ($ 3.2 per day) and estimated that the poverty ratio in Pakistan stood at 39.3 per cent in 2020-21 and is projected to remain at 39.2 per cent in 2021-22 and might come down to 37.9 per cent by 2022-23. By using the upper middle-income poverty rate ($ 5.5 per day) methods, the World Bank estimated that poverty stood at 78.4 per cent in 2020-21 and that it would be standing at 78.3 per cent in 2021-22 and is projected to come down to 77.5 per cent in 2022-23.

Food Insecurity

One of the critical areas of the impact of the development of the Pak economy is food availability. As per the 2019 Global Hunger Index released by the

International Food Policy Research Institute (IFPRI), Pakistan was ranked 94th out of 117 countries that put it among those suffering from serious levels of hunger.[84] In 2021, Pakistan was ranked 106th among 119 countries surveyed for the Global Hunger Index, and has been characterised as facing a "serious" level of hunger. More worryingly, almost half of the children under five years were stunted (low height-for-age) and one in ten was suffering from low-weight-for-height (wasting). According to the report, the cost of under-5 malnutrition was heavy: about $ 2.24 bn is estimated as the loss of the future labour force; $ 1 bn is the estimated healthcare expense, which families incur to address diarrhoea and respiratory infection among children; $ 3.7 bn was the estimated cost of low labour productivity emanating from stunting, anaemia or iodine deficiencies in childhood; and $ 657 m was the estimated cost of prevalence of chronic weakness and fatigue among 10 million working adults with anaemia experience. According to the SBP: "In the case of Pakistan, estimates suggest that malnutrition and its outcomes cost the economy 3 per cent of GDP ($ 7.6 billion) every year. Per capita consumption of food products that possess high-nutritional value like beef, chicken, fish, milk, vegetables, and fruits is almost 6-10 times lower than that of developed countries."[85]

According to *The Express Tribune*, Pakistan with more than 220 million mouths to feed is in need of 125 kg per capita per annum of wheat; and, at the same time, adds around three million more people to its grain basket annually. This requires the formulation of a strategic food security policy that Pakistan has not been able to devise yet. It quotes the Federal Committee on Agriculture estimates that around 30 million tonnes of wheat flour was needed annually to remain self-reliant. However, there were inherent drawbacks as more than a million tonnes went for seed usage, another million or two to retain strategic reserves, coupled with more than 1.5 million Afghan refugees to feed and an unending smuggling of around 400,000 tonnes of wheat to Afghanistan.[86]

In a nutshell, despite its huge irrigation and agricultural network and using 95 per cent of its total water resources for agriculture, Pakistan has become a net importer of key food items such as wheat, sugar, edible oil and pulses. This is likely to increase food inflation in the near term, given the escalating global commodity markets. Consequently, things will get worse for the poor, as they will find it harder to feed their families.[87]

In 2020, the government informed the National Assembly that Pakistan was no longer self-sufficient in wheat as the per acre yield had declined. Nearly 25 million tons of wheat was produced in the year against the target of 27 million tons. Accordingly, the private sector has been allowed to import wheat. Likewise, the production of cotton, maize and sugarcane had also declined. In the case of cotton, the production had declined to 7.3 million tons from 15 million tons. [88]

Debt

Data released by the State Bank of Pakistan (SBP) in September 2021 revealed that the public debt had increased to Rs. 39.9 trillion by June, an addition of Rs. 14.9 trillion within three years. Over the past three years, the total public debt had increased by about 60 per cent, which averaged out to a massive 20 per cent increase each year. Such a large debt means that this year too, just like every fiscal year, the development budget will have to be revised downward to meet repayment obligations as and when they become due.[89]

Under the 2005 'Fiscal Responsibility and Debt Limitations Act' the debt-to-GDP ratio was to be brought down to 60 per cent within two financial years and then to 50 per cent of GDP within five financial years. Under the PPP government (2008-2103), the debt-to-GDP ratio hovered around 66 per cent; under the PML-N government (2013-2018), the debt-to-GDP ratio deteriorated to 73 per cent. Under the PTI (2018-2021), the debt-to-GDP ratio has gone up to 107 per cent. Putting it starkly, Dr. Farrukh Saleem estimates that in 1970, every man, woman and child in Pakistan was indebted to the tune of Rs. 500. In 2008, when the PPP came to power the per capita debt was Rs. 36,000. In 2013, when the PML-N came to power the per capita debt was Rs. 88,000. In 2018, the PTI came to power, and in 31 months it has taken the per capita debt to Rs. 200,000. Overall, the per capita debt has risen from Rs. 500 to Rs. 200,000 in a matter of 51 years. In 2018, when the PTI formed the government, 39 per cent of total taxes were allocated for debt servicing. In 2021, a massive 74 per cent of total taxes had to be allocated towards debt servicing. It is estimated that by 2025, 100 per cent of taxes would go towards debt servicing. In other words, by 2025, there will be no money for the defence budget or for running the civil government. As he aptly puts it: "Modern slaves are not in chains; they are in debt."[90] Thus, under the PTI government, foreign debt is piling up with the share of short-term expensive borrowings growing rapidly, and exports slowing down.

In the Federal Budget 2020-21, for example, interest on loans was the single largest expense, greater than "defence affairs and services" and also greater than the whole of "development expenditure." According to an April 2021 report prepared by the Institute for Policy Reforms (IPR), a Lahore based research entity, the "most critical problem faced by the Pakistan economy is repayment and servicing of external debt" and that instead of bringing economic growth, "borrowing creates more borrowing with an external account crisis waiting to happen." Pakistan's debt would have helped if it were invested to build the productive capacity of the economy, generating returns greater than the interest rate and earning forex through growing exports. However, the fact was that Pakistan was taking on more debt to manage previous debt and its exports-to-GDP ratio had declined showing that this had not been the case. The high degree of indebtedness has made Pakistan more vulnerable to economic shocks and weakened it politically vis-a-vis powerful external lenders. It has also greatly reduced Pakistan's ability to invest in the social sector.[91]

The debt situation has come to such a pass that during his February 2022 visit to China, Imran Khan requested China for financial support of about $ 21 billion through rollover of existing loans of $ 10.735 billion and $ 10 billion as deposit fund, to meet future financial needs and deal with financial challenges. This was required to prevent a possible default on external payments worth $ 8.6 billion that come due at the end of June. Pakistan owed $ 1.3 billion to Chinese companies but had only paid $ 286 million in the days before Khan's Beijing visit. The Chinese leadership were reported to have 'taken note' of the request but had not yet replied at the time of writing.[92]

It is obvious that Pakistan has been 'trapped in a vicious debt circle and needs a constant dollar inflow to retire a perpetually inflating debt burden,' *Asia Times* quoted economist Farrukh Saleem stating. He further said that Pakistan needed a continuous current account surplus of $ 15 billion on average to avoid taking out new loans or major currency depreciation. China had already loaned $ 4 billion to the State Administration of Foreign Exchange (SAFE) deposit to shore up the country's fast-depleting foreign exchange reserves. In a recent country report, the International Monetary Fund (IMF) said Pakistan owed China $ 18.4 billion, equal to 20 per cent of the country's total external debt liabilities of $ 92.3 billion. This represented one of the highest contributions by any single country or institution ever to Pakistan. Based on a 4 per cent GDP growth during the current fiscal year, the IMF predicted total foreign debt would jump to $ 103 billion by the end of the next fiscal year. Pakistan has recently received $ 3 billion from Saudi Arabia, $ 2 billion from the United Arab Emirates and $ 4 billion from China to shore up its declining foreign reserves. In addition to that, the IMF has given more than $ 2 billion, while another $ 1 billion has come from Sukuk bonds. Pakistan needs to pay $ 8.6 billion this year and $ 16.9 billion in the next financial year to pay off external debts.[93]

In a nutshell, the kind of borrowing that Pakistan has indulged in is unsustainable and together with declining exports and fluctuating remittances from overseas workers, the Pakistani economy will continue to face a tough balance of payments situation.

Foreign Direct Investment (FDI)

The net Foreign Direct Investment (FDI) decreased by 28.9 per cent in the year 2021. The net FDI stood at $ 1.847 billion during the period of 2020-21.[94] State Bank data for the last four years shows that inward FDI flows were either falling or stagnating while outward flows of profits had jumped up by 115 per cent in July 2021. While FDI in South Asia spiked by 20 per cent to $ 71 bn in 2020 despite COVID-19, Pakistan saw these flows come down sharply to less than 0.75 per cent of its GDP. FDI flows to India rose by 27 per cent to $ 64 bn in various sectors of its economy during the same year. Indonesia and Vietnam received FDI flows of $ 18.6 bn and $ 15.8 bn.[95]

Inflation

According to Dr. Farrukh Saleem, food inflation is perhaps the most critical issue today since 80 per cent of Pakistani families spend roughly 80 per cent of their incomes on food items. Thus, two years ago, an average family spent around Rs. 27,000 a year on wheat flour. Today, the same family, in order to buy the same amount of wheat flour, would have to come up with Rs. 58,000; a difference of Rs. 31,000 per family. This is unprecedented because never ever in the past 70 years has there been a two-year period during which wheat flour had gone up by 100 per cent. Two years ago, electricity consumers in Pakistan were charged Rs. 1.1 trillion. Today, the same electricity consumers would have to cough out Rs. 3 trillion; that is an additional Rs. 66,000 a year for an average consumer. This is unprecedented because never ever in the past 70 years has there been a two-year period during which the electricity tariff had gone up by a whopping 300 per cent.[96]

Energy Security

Pakistan's warped economic development has also ensured that in a critical element of national energy security, Pakistan is insecure. In fact, if anything, energy security continues to be a seriously neglected dimension of national security. Pakistan's current energy mix is 35 per cent indigenous gas, 31 per cent oil, 12 per cent coal, 8.7 per cent LNG, 7.7 per cent hydroelectricity, 2.7 per cent nuclear, 1.1 per cent renewables and a small fraction from imported electricity. Pakistan imports over $ 20 billion worth of petroleum products, petroleum crude, liquefied natural gas and liquefied petroleum gas; $ 2.5 billion a year of coal. More than 80 per cent of its export earnings are spent on importing fuel. In the next four years, local gas production is projected to fall from 4 billion cubic feet per day to 2 billion cubic feet per day. This would mean even greater energy insecurity.[97]

Current Situation

The economic situation of Afghanistan that is fast deteriorating with supply shortages of basic necessities being reported is also impacting Pakistan. The Taliban government is increasingly facing a shortage of funds as earlier over 80 per cent of the cost of public services was financed by external sources, especially the USA. Deterioration of living conditions could lead to migration, especially to Pakistan. The post-US withdrawal situation in Afghanistan is also a factor behind increased pressure on the PKR. In 2021, Afghanistan's imports of close to $ 6 billion were financed by dollars from within the country. Now, however, most of the Afghan imports are being routed through Pakistan with traders in Pakistan importing in USD and exporting to Afghanistan in PKR. There is thus an additional pressure on the currency to feed Afghani imports.[98]

The IMF had approved a $ 6 billion Extended Finance Facility (EFF) for Pakistan in July 2019, enabling Pakistan to partially stabilise the economy. Pakistan had agreed to undertake numerous strategic, technical and legislative changes. Since then, the disbursement of tranches has been delayed due to Pakistan's non-performance of commitments. In February 2022, Pakistan completed the sixth EFF review and the earlier withheld $ 1 billion tranche was released. This was after the government undertook aggressive revenue measures by introducing amendments in indirect tax legislation and autonomy of the State Bank. Pakistan has now obtained the $ 3 billion from the IMF under the current programme with $ 3 billion to be issued subject to successful completion of the remaining reviews.[99]

The declining value of the rupee also reflects higher economic uncertainty.[100] Between May and September 2021, the rupee fell from Rs. 152-to-a-dollar to Rs. 173-to-a-dollar, i.e., a steep fall of Rs. 21, something that has not happened in the past four decades (since the rupee was delinked in 1982). Between mid-June and the first week of September, the SBP was reported to have injected $ 1.2 billion into the interbank market in an attempt to stabilise the rupee—but to no avail. The rupee has kept on falling. At the time of writing, it is hovering around Rs. 175-180. Additionally, in July-August, imports increased by 73 per cent to $ 12 billion that is a new two-month record in Pakistan. In the same period, exports amounted to a paltry $ 4.5 billion. That meant a trade deficit of $ 7.5 billion—another record in Pakistan's 74-year financial history.[101]

The distorted nature of Pakistan's economy and policy-making can be gleaned from the fact that in 2018 Pakistan was forced to borrow $ 35 billion while over the same period it imported cars, SUVs, extra petroleum to run the new autos, and mobile phones totalling $8 bn! This staggering amount is equal to nearly 25 per cent of the total gross foreign loans contracted by Pakistan during this period. Likewise, during 2019-21, new franchises of foreign fast food outlets and cafes and restaurants were opened that not only imported a range of expensive ingredients, but also paid hefty franchise fees and remitted profits in US dollars. Data compiled from the State Bank and the Pakistan Bureau of Statistics shows that a staggering $ 13 bn was cumulatively spent on these imports since 2019. As per annual data from the State Bank, Pakistan has imported cars/SUVs and mobile phones alone worth $ 30 bn cumulatively since 2006! With franchise fees and profit repatriation, the import of non-essential foreign consumer goods and services totals scores of billions of US dollars over this period. According to Sakib Sherani 'for a country running out of dollars to import essential energy, machinery and capital goods, food and raw materials, such poor choices made by Pakistan's elitist policymakers represent both capacity and mindset issues, as well as a Herculean ignorance of the path of development taken by high-performing developing economies.'[102]

Bottom Line

Pakistan has been avoiding economic collapse narrowly not because of structural changes or policy initiatives but by monetising its geographical position due to the international situation. Thrice in the last 70 years, Pakistan has been bailed out by the USA just as it was going over the brink, all three times when the army was ruling. And all three times, the rulers have not used the opportunity provided by foreign bailouts to make the necessary structural changes to put Pakistan on the path of sustainable growth. There may or may not be a fourth bailout but the crucial question is whether the leaders, civilian and military, have begun to recognise how deep-rooted the problem is and how the already yawning gap between Pakistan and the rest of the world, including its neighbours, is widening?

Population

Demographic change shapes political power like water shapes rock. Up close, the force looks trivial, but viewed from a distance of decades or centuries it moves mountains.[103]

Demographic trends, especially age structures, are one of the key components of any country's future. Such trends have a long gestation period just as their impact is also long-term. If such trends are anticipated and planned for, rich economic dividends can be reaped as demonstrated by the East Asian economies. If the necessary measures are not taken early, the consequences will manifest themselves after decades by which time it may be too late to rectify the situation.

Numbers

The overall growth rate of Pakistan's population, according to the Population Situation Analysis (PSA) report of December 2020 of 2.4 per cent in 1951 increased to 3.6 per cent during the 1961-72 period; it then gradually declined to 2.4 per cent for the 1998-2017 inter-census period. Pakistan's population increased six fold between 1951 and 2017 from 34 million to 208 million and is projected to reach 263 million by 2030 and 383 million by 2050—an increase by 84 per cent during the period 2017-2050 if serious and sustained actions are not taken to halt the growth.[104] More than 106.4 million people in Pakistan are men, while 101.3 are women. Over 60 per cent of the population resides in rural areas. Currently, in 2022, the population is estimated to be around 225 million. Former Special Assistant to the Prime Minister, Dr. Zafar Mirza stated that at the current rate Pakistan's population would double in the next 30 years, compared with an average doubling time of 60 years for other South Asian countries.[105]

Since its creation Pakistan has made very little progress in family planning. This is an area critical to maternal, newborn, infant and child health and survival. It has major spinoff effects on women's health, education and labour force participation as well as impacting environment and quality of life, although a few sexual and reproductive health areas have witnessed notable progress. The report also noted that Pakistan suffered not only from a low economic growth but also an inequitable distribution of the gains from such growth and associated opportunities of education, employment and income. This is particularly true for the female population.

Another issue is of female labour participation. Though these rates have increased from 13.7 per cent in 1990 to 20.3 per cent in 2020, they are still very low. The status of women remains a challenging issue and the country ranks near the bottom of the world's countries on indicators such as women's health and survival, education attainment and equal economic participation and opportunity. Moreover, women and children are showing one of the highest levels of malnutrition, undernourishment and childhood stunting in the world and only 15 per cent of children consume a minimally acceptable diet. Alarmingly, Pakistan has the highest percentage of population experiencing dietary energy consumption poverty, compared to India, Bangladesh and Sri Lanka. In 2019, 24 per cent of Pakistan's population had insufficient food intake to meet dietary energy requirements.[106]

Province-wise, the population of Punjab is slightly less than 110 million, followed by Sindh with 47.8 million, Khyber Pakhtunkhwa 34 million and Balochistan 11.3 million. According to research conducted by several reputed organisations, including the UN Population Division, Pakistan would require more than 117 million jobs, 19 million houses, and 85,000 primary schools in the next two decades to meet the demands of its rapidly increasing citizen count. It is apprehended that if the numbers continue to grow at the same rate, the population of Punjab, already the most populous province, will be equal to the current national headcount by the time Pakistan marks its centennial.[107] Karachi is the largest city with more than 15 million people, followed by Lahore with 11 million. Experts and politicians, however, appear to be sceptical about population figures for Karachi, claiming the city's actual population is somewhere around 25 million.

(i) According to the 2020-21 Economic Survey:[108] life expectancy at birth in 2019 was 67.3 years against India's 69.7 years, Bangladesh's 72.6 years, Sri Lanka's 77 years, Indonesia's 71.7 years, Malaysia's 76.2 years with only Afghanistan statistics worse than Pakistan's at 64.8 years; infant mortality rate was 55.7 per 1,000 live births in Pakistan, as compared with India's 28.3, Bangladesh's 25.6, Sri Lanka's 6.4, Indonesia's 20.2, Malaysia's 7.3 with even Afghanistan performing better than Pakistan with 46.5 deaths per 1,000 live births; and

(ii) Under-five mortality was at 67.23 per 1,000 in 2019, as compared with India 34.3, Bangladesh 30.8, Sri Lanka 7.1, Indonesia 23.9, Malaysia 8.6 and Afghanistan at 60.3.

Experts believe that Pakistan is going through a demographic transition and is experiencing a 'once-in-a-lifetime' window of opportunity of a 'demographic dividend' as the working-age population bulges and the dependency ratio declines. The crux of a demographic transition is the nature of the age structure of a country's population based on the reality that while the young and the old tend to consume more than they produce, the working-age population tends to produce more than it consumes. Thus, countries that have a larger proportion of working-age population relative to the young and elderly dependents is said to be undergoing a demographic transition that creates the condition for a demographic dividend. However, a demographic dividend is a time-specific window of opportunity, and does not last indefinitely. To actualise demographic dividend, the basic question is whether those entering the labour market can be absorbed productively against the backdrop of an increasingly globalised and technologically advanced world. Over time, the age structure changes again, as the large adult population starts ageing and becomes less productive. Thus, the demographic dividend only creates the conditions for an economic spurt that has to be harnessed. If harnessed, it could lead to potentially greater economic activity. If it is not capitalised upon, it could lead to massive unemployment and its attendant consequences.

Pakistan's working age population of 15–64 years reached 52 per cent in the early 1990s, 59 per cent in 2006 and is currently estimated to be 60.4 per cent, creating the possibility of a demographic dividend. The current share of 60 per cent of the working-age population would peak at 68 per cent around 2045 by when it will start declining again as the population begins to age and moves out of the working age group. Thus, the once-in-a-lifetime window for Pakistan for a potential 'demographic dividend' is roughly between 1990 and 2045. Of these 55 years, 30 have already passed without any visible pick-up in economic activity.[109]

Pakistan has the tenth largest labour force in the world. According to the Labour Force Survey 2013–14, the total labour force in the country was 60.09 million, increasing to 61.04 million in 2014–15. (This low figure compared to the total population is due to low female employment rates). According to one estimate, by 2030, there are likely to be 175 million potential workers of which 90 million will be males and 85 million females. This is likely to increase to 221 million individuals in working ages by 2050. Given the low female employment rates, conservative estimates are a total of roughly 105 million in the labour force by 2030, increasing to 140 million by 2050.[110] According to another projection, the working-age population will rise from 85 million in 2010 to 178 million in 2050.[111]

Based on Pakistan's population projections, 3.1 million persons are expected to enter the labour force every year over the next four decades. As mentioned in the section on the economy, at 5 per cent growth rates, the economy can absorb only around 1 million people. "Pakistan needs a high economic growth rate, 7-8 per cent, for the next 30 years to absorb the new entrants to the labour force," said a summary of the Population Situation Analysis (PSA) launched by the Ministry of Planning and Development, which was finalised with the support of international development partners.[112] So what happens to the 2.1 million year on year for the next four decades and beyond who would not find employment?

With the female half of the population not able to fully participate in the labour market due to a variety of reasons, it is debatable whether the age structure itself can be called a window of opportunity. Not surprisingly, Pakistan ranks 123rd in the world on the Gender Development Index, even lower than its Human Development Index ranking, indicating that access to opportunities, resources and benefits by men and women are skewed. It is fairly clear that the advantages of a demographic dividend cannot be secured without the wholesome participation of half the population.

The second issue is of education and an educated workforce. A major factor inhibiting Pakistan's economic prospects is the low level of education and technical skills of the workforce. As noted in the chapter on Education, Pakistan's education system is both quantitatively and qualitatively poor. With one-third of the youth labour force being illiterate and the rest possessing very low levels of technical education in 2010-11, not surprisingly, Pakistan, it has been argued, is stuck in a 'low-level skills equilibrium trap' which severely restricts its move into higher value-added sectors essential for raising productivity and increasing economic growth.[113] This is the snowballing effect of insufficient investment in the education sector over the decades, which has manifested itself at a time when the need for an educated work force is the most in order to reap the demographic dividend. Moreover, these consequences will last for years, if not decades, to come, even if Pakistan were to launch a crash investment programme today.

What happens if the demographic dividend is not realised? The flip side of an unrealised demographic dividend is that the massive 'youth bulge' could pose a serious threat to law and order including, in Pakistan's case, of terrorism. The danger for Pakistan is that without sustained economic growth and without investment in education, the demographic dividend would degenerate into a 'demographic horde' with all its attendant consequences of frustration, alienation and violence.

The other problem with an unrealised demographic dividend is that an unproductive population would pose huge pressures on resources like food, water, and energy. A country that was near to being self-sufficient in food in the early 1980s has a food security issue today largely due to increased population.

One sign of an unrealised demographic dividend is already visible. According to the 'National Nutrition Survey, approximately 60 per cent of the country's population is facing food insecurity and nearly 50 per cent of the women and children are malnourished. It warned: 'The growing population in Pakistan poses a significant threat to food security, Pakistan's development and social indicators and stability.'[114] The Planning Commission of Pakistan and the World Food Programme in a report titled 'Minimum cost of diet in Pakistan', put the figure of lack of access to proper recommended nutrition at 67.6 per cent of households across the country. This was particularly prevalent in the rural areas of Balochistan, where as many as 83.4 per cent households were unable to pay for adequate nourishment, closely followed by that in Sindh (70.8 per cent), Khyber Pakhtunkhwa (67.4 per cent) and Punjab (65.6 per cent).[115]

A more widespread risk is of youth radicalisation—the threat of millions of young, impoverished and unemployed Pakistanis succumbing to extremism. As the Government's own Pakistan Vision 2025 puts it, 'A large set of Pakistani youth is dissatisfied, frustrated and in a state of disarray due to low education levels and large-scale unemployment. This has led to serious social problems including drug abuse, crime, mental disorder, terrorism and religious fanaticism.'[116]

Finally, it is worth noting that after the period of demographic dividend, there would be rapid population ageing. Given the anticipated rapid fertility decline in the future, the size of the population aged over 65 will rise from 7.5 million in 2010 to 30 million in 2050, representing 10 per cent of the country's population at the latter year. While in the South Asian context, older parents are looked after by the grown-up children, yet a rapidly ageing population will pose societal challenges including those of health and care for the elderly. Pakistan then could be caught between a large uneducated and unskilled young population and a significant older population, which would place an extraordinary burden on Pakistan's economy. Durr-e-Nayab warns: 'Aging of population is the inevitable end of demographic transition, and Pakistan, albeit slowly, is moving towards it. In the absence of any state planned old-age security system and the existing low saving rates in the country, the demographic dividend can turn into a demographic nightmare for majority of the elderly.'[117]

Bottom Line

Thirty years of the once-in-a-lifetime demographic dividend window of opportunity have already passed it by without any visible signs of an economic upsurge. No thinking seems to have gone into understanding the needs of a changing age structure. The lack of investment in the education sector for decades is showing results today in terms of the quantity and quality of education and literacy rates and especially the poor statistics for female education. The latter is perhaps one of the most important factors that has hampered Pakistan's development. There is a serious danger of youth bulge becoming a nightmare for Pakistan and its neighbours.

Time clearly is not on Pakistan's side. The demographic transition Pakistan is undergoing can have explosive social and political consequences due to past failure to make timely investments in education, health and a developmental economy. The inability to generate the required number of jobs through a sustained, high GDP growth, will result in the streets being crowded with young men and women seeking jobs, justice, education, and medical care for themselves and their families, leaving them vulnerable. This could pose a serious threat to the country's stability.[118]

Conclusion

The NTST show how vulnerable Pakistan has made itself over the decades. None of these threats are a product of a few years but due to lack of governance over decades. It is obvious that Pakistan is faced with hydra-headed problems—increasingly diminishing water supplies, an uneducated horde of young people, an economy on the drip, demographic pressures, lack of jobs, and a growing radicalised population.

Such a combination will lead to unacceptable social chaos and anarchy that the army too will not be able to control or be immune from. No amount of nuclear weapons, non-state actors or Chinese assistance will help Pakistan in tackling these non-traditional security threats.

Pakistan thus stands at a critical moment in its history. Ultimately, the question boils down to whether or not the Pakistani leadership, especially the military, continues to see Pakistan's security purely in military terms. If it does, Pakistan will sink deeper into the quagmire. Even if it changes its mindset and sees security in broader terms to encompass the NTST, it will take a Herculean effort to pull Pakistan from the brink of the abyss, but at least Pakistan will have a chance.

Only a leadership that has vision and comprehension of the multiple crises facing the country can deal with these NTST. Such a leadership will also have to have the courage and willingness to take resolute action to tackle each of the problems. Without this, Pakistan is headed towards the abyss. However, in the short or medium terms, such a leadership does not seem to be on the horizon. The policies that Pakistan adopts or does not adopt today, the investment that it makes or does not make today will determine the kind of country that Pakistan will be in the next three decades. With such a huge focus and investment on defence and other priorities, tackling the demographic challenge is indeed difficult, especially because results are barely visible during the relatively short attention span of a politician or a general. Not surprisingly, experts have lamented that there is no sustained attention on the demographics of Pakistan.[119]

In this context, Pakistan would do well to heed the warning: 'If, in 10 or 20 years, Pakistan still has a large number of unemployed or underemployed people, including tens of millions of young people, the country may face crises that dwarf those it has experienced to date.'[120] The Centre for International and Strategic Studies has an even more dire warning: 'Many nations in North Africa, the Middle East, South and East Asia, and the former Soviet bloc—including China, Russia, Iran, and Pakistan—are now experiencing a rapid or extreme demographic transition that could push them toward civil collapse, or (in reaction) toward "neo-authoritarianism."'[121]

ENDNOTES

1. Parts of this chapter have been extracted from the Author's book, *Pakistan: Courting the Abyss*, NOIDA: Harper Collins Publishers, 2016.
2. Cabinet Mission Plan, 16 May 1946. Notes 431.
3. Craig Baxter (ed.), *Diaries of Field Marshal Mohammed Ayub Khan, 1966–72*, Karachi: OUP, 2007, p. 271.
4. Tilak Devasher, *Pakistan: Courting the Abyss*, NOIDA: Harper Collins Publishers, 2016.
5. Mushtaq Ahmed, 'Water saga', *The Nation*, 31 May 2016.
6. Ashfak Bokhari, 'Forgotten water policy initiatives', *Dawn*, 13 June 2016.
7. Dr. Zaigham Habib, 'Water Worries', *The Friday Times*, 24–30 April 2015.
8. Cited in 'The Indus Equation', Strategic Foresight Group, Mumbai, 2011.
9. Crops at risk: Editorial in *Daily Times*, 25 August 25 2021, https://dailytimes.com.pk/807571/crops-at-risk/
10. Tarbela Dam water level drops alarmingly, *Dawn*, 13 March 2022, https://www.dawn.com/news/1679675
11. Osama Farooq, 'Looming crisis of water scarcity over Pakistan; Challenges, implication and way forward', in *Business Recorder*, 21 November 2021, 2020, https://www.brecorder.com/news/40034295/looming-crisis-of-water-scarcity-over-pakistan-challenges-implication-and-way-forward
12. 'Is the Glass Half Empty or Half Full? Issues in Managing Water Challenges and Policy Instruments', IMF, June 2015, p. 12.
13. 'Per capita water availability alarming: minister', *The News*, 29 June 2013.
14. Simi Kamal, op. cit.; 'Pakistan losing water resources due to poor infrastructure: experts', *Pakistan Today*, 22 March 2013.
15. Economic Survey of Pakistan 2013-2014, Government of Pakistan, p. 250.
16. Osama Farooq.
17. Simi Kamal, 'Pakistan's Water Challenges: Entitlement, Access, Efficiency, and Equity,' in Michael Kugelman and Robert M. Hathaway (eds.), *Running on Empty: Pakistan's Water Crisis*, Washington DC: Woodrow Wilson International Centre for Scholars, 2009, pp. 28-44.

18. Osama Farooq.
19. Syed Mohammad Ali, 'IMF's advice for our water woes', *Express Tribune*, 10 July 2015.
20. 'Looming water crisis', editorial, *Daily Times*, 12 June 2015.
21. Saving water: editorial in *The Express Tribune*, 11 August 2021.
22. Simi Kamal, op. cit.
23. FAO, AQUASTAT database, 2013, cited in Daanish Mustafa, Majed Akhter, and Natalie Nasrallah (eds.), op. cit.
24. Contaminated water: Editorial in *Dawn*, 11 August 2021, https://www.dawn.com/news/1640026/ontaminated-water
25. Unsafe Drinking Water: editorial in *The Nation*, 11 August 2021, https://nation.com.pk/11-Aug-2021/unsafe-drinking-water
26. 'No safe drinking water in major cities, NA told.' Amir Wasim in *Dawn*, 10 August 2021, https://www.dawn.com/news/1639701/no-safe-drinking-water-in-major-cities-na-told
27. Water distribution: editorial in *The Express Tribune*, 22 August 2021, https://tribune.com.pk/story/2316621/water-distribution-1
28. Drought conditions may worsen in Balochistan, Sindh, report in *The Express Tribune*, 9 June 2021, https://tribune.com.pk/story/2304240/drought-conditions-may-worsen-in-balochistan-sindh
29. Khaleeq Kiani, 'Water Shortage Worsens for Rabi Crops', *Dawn*, 14 October 2015.
30. Pakistan likely to face 30 to 40 pc water shortage, by Fawad Yousafzai, *The News*, 15 March 2021.
31. Khaleeq Kiani, IRSA finalises water shares for Rabi amid Sindh's protest, *Dawn*, 6 October 2021, https://www.dawn.com/news/1650351/irsa-finalises-water-shares-for-rabi-amid-sindhs-protest
32. Shaheen Akhtar, 'Emerging Challenges to Indus Waters Treaty: Issues of Compliance and Trans-boundary Impacts of Indian Hydroprojects on the Western Rivers', *Focus*, vol. 28, no. 3, 2010, cited in Daanish Mustafa, Majed Akhter, and Natalie Nasrallah, op. cit.
33. Anwar Iqbal, 'Water scarcity may threaten national economy: IMF', *Dawn*, 9 June 2015.
34. CCI unanimously approves country's first water policy, *The Express Tribune*, 24 April 2018.
35. 'Partnering with Pakistan', *Washington Post*, 28 January 2009.
36. 'Indus Waters Treaty', editorial, *Dawn*, 9 March 2016.
37. Zafar Bhutto, 'Clearing the air: India not behind water shortage in Pakistan', *The Express Tribune*, 10 July 2015.
38. 'The Big Problem with Water', *The Express Tribune*, 27 September 2017.
39. Pervez Hoodbhoy, 'Can Pakistan Work? A Country in Search of Itself', *Foreign Affairs*, November/December 2004.
40. 'Education Emergency in Pakistan', *Dawn*, 9 March 2011.
41. 'Pakistan: Education For All, Review Report 2015', Ministry of Education, Government of Pakistan, June 2014, in collaboration with UNESCO.
42. Single National Curriculum launched, by Kashif Abbasi in *Dawn*, 17 August 17 2021, https://www.dawn.com/news/1641105/single-national-curriculum-launched
43. 'National Internal Security Policy', Ministry of Interior, Government of Pakistan, p. 28.
44. Alif Ailaan, '25 Million Broken Promises: The crisis of Pakistan's out-of-school children', 2014.
45. Ibid.
46. Azam Khan, 'Why 25 million children are out of school', *The Express Tribune*, 31 August 2015.
47. 'Pakistan: Education for All, Review Report 2015.'
48. 'Financing Education in Pakistan, Opportunities for Action', Country Case Study for the

Oslo Summit on Education for Development, 6–7 July 2015, p. 12.; 'Education for All, Review Report, 2015', p. 17.

49. Pakistan Economic Survey 2020-21.
50. Ibid.
51. Alif Ailaan, op. cit.
52. 40% educated women jobless, Senate body told, Report in *The News*, 28 September 2021, https://tribune.com.pk/story/2322309/40-educated-women-jobless-senate-body-told; 24% educated Pakistanis unemployed, Senate body informed, *Geo News*, 27 September 2021, https://www.geo.tv/latest/372784-24-educated-pakistanis-unemployed-senate-body-informed
53. Kashif Abbasi, 44pc of fifth graders unable to read English properly, survey reveals, *Dawn*, 11 March 2022, https://www.dawn.com/news/1679314/44pc-of-fifth-graders-unable-to-read-english-properly-survey-reveals
54. Economic Survey, 2013–14, op. cit.
55. 'UN report: Pakistan's education 50 years behind world', *The Express Tribune*, 7 September 2016.
56. 'Pakistan among the least innovative countries in the world, report says', *The Express Tribune*, 8 September 2016.
57. A.H. Nayyar, 'Insensitivity to the Religious Diversity of the Nation', in A.H. Nayyar and Ahmad Salim (eds.), *The Subtle Subversion: The State of Curricula and Textbooks in Pakistan*, Islamabad: Sustainable Development Policy Institute, 2004.
58. Cited in United States Commission on International Religious Freedom, 'Connecting the Dots: Education and Religious Discrimination in Pakistan. A Study of Public Schools and Madrassas', November 2011, p. 13.
59. Cited in Stephen Cohen, The Idea of Pakistan, New Delhi: OUP, 2004, p. 171.
60. Tariq Rahman, 'Denizens of Alien Worlds', cited in Haroon Mustafa Janjua, 'Curricula of deception', *The Nation*, 3 January 2015.
61. United States Commission on International Religious Freedom, op. cit., p. 16.
62. A.H. Nayyar, Dissecting The Single National Curriculum 9 August 2020, https://www.dawn.com/news/1572130
63. The education paradox: Op-ed by Iftikhar Durrani in *The News*, 26 February 2022, https://www.thenews.com.pk/print/936752-the-education-paradox
64. A.H. Nayyar, op cit.
65. Education emergency: Editorial *The News*, 12 September 2021, https://www.thenews.com.pk/print/891202-education-emergency
66. Curriculum controversy: editorial in *The News* 3 August 3, 2021, https://www.thenews.com.pk/print/872279-curriculum-controversy
67. A great leap backward, by Zahid Hussain, *Dawn*, 15 September 2021, https://www.dawn.com/news/1646467/a-great-leap-backward
68. Curriculum debate: Editorial *Dawn*, 9 August 2021, https://www.dawn.com/news/1639582/curriculum-debate
69. A.H. Nayyar, op. cit. 2020.
70. Aitchison rejects the SNC, by Intsab Sahi in TNS, 19 September 2021, https://www.thenews.com.pk/tns/detail/893427-aitchison-rejects-the-snc
71. Education: PTI's plan exposed, by Pervez Hoodbhoy in *Dawn*, 18 July 2020, https://www.dawn.com/news/1569679/education-ptis-plan-exposed
72. A.H. Nayyar, op. cit. 2020.
73. Ibid.
74. The world beyond SNC: by Muhammad Hamid Zaman in *The Express Tribune*, 24 August 2021, https://tribune.com.pk/story/2316871/the-world-beyond-snc

75. Education emergency: Editorial *The News*, 12 September 2021, https://www.thenews.com.pk/print/891202-education-emergency
76. William Easterly, 'The Political Economy of Growth Without Development: A Case Study of Pakistan', paper for the Analytical Narratives of Growth Project, Kennedy School of Government, Harvard University, June 2001, p. 10.
77. Pakistan Economic Survey 2020-21.
78. IMF forecasts 1.5 pc growth rate for Pakistan, by Khaleeq Kiani in *Dawn*, 7 April 2021, www.dawn.com/news/1616843/imf-forecasts-15pc-growth-rate-for-pakistan
79. Economy review: Editorial in *The News*, 16 August 2021, https://www.thenews.com.pk/print/878725-economy-review
80. Joblessness jumped in 2018-19: labour survey, by Nasir Jamal in *Dawn*, 17 September , 2021, https://www.dawn.com/news/1646761/joblessness-jumped-in-2018-19-labour-survey
81. WB Growth Forecast: Editorial in *The Express Tribune*, 19 January 2022, https://Tribune.Com.Pk/Story/2339330/Wb-Growth-Forecast
82. Oxford Poverty and Human Development Initiative, 'Pakistan Country Briefing', Multidimensional Poverty Index Data bank, University of Oxford, June 2015.
83. Poverty in Pakistan up from 4.4 pc to 5.4 pc: WB, by Mehtab Haider in *The News*, 20 June 2021, https://www.thenews.com.pk/print/852321-poverty-in-pakistan-up-from-4-4pc-to-5-4pc-wb
84. Pakistan's hungry, angry people; Editorial in *Daily Times*, 18 October 2019, https://dailytimes.com.pk/485039/pakistans-hungry-angry-people/
85. SBP report shines light on food insecurity, by Shahid Iqbal in *Dawn*, 16 July 2019, https://www.dawn.com/news/1494372/sbp-report-shines-light-on-food-insecurity
86. Path to food security, Editorial in *The Express Tribune*, 4 October 2021, https://tribune.com.pk/story/2323171/path-to-food-security
87. Food out of reach: Editorial in *Dawn*, 11 August 2021. https://www.dawn.com/news/1640028/food-out-of-reach
88. Country no more self-sufficient in wheat, NA told, Amin Ahmed, 26 June 2020, https://www.dawn.com/news/1565264
89. Mountain of debt: Editorial in *Daily Times*, 1 September 2021, https://dailytimes.com.pk/810327/mountain-of-debt/ ; Rising Public Debt: Editorial in *The Nation*, 1 September 2021, https://nation.com.pk/01-Sep-2021/rising-public-debt
90. Dr. Farrukh Saleem, When will the 'debt bomb' explode? 6 April 2021, https://pakobserver.net/when-will-the-debt-bomb-explode/
91. Is Pakistan's public debt sustainable? Usman Hayat, 3 November 2021, https://www.dawn.com/news/1652968/is-pakistans-public-debt-sustainable
92. Mushtaq Ghumman, $21 bn support request: Ministry seeks update from Pak envoy in Beijing, *Business Recorder*, 17 March 2022, https://www.brecorder.com/news/40161301/21bn-support-request-ministry-seeks-update-from-pak-envoy-in-beijing
93. F.M. Shakil, Debt-ridden Pakistan begs China for a bailout, *Asia Times*, on line, 10 February 2022, https://asiatimes.com/2022/02/debt-ridden-pakistan-begs-china-for-a-bailout/?mc_cid=da5057a34f&mc_eid=a748d84c85
94. FDI plunges by 28.9 pc in FY21, by Naveed Butt, Zulfiqar Ahmad in *Business Recorder*, 3 August 2021, https://www.brecorder.com/news/40110796/fdi-plunges-by-289pc-in-fy21
95. Decreasing FDI flows: Editorial in *Dawn*, 19 August 2021, https://www.dawn.com/news/1641482/decreasing-fdi-flows
96. Dr. Farrukh Saleem, Real issues, 28 March 2021, https://www.thenews.com.pk/print/810814-real-issues
97. Energy security, by Dr. Farrukh Saleem, 26 December 2021, https://www.thenews.com.pk/

print/919861-energy-security

98. Woeful PKR slide: Editorial in *Business Recorder*, 31 December 2021, https://www.brecorder.com/news/40143752/woeful-pkr-slide
99. Abdul Rauf Shakoori & Huzaima Bukhari, 'PTI and the bitter IMF pill', *The News*, 13 February 2022, https://www.thenews.com.pk/tns/detail/932991-pti-and-the-bitter-imf-pill
100. Economy: rising uncertainty, by Dr. Hafiz A. Pasha in *Business Recorder*, 7 September 2021, https://www.brecorder.com/news/40118457/economy-rising-uncertainty
101. The falling rupee, Dr. Farrukh Saleem, 3 October 2021, https://www.thenews.com.pk/print/897115-the-falling-rupee
102. Sakib Sherani, Elite illusions and delusions, 9 December 2021, https://www.dawn.com/news/1662756
103. Richard Jackson and Neil Howe, The Greying of the Great Powers: Demography and Geopolitics in the 21st Century, Washington, DC: Centre for Strategic and International Studies (CSIS), 2008, p. 15.
104. Pakistan Population Situation Analysis 2020, Ministry of Planning & UNFPA, https://pakistan.unfpa.org/sites/default/files/pub-pdf/pakistan_psa_2020_final_report.pdf
105. 'Pakistan's population may double in next 30 years', *Dawn*, 25 December 2019, https://www.dawn.com/news/1524251
106. Ibid.
107. Soaring national headcount poses greater threat, by Asif Mahmood/Razzak Abro/Wisal Yousafzai/Zafar Baloch in *The Express Tribune*, 11 July 2021, https://tribune.com.pk/story/2310004/soaring-national-headcount-poses-greater-threat
108. Cited in 'Balance in population growth', Editorial in *Business Recorder*, 13 July 2021, https://www.brecorder.com/news/40106811/balance-in-population-growth
109. Durr-e-Nayab, 'Demographic Dividend or Demographic Threat in Pakistan', Islamabad: Pakistan Institute of Development Economics, Working Papers, 2006.
110. Ibid.
111. Rabbi Royan and Zeba A. Sathar, 'Overview: The Population of Pakistan Today', in Zeba A. Sathar, Rabbi Royan & John Bongaarts (eds.), op. cit., pp. 3–12.
112. Khaleeq Kiani, Updated Next five years' economic growth not encouraging, 10 December 2020, https://www.dawn.com/news/1594909, https://pakistan.unfpa.org/sites/default/files/pub-pdf/pakistan_psa_2020_final_report.pdf
113. Rashid Amjad, op. cit., p. 48.
114. Pakistan Vision 2025, Planning Commission, Government of Pakistan.
115. 'The issue of malnutrition of children in Pakistan', Editorial in *Daily Times*, 18 July 2016.
116. Pakistan Vision 2025, Planning Commission, Government of Pakistan.
117. Durr-e-Nayab, 'Demographic Dividend or Demographic Threat in Pakistan', Islamabad: Pakistan Institute of Development Economics, Working Papers, 2006.
118. Pakistan Vision 2025, Planning Commission, Government of Pakistan.
119. Zeba A. Sathar, et al, op. cit.
120. David E. Bloom, Foreword, in Zeba A. Sathar, Rabbi Royan, & John Bongaarts (eds.), *Capturing the Democratic Dividend In Pakistan*, Islamabad: The Population Council, 2013.
121. Richard Jackson & Neil Howe, The Greying of the Great Powers: Demography and Geopolitics in the 21st Century, Washington DC: Centre for International and Strategic Studies, 2008.

5

Pakistan's National Security Policy: Much Ado About Nothing*

Amb Satish Chandra

Pakistan's recently-released National Security Policy (NSP) 2022-2026 is essentially an exercise in image building necessitated by its being in the doghouse internationally because of its abominable human rights record, an economy perpetually in shambles largely due to the prioritisation of military spending over development, dicey democratic credentials, and being a breeding ground for terror. Accordingly, the NSP projects Pakistan as a much-maligned peace-loving state determined to pull itself up by its boot straps by focusing more than ever before on the economy and on human security.

For a document that has purportedly been under preparation since 2014, the NSP disappoints, as it is long on rhetoric and short on specifics, fails to transcend the banal, and displays the customary animosity towards India. It is unlikely to lead to any meaningful policy change and is no more than an effort to blunt Pakistan's negative image.

The full text of the NSP, reportedly running into over 100 pages, has not been made public and the abbreviated text that has been released exclusive of the messages and executive summary is about 48 pages which gets further reduced to only 36 pages if one deducts the numerous blank and cover pages for each of its eight sections. The Government's bashfulness in sharing the NSP in totality with its people is inexplicable. Does it arise from a fear that the details would be divisive or that they lack gravitas?

*First Published in *National Security Review*, Vivekananda International Foundation.

The NSP as released has a section each devoted to Policy Formulation, National Security Framework, and National Cohesion, Securing the Economic Future, Defence, Internal Security, Foreign Policy, and Human Security.

The Policy Formulation section asserts that the absence of a comprehensive national security policy, covering both traditional and non-traditional security, necessitated a NSP, which was developed under the guidance of the National Security Committee on the basis of extensive consultations over a period of seven years. It further mentions that the NSP is for five years and would be subject to monitoring as well as annual review and updates by the National Security Division.

The National Security Framework section provides an overview of the NSP including its vision, conceptualisation, and implementation principles. The vision projects Pakistan as an Islamic welfare state aligned with the universal principles of justice, equality, and tolerance, seeking a peaceful neighbourhood, ensuring fundamental rights and social justice without discrimination on the basis of caste, creed, or belief and promoting good governance. This is a motherhood and apple pie formulation designed to win over the gullible, far removed from the nasty brutish reality that is Pakistan.

In terms of conceptualisation, it makes the well accepted point that national security must be viewed in a comprehensive manner, inclusive of traditional and non-traditional security. However, it further projects that "Pakistan's vital national security interests are best served by placing economic security as the core element of national security. The country's security imperatives in the next decade will be driven by the need to realise its economic potential while ensuring national cohesion, territorial integrity, internal security, and citizen welfare." The importance of paying attention to the economy and citizen welfare is widely acknowledged but has historically been ignored by Pakistan. Whether any change will actually be made is highly debatable but flagging it serves an important purpose as a PR exercise at a time when Pakistan is doing the rounds of all manner of countries and institutions with a begging bowl.

On implementation principles, too, the NSP does not rise beyond the mundane by calling for a whole-of-government approach, inclusivity, introspection, pragmatism, prioritisation, consistency, etc. However, comments such as "Pursuing our vital national security interests unapologetically will be a cornerstone of our approach to the world" display a pervasive sense of insecurity that suffuses the entire paper.

The National Cohesion section also reveals Pakistan's sense of insecurity by acknowledging concerns about its unity being affected by "divisive discourse." It, however, as is its wont, shifts the blame for this to "disruptive external support." Simultaneously, it indulges in creative narrative building projecting that Pakistan has a "coherent national identity" based on "unity in diversity" and that it will promote national cohesion by cherishing its diversity and inculcating tolerance. The section is more upfront in acknowledging the socio-economic and geographic inequalities and of the need to address them. It, similarly, makes a pitch for improved governance and institutional capacities but, wary of ruffling feathers, makes out that existing reforms are geared to delivering results.

The section on securing Pakistan's "Economic Future" identifies the three main challenges facing the country as "external imbalance, vertical inequalities and horizontal inequalities." On the first, no detailed policy solution is offered other than an anodyne assertion, which could be made by any school child, that there must be an increase in exports, remittances, and revenues. Similarly, on vertical inequalities representing socio-economic inequalities and on horizontal inequalities representing inter provincial inequalities, also referred to in the earlier section, apart from stressing the need to address them effectively, not only are no specific suggestions offered but it is blandly contended that reforms are already in place to deal with them.

In addition to the three challenges cited above, the section focuses on the following issues that have an impact on the economy:

1. **Growth and Development:** While recognising the need for "sustainable growth and inclusive development", Pakistan is actually commended with references to its "economic resilience", "positive growth trajectory" and "vibrant economy." Such enunciations, totally at variance with facts, impinge adversely on the credibility of the NSP and have clearly been incorporated as an image building exercise. Other than exhortations for the need for rapid growth, enhanced productivity in agriculture and industry, consolidation of industry, increased savings rate, etc., there is no going into the nitty gritty of how these commendable objectives are to be realised.
2. **Trade, Investment, and Connectivity:** Like the entire paper, this sub-section too is rich in high sounding rhetoric of which a classic example is the very first sentence which reads "As Pakistan supplements its geo-strategic focus with an added emphasis on geo-economics, it envisions itself as a melting pot of global economic interests offering economic bases to its partner countries for development partnerships." Behind all

this fanciful rhetoric the short point is that Pakistan has a great opportunity to leverage its location for creating connectivity, which would help promote its economic development. This is a well-worn theme in the Pakistani narrative and is by no means new. Interestingly, while the subsection, on the one hand, refers to the possibility of promoting connectivity between Central Asia and South Asia it, on the other, virtually rules out "eastward connectivity" on account of India's "regressive approach." This is a clear indicator that Pakistan's negativity towards India will trump any effort to make its economy the core concern of its security policy. The section is, however, significant in terms of indicating an intent to harness Pakistan's EEZ and coastline to develop its economy, as also to evolve a comprehensive maritime policy to optimise the nation's blue economy.

3. **Fiscal Management:** While expressing a concern on the mounting debt, the section makes out that "efforts are being directed to ensure that public debt remains at a sustainable level while increasing the government's ability to generate revenues through a transparent, responsive, and progressive tax regime." No details in this regard are, however, provided and the reader is expected to accept such bland assertions as gospel truth.
4. **Energy Security:** Here again, while concerns are expressed about the negative performance of the energy sector and the problems of circular debt, bland commitments are made that by 2030, renewables and clean energy will account for 30 per cent and 60 per cent, respectively, of the country's energy mix and that energy production will increasingly be indigenised.
5. **Education, Technology and Innovation:** The projection in regard to these issues, which are dealt with together in one para, is essentially that education will be modernised making it technology based and innovation friendly. But how this is to be done and how it would gel with the madrassa-based education in the country is left unexplained.

The Defence section is on expected lines with commitment to maritime and airspace surveillance, fencing of the western border, modernisation of armed forces, indigenisation of defence production, strengthening of naval capabilities, the criticality of nuclear deterrence and continued adherence to full spectrum deterrence. As expected, it engages in much India bashing of which the following are some instances:

- "Special attention is required to manage lingering border disputes which continue to pose security threats, particularly along the Line of Control and Working Boundary where ceasefire violations by India threaten civilian lives and property while endangering regional stability."
- "The Indian Ocean is fast becoming a space for contestation. The self-professed role of any one country as a so-called net-security provider in the wider Indian Ocean would affect the region's security and economic interests negatively."
- "The expansion of India's nuclear triad, open-ended statements on nuclear policy, and investments in and introduction of destabilising technologies disturb the strategic balance in the region. Pakistan's deterrence regime is vital for and aimed at regional peace."

The Internal Security section, while noting that terrorism is one of the most "acute form of efforts to undermine stability and national harmony", would have one believe that Pakistan has zero tolerance for terrorist activities, has fought one of the most successful wars against terrorism, and is globally acknowledged for "taking positive strides towards creating a strong financial monitoring system to prevent terror financing." Continuing in a similar vein of palpably false narrative building, it projects that Pakistan is committed to "strengthening police forces and associated counter-terrorism agencies, undertaking intelligence-based operations against all terrorist groups, preventing any use of financial sources for terrorism, addressing structural deficiencies and sense of deprivation in recruitment areas, and promoting a pluralistic anti-terror narrative." Interestingly, as a slip or a rare moment of honesty there is no denial in this section of Pakistan's use of terror as an instrument of foreign policy!

While expressing concern about violent sub-nationalism, it is projected that there is an external hand behind it. Attention is also invited to the dangers of radicalisation and extremism. In this context, while projecting that those promoting it would be firmly put down, it is also suggested that "inculcating interfaith and intersectarian harmony and societal tolerance in all its forms will be prioritised." If actually undertaken, this would be the seventh wonder of the world and the Pakistan as we have known it would be unrecognisable!

The Foreign Policy section is characterised by much high sounding rhetoric, a re-run of themes earlier touched upon, an unintended display of insecurity, an unwitting revelation of the rationale of the nature of the NSP, and, of course, the staple of India bashing.

Accordingly, there is not only a call for a greater focus on economic diplomacy but also a reiteration of the need for connectivity initiatives leveraging the country's geo-economically pivotal location.

The reference to Pakistan having adopted a "dynamic and self confident approach to a fast changing world order" smacks of a deep-seated sense of insecurity, which is also evident from similar quite unnecessary assertions elsewhere in the paper.

The section is also indicative that Pakistan is, in fact, hurting greatly on account of its reputation being in tatters the world over by its calling for an image makeover based upon "Pakistan's reality as a responsible state that offers an economic hub for regional and global activity while striving for peace within and beyond its borders." On the same pattern as elsewhere in the paper, it conveniently pins the responsibility for its negative image on the "sustained disinformation and influence operations by adversaries." Indeed, quite unwittingly the section also reveals the real rationale of the NSP by categorically stating that Pakistan will "reverse" the "unfair negativity" attached to its image by emphasising its "economic and human security-centric outlook" and projecting it "as a responsible state that offers an economic hub for regional and global activity while striving for peace within and beyond its borders." Clearly, the call for a greater economic focus in the NSP has little purpose other than an image makeover.

The comments in the section relating to India as detailed below are a mix of image building and vitriolic criticism of the latter and indicate that the basics of Pakistan foreign policy remain unchanged:

> "Pakistan, under its policy of peace at home and abroad, wishes to improve its relationship with India. A just and peaceful resolution of the Jammu and Kashmir dispute remains at the core of our bilateral relationship. The rise of Hindutva-driven politics in India is deeply concerning and impacts Pakistan's immediate security. The political exploitation of a policy of belligerence towards Pakistan by India's leadership has led to the threat of military adventurism and non-contact warfare to our immediate east. Growing Indian arms build-up, facilitated by access to advanced technologies and exceptions in the non-proliferation rules, is a matter of concern for Pakistan. Besides impacting regional stability, such policies of exceptionalism also undermine the global non-proliferation regime. India's pursuit of unilateral policy actions on outstanding issues is an attempt to impose one-sided solutions that can have far-reaching negative consequences for regional stability. India is also consistently engaged in an effort to spread disinformation targeting Pakistan. Pakistan continues to

> believe in resolving all outstanding issues through dialogue; however, recent Indian actions remain significant hurdles in this direction."

Additionally, asserting that India's "illegal and unilateral actions of August 2019 have been rejected" by the people of Kashmir, it accuses it of human rights abuses, war crimes and genocide in the State. It goes on to state that "Pakistan remains steadfast in its moral, diplomatic, political, and legal support to the people of Kashmir until they achieve their right to self-determination guaranteed by the international community as per United Nations Security Council (UNSC) resolutions...."

The Human Security section has a few anodyne paragraphs on population growth, health security, food security, climate and water stress, and gender security. One gets the impression that these have been included merely to tick the boxes. In most of these, it makes all the right noises but, as elsewhere, it does not get into the specifics of how the desired outcomes will be realised. The basic lack of attention to specifics is illustrated by the assertion in the paragraph on water wherein it makes a case for access to transboundary watercourses in the Indus Basin as a national security imperative since nearly 80 per cent of its waters originate from outside. Such assertions are *prima facie* ridiculous as they have no basis in law and in the instant case they are groundless as Pakistan receives 80 per cent of the flows of the Indus Waters by virtue of the Indus Waters Treaty.

In the context of the foregoing, it would be reasonable to conclude that Pakistan's NSP is an exercise of much ado about nothing and essentially a thinly disguised effort at countering its negative image the world over. Those expecting any marked policy shift will be disappointed.

6

Pakistan National Security Policy 2022-26: Some New Elements But No Shift on India*

Dr. Arvind Gupta

The Imran Khan government has produced the country's first ever National Security Policy (NSP) document that outlines Pakistan's approach to national security and provides guidance to the government departments. A public version of the document has been published. Pakistan joins a select group of countries to have a formal national security policy document. Even India, which has had a national security council since 1999, has so far not produced such a document.

The document has been produced by the National Security Division of the Pakistan government after consultations with civilian and military stakeholders as well as think tanks and other institutions. It has been approved by the National Security Committee, which includes various ministers and the Chief of Army Staff. It is not clear whether the document has been approved by the Cabinet. The opposition parties have criticised the government for not consulting them before releasing the policy.

The document lays down the conceptual framework of the government's national security approach and has chapters on national cohesion, economic security, defence, internal security, foreign policy, and human security. The rationale of the new national security policy approach has been described in the following words: "The Policy places economic security at the core of

---

*First published by Vivekananda International Foundation https://www.vifindia.org/article/2022/january/17/pakistan-s-national-security-policy-2022-26-some-new-elements-but-no-shift-on-india 1/6.

comprehensive national security, emphasising a geo-economic vision to supplement the focus on geo-strategy, and recognises that sustainable and inclusive economic growth is needed to expand our national resource pie. This will in turn allow greater availability of resources to bolster traditional and human security."

PM Imran Khan writes in the Foreword that Pakistan's National Security approach must be "citizen centric." In National Security Adviser Moeed W Yusuf's words, the policy is "a clear and bold vision, emphasising a geo-economic paradigm that supplements our geo-strategic approach."

The policy is supposed to provide guidance to the other departments. It lays down a roadmap of implementation, which is not mentioned in detail in the public version.

A Broad Framework for National Security

The document conceptualises National Security in the broader context integrating non-traditional and traditional dimensions. It says, "The challenge before us is to move away from the traditional guns versus butter debate, instead recognising that traditional and non-traditional aspects of national security must be linked through a symbiotic relationship."

The policy holds that Pakistan can take advantage of the new opportunities that are arising in the emerging world order provided it follows a geo-economic approach aimed at exploiting its geostrategic location, connecting with the surrounding regions, making Pakistan hospitable for foreign direct investment, increasing Pakistan's exports, tapping into new technologies, investing in human resource development and skills, improving coordination amongst institutions and following a whole-of-government approach in the implementation of the policy.

There is candid admission that Pakistan's deplorable economic situation has impacted its security adversely. The document acknowledges the country's weaknesses quite frankly: low productivity, mounting debt, inadequate skills base, poor education system, inefficient use of resources, massive disparities, income inequalities, and growing stress on food, water, and energy resources, and many others.

The document seeks to correct Pakistan's image as a terrorism supporting, intolerant country. The policy says that "Continuous and dedicated efforts will be made through an approach centred on cherishing the diversity of Pakistan, inculcating tolerance, and promoting national cohesion through educational and cultural institutions and an inclusive national discourse."

There is an entire chapter on human security, which mentions the challenges arising out of "population and migration, health security, climate and water security, food security, and gender security." The document mentions gender equality, preventing structural violence, and ensuring equal participation of women as issues of "paramount importance."

The policy also talks about inter-faith harmony and minority rights, and recognises the need for "intellectual expression and thought based on openness and equal opportunities, irrespective of caste, creed, religion, gender, or socio-economic standing."

The internal security chapter deals with terrorism, violent sub-nationalism, extremism and sectarianism, and drugs and narcotics nexus with politics and business. It claims, rather disingenuously, that "Pakistan's efforts at creating a strong financial monitoring system to prevent terror financing have been globally acknowledged." It talks about "undertaking intelligence-based operations against all terrorist groups, preventing any use of financial sources for terrorism." A multi-dimensional approach consisting of targeted socio-economic interventions and governance-related initiatives in regions where "violent sub-nationalist elements operate."

India

In India, the document would be perused with keen interest to see whether Pakistan's hostile approach to India will change under the geo-economic paradigm.

The NSP stresses that Pakistan wants peaceful relations with India but then goes on to make the improvement in relations dependent upon a "...just and peaceful resolution of the Jammu and Kashmir dispute", which "remains at the core of our bilateral relationship." It holds India responsible for the sorry state of bilateral relations. "...bilateral ties have been stymied as a consequence of the unresolved Kashmir dispute and India's hegemonic designs."

As if that was not enough, the document directly interferes in India's internal affairs when it expresses concern at the rise of so-called "Hindutva-driven policy" that "impacts Pakistan's immediate security."

The anti-India rant goes on. India is blamed for "military adventurism", "non-contact warfare", "arms build-up", "belligerence towards Pakistan" and policies of "exceptionalism that undermine the global non-proliferation regime." It is also accused of "imposing one-sided solutions that have negative consequences for regional stability." The document says that India is consistently engaged in "spreading disinformation to target Pakistan." There are veiled references to surgical strikes, air strikes against terrorist hideouts after the Pulwama terror attack, the abrogation of Article 370 and India's effort to highlight Pakistan's consistent support to terrorism and terror financing. Recent Indian actions are considered to be "hurdles" to dialogue.

There is no sign of a rethink on Jammu and Kashmir. The Indian Armed Forces in Jammu and Kashmir are described as "occupation forces" and accused of carrying out "human rights violations" and "genocide." The document repeats Pakistan's usual refrain that it "remains steadfast in its moral, diplomatic, political, and legal support to the people of Kashmir until they achieve their right to self-determination guaranteed by the international community as per the United Nations Security Council (UNSC) resolutions."

Without specifying Article 370, the document asserts that "India's illegal and unilateral actions of August 2019 have been rejected by the people of Indian Illegally Occupied Jammu and Kashmir (IIOJK)", and that "India continues to create false propaganda around the Kashmiri resistance to hide its illegal actions."

India is regarded as a threat. The document warns that "With a regressive and dangerous ideology gripping the collective conscience in our immediate neighbourhood, the prospects of violent conflict have grown immensely.... The possibility of use of force by the adversary as a deliberate policy choice cannot be ruled out." And, to meet this threat, "Requisite conventional capabilities will be ensured through astute investment in constant modernisation of our armed forces without embroiling in any arms race." The country would increase its "capabilities in network centricity, battlefield awareness, electronic warfare capabilities, and other force multipliers."

In the light of such uncompromising formulations, it is difficult to conclude that Pakistan's India policy will change in the near future even as it tries to tell the world that it is adopting a new paradigm in its national security approach.

Foreign Policy

There is nothing startlingly new or unexpected in the document in as far as Pakistan's relations with other countries are concerned.

Pakistan would expand its "deep-rooted historic ties with China" based on "trust and strategic convergence, across all areas of mutual engagement." The China-Pakistan Economic Corridor (CPEC) will provide "impetus to Pakistan's economy and jumpstart domestic growth, alleviate poverty and improve regional connectivity." Pakistan would invite other interested countries to invest in "CPEC-related and other special economic zones."

Pakistan would like to broaden its relationship with the USA beyond the narrow focus on counter-terrorism.

The importance of Central Asia in Pakistan's geo-economic paradigm is recognised explicitly. Russia and Central Asia get a favourable mention. The document says, "Pakistan is committed to reimagining its partnership with Russia in energy, defence cooperation, and investment", and, "Under Vision Central Asia, Pakistan is working towards actualising agreements on energy and transit with the Central Asian Republics."

On Afghanistan, the document talks of Pakistan's commitment to "facilitating and supporting peace and stability in Afghanistan in close collaboration with the international community through addressing economic, humanitarian, and security issues." Afghanistan is regarded as a potential "gateway for economic connectivity with Central Asian states." This would be the "key driver for Pakistan's support for peace in Afghanistan." Russia and Central Asian countries are described as "important partners in our shared objectives of peace and stability in Afghanistan."

Assessment

The target of the document is not so much India as the rest of the world.

Through this document, Pakistan is trying to project to the rest of the world that it is a progressive, moderate country with a huge economic potential and not an intolerant, bankrupt, dysfunctional, terrorist-infested country as India would have the world believe.

Pakistan would like to correct that perception through the new understanding of national security that it is presenting to the world.

The fact is that Pakistan is hurtling towards economic bankruptcy. Pakistani leaders and officials are openly admitting that the mounting debt crisis has impacted Pakistan's sovereignty as every now and then the country has to rush to the IMF for loans on stringent conditionalities. Every year, Pakistan borrows USD 15 billion to repay its debt obligations. Its external debt has ballooned to USD 130 billion while its foreign exchange reserves are about USD 24 billion.

Pakistan is desperate to have foreign direct investment and external funding without which its economy cannot improve. The National Security Policy document seeks to project a benign image to the world.

The National Security Policy has steered clear of giving any major prescriptions on traditional security issues. That is the preserve of the Pakistan Army. It is not clear to what extent the Army is on board. However, going by Bajwa's remarks last year at the Islamabad Security Dialogue in which he had also talked about geo-economics and a new paradigm for national security, it would seem that the document has the Army's tacit approval at least.

Imran Khan mentions in the Foreword that Pakistan would become a welfare state in the image of Riyasat-e-Medina. The document also says that Pakistan would fight Islamophobia internationally. But, religious fundamentalist groups are likely to see the geo-economic paradigm and pandering to the world for foreign direct investment as capitulation.

It would be a welcome move if Pakistan actually puts economics at the heart of its policies. That will be good for India, the region and the world. But, whether Pakistan has the intention to do so is not clear, given the fact that it continues to regard India as the main threat. There is no hint of any impending change in Pakistan's India policy.

Talking about geo-economics and the broad-based security is one thing, implementing the words in deeds is an entirely different matter. The document implicitly accepts that the Pakistani state is becoming increasingly dysfunctional. It does not hide the fact that the country is facing many serious problems. The drafters of the document themselves say that many of the goals and objectives mentioned in the document are "aspirational", which means that implementing them would not be easy.

As for India, the proof of the pudding would be in its eating. For India, the document is not likely to be more than a sophisticated PR exercise. However, the rest of the world may not see it so. At least Pakistan would hope that other countries would be impressed with the charm of human security and geo-economic concepts that the NSP emphasises so much.

7

Media Under Siege

Aakriti Vinayak

Introduction

Dynamic media, today, is the centrepiece of information and misinformation, and its place in governance is more complex than ever. The media is a watchdog of public interest and carrier of information in the most dynamic institution of civil society and can flourish in a democratic and tolerant culture[1]. Its watchdog role in a democracy is crucial to the voice of the people, giving them the power to be informed, aware, and better educated in all spheres of public affairs. However, the media in Pakistan in the last 72 years has remained 'under siege' and 'in chains.' Though liberalisation of the media in Pakistan has mainstreamed it as a stakeholder, almost on par with the judiciary and Parliament, the country's transitional and fragile democracy has prevented it from playing a watchdog role for society. More importantly, Pakistan's chequered political history of long stretches of martial law, the subjugation of representative governments by the deep state, and a brutal domination of the media landscape ownership for most part of the country's existence almost ensures that media independence has been mostly fiction[2]. In fact, the media remains under a state of crisis and stress in Pakistan.

Recently, independent media watchdogs have declared Pakistan as one of the most dangerous countries in the world for journalists. According to the International Federation of Journalists, Pakistan is the world's fifth-most dangerous country for journalists and in its 2020 World Press Freedom Index, Reporters Without Borders ranked Pakistan 145th out of 180 countries.[3]

This chapter aims to understand and expose the fettered state of the Pakistani media. Firstly, the chapter traces the origins of the Pakistani media from the pre-partition times to its liberalisation in 2002. It also looks at the Pakistan media's convoluted history of setbacks over the years from strict military censorship to unconstitutional curbs on free expression. Secondly, it tries to understand that though there is a vibrant media landscape in Pakistan, the idea of a free media remains an elusive dream as it remains under a strict control of various regulatory mechanisms and draconian laws. It also remains under a strict control of the power-holders of the state. The Pakistani media continues to face suppression by the military, intelligence agencies, politicians and the judiciary. Thirdly, this chapter analyses how journalists face physical, psychological, and financial threats in the line of their duty. Fourthly, it examines how, under the current regime of Imran Khan, the media is going through the worst forms of censorship and crackdowns and how the influence of the military "establishment," has increased dramatically since Imran Khan became prime minister in July 2018. In conclusion, the chapter highlights that the freedom of the Press and expression exists only on paper and those who transgress boundaries, problematise the given narrative and raise uncomfortable questions are persecuted, harassed, and vilified.

History of Media in Pakistan

As far as the print media in Pakistan is concerned, it dates back to the pre-partition years of British India, when a number of newspapers were established to promote a partition agenda.[4] The country's founder, Muhammad Ali Jinnah, the Quaid-i-Azam, was the founder of one of the country's most influential newspapers, *Dawn*, in 1941. *Dawn*, begun as a weekly newspaper in 1941 and transformed into a daily in 1942, was the main avenue through which Muhammad Ali Jinnah (1876-1948), and the All-India Muslim League, advocated the creation of Pakistan when the partition of India became the party's demand after the Lahore Resolution of March 23, 1940.[5] In a sense, the Pakistani print media came into existence with a mission to promulgate the idea of Pakistan. There was also a conservative newspaper, *Nawa-e-Waqt*, established in 1940, which was the mouthpiece of the Muslim elites who were among the strongest supporters for an independent Pakistan. There were a few other newspapers; these included *Pakistan Times*, *Zamindar*, *Civil and Military Gazette*, *Morning News* and *Jang*, which later moved into the newly created Pakistan. With this humble beginning in 1947, 103 dailies were added during the first decade of independence. In 1970, the number of dailies rose to 117 and 121 by 1986.

However, under Pakistan's first military dictator, General Ayub Khan (1958-

69), the centralised media control was properly institutionalised. General Ayub passed the Press and Publication Ordinance in 1960, which enabled the state to dictate and censor content and take over media institutions, such as the Associated Press of Pakistan (APP) news agency, and Progressive Papers Limited (PPL), which published the *Pakistan Times*, *Imroze* and the weekly *Lailo Nahar.*[6] In 1964, the PPL was converted into the National Press Trust media group, which went on to acquire additional newspapers that supported the actions of successive military regimes. The government also began to exert greater control over privately-owned outlets by establishing quotas for newsprint and by restricting distribution in order to keep newspapers in check. It is interesting to note that with the opening of new universities and improvements in literacy, the growth of Urdu-language dailies was three times that of the English press.[7] In fact, the process of nationalisation of the independent newspapers during the General Ayub era, and the gradual Islamisation of the media during successive military regimes, were instrumental in allowing the infiltration of right-wing ideologies into mainstream journalism, while left-wing influences gradually weakened.[8]

As far as radio is concerned, the state maintained a position of monopoly until the 2002 liberalisation of the media. Independent Pakistan inherited a basic radio infrastructure comprising three radio stations in Lahore (established in 1928), Peshawar (1935) and in Dhaka (1938). The government continued to own and operate these three stations with AM operations while adding several more stations in the network that was called 'Radio Pakistan.' In 1972, the government converted 'Radio Pakistan' into 'Pakistan Broadcasting Corporation (PBC).' The radio became a popular medium not only in the rural but also in urban centres by 1970. The apparent objectives of radio broadcasting in Pakistan were to promote "democratic, religious, moral, and social values and projecting the state policies on national issues both in its home and external broadcasts."[9]

The introduction of TV in Pakistan primarily contributed to undermining radio broadcasting, especially in urban areas. The Pakistan Television Corporation, commonly known as PTV, became a commercialised state organisation. Although a corporation, the government controls most of its shares, while it works under the Ministry of Information, Broadcasting, National History, and Literary Heritage.

The state-owned PTV was established in 1964 and by 1974 was broadcasting from Karachi, Rawalpindi, Islamabad, Peshawar and Quetta.[10] Due to its statutory configuration, it is the government that determines its editorial and administrative policies. The government, for instance, appoints PTV's Board of Directors. The

Board, in turn, elects a chairman, and a managing director, who are eventually responsible for the implementation of the corporation's policies.

Interestingly, it was in 2002 that the Pakistan government under General Musharraf liberalised the broadcast media sector, leading to an explosion of local, privately owned satellite television channels distributed via cable networks. The General permitted the deregulation of satellite channels and FM radio stations, but retained the state's monopoly over domestic terrestrial broadcasting, which had the widest reach. Between 2002 and 2010, nearly 89 television channels were launched and 26 foreign channels granted broadcasting rights. On the radio front, 138 FM radio licences were granted during the same period, of which about 115 had become operational by 2012. The Musharraf government also created the Pakistan Electronic Media Regulatory Authority (PEMRA) to regulate this newly liberalised sector.

The military's motivation for liberalising media licensing was based on an assumption that the Pakistani media could be used to strengthen national security and counter the threat from India. What prompted this shift was the military's experience during two past confrontations with India. One was the Kargil War and the other was the hijacking of an Indian airliner by Pakistan-based militants. In both these instances, the Pakistani military felt that it had lost the media war to India.[11] In an increasingly media-saturated region, the Pakistani military thus saw licensing privately owned media as an efficient way to strengthen Pakistan's capacity to compete in a "media war" with India.

Convoluted History: Uneasy Relations between Press and Government Regimes in Pakistan

Pakistan's Press has had a complex relationship with successive governments and the powerful military over many years. The media could not get its due status because of two martial laws announced by Field Marshal Ayub Khan in 1958 [by introducing Press and Publication Ordinance (PPO)] and General Yahya Khan. However, the mass media not only became an easy target of military dictators, but was also widely and comfortably suppressed by political leaders. Zulfikar Ali Bhutto (ruled 1972–77), the first democratically elected leader who championed democratic values, human rights, and freedom of expression, not only continued the existing legal framework but also introduced new measures.[12] Two martial law orders were issued to bring the NPT publications under his direct control when he assumed responsibility as Martial Law Administrator in 1972. Bhutto targeted the press, the chairman of the National Press Trust, Gen

Habibullah Khan (retd), who was dismissed, put in prison and humiliated by being handcuffed like a common criminal in public; the editor-in-chief of the *Pakistan Times*, Z.A. Suleri, who was dismissed; the editor of *Dawn*, Altaf Gauhar, who was arrested; the printer, publisher and editor of *Urdu Digest*, *Zindagi* (Urdu), and *Punjabi Punch* (English) who were arrested; Shorish Kashmiri of the weekly *Chattan*, who was jailed; the newspapers *Hurriyat* and *Jasarat* that were banned and their editors, Anwar Khaleel and Salahuddin, imprisoned; the *Mehran* which was banned while Iqbal Burney's weekly *Outlook* was forced to shut down as was the daily *Sun*.[13]

In 1977, General Zia-ul-Haq imposed martial law, which took the nation to an unprecedented level of coercion and censorship. It is considered to be the worst in the history of Pakistan. The Press was under siege and censorship was imposed by the military authority. Zia-ul-Haq tightened the grip on news and current affairs programmes, with stringent policies to control the state media, especially television. The civilian governments of Benazir Bhutto and Nawaz Sharif allowed freedom of the Press to some extent.[14] Despite this openness, however, state-controlled radio and TV started excluding major news stories from their news shows, while the private press was reporting them. Overall, the media has never been totally free, as the various regimes in Pakistan have operated indiscriminately attempting to dominate the system and socio-political narratives.

Media Landscape

Pakistan's media industry is quite vibrant. Particularly, television and radio bloomed in the last two decades after the broadcasting sector was opened to private players in 2002. The privatisation spree in 2002 changed the media dynamics so fast that by 2018 the Pakistani media industry became a mix of state-controlled radio and TV and privatised electronic media, which included a variety of TV outlets and FM radio stations, in addition to Internet-based social media outlets.[15]

Television and FM Radio

As of December 2020, the Pakistan Electronic Media Regulatory Authority (PEMRA) had issued a total of 106 Satellite TV licences and 4,062 Cable TV licences. The PEMRA has also issued 257 FM Radio licences along with 61 other licences including for Mobile TV, Internet Protocol TV (IPTV) and Direct-to Home (DTH) licences.[16] As per a Gallup Pakistan survey, average TV viewership was on a declining trend, falling from ~205 minutes per day per viewer in 2002 to ~112 minutes in 2018. This is likely due to the growing popularity of digital platforms and increasing usage of mobile phones, which provide easy access to social media apps.[17]

Internet/Digital Media

Digital media has grown exponentially in recent years alongside growth in Internet and social media usage. There are approximately 61 million Internet users and approximately 46 million social media users in Pakistan that makes up almost ~27 per cent and ~20 per cent of the population, respectively. In terms of social media usage, YouTube leads the way with ~44 million monthly active users (MAU). Meanwhile, Facebook has ~36 million MAU followed by TikTok with ~24 million MAU. Instagram and Twitter have ~6 million and ~4 million MAU, respectively.[18]

Proliferation of Internet connectivity has facilitated users' access to conventional media and social media. However, growing Internet penetration has not necessarily led to Internet freedom. According to the annual Freedom on the Net Report 2021, released by Freedom House, Pakistan's score on Internet freedom declined one point to 25 this year. Pakistan joined China, Iran, Myanmar, Cuba, Vietnam, Saudi Arabia, Egypt and Ethiopia on the listing of 10 bottom countries on Internet freedom.[19]

Print

According to the Pakistan Bureau of Statistics (PBS), the number of newspapers in the country stood at approximately 707.[20] The All Pakistan Newspapers Society (APNS) reported 466 total publications in 2018, based on its membership, comprising 384 dailies, 60 monthlies, 18 weeklies, and 4 fortnightly magazines. Of the total number of dailies (384), the overwhelming majority of newspapers (252) are published in the national language, Urdu. Next come the English dailies at 84, followed by Sindhi 43, Pushto 3, Seraiki 1, and Balochi 1.

However, there has been low circulation of the print media. The reason is increasing competition from TV, radio and news websites on the Internet. Reliable circulation figures for newspapers in Pakistan are hard to come by. According to the Federal Bureau of Statistics in Islamabad, the average daily sale for all Pakistani daily newspapers fell to 6.1 million in 2008 from a peak of 9.9 million in 2007.[21] Pakistan's largest circulation newspaper is the conservative *Daily Jang* (www.jang.com.pk), an Urdu-language paper that claims a daily sale of 850,000. It is followed by *Nawa-i-Waqt* (www.nawaiwaqt.com.pk), a right-wing Urdu daily that claims to sell about 500,000 copies per day. The largest circulation

English language paper is *Dawn* (www.dawn.com) which claims a daily sale of 138,000, mostly in and around Karachi.[22]

Media Freedom: An Elusive Dream?

The media landscape remains deeply complex. Though there are more than 40 news channels on television and as many as 700 newspapers in print, the overall media environment in Pakistan remains fraught with dangers. Where the establishment has not been able to completely subjugate the media, or at least keep its most vocal critics under control, it has always been able to resort to an alternative, very effective method—repression.

Though Article 19 of the Constitution of Pakistan and Universal Declaration of Human Rights (UDHR) guarantee freedom of expression and a free media, the media in Pakistan continues to be in chains or under strict regulation. The rapid reconfiguration of Pakistan's media landscape remains contradictory as it remains vulnerable to state control. Further, the media remains vulnerable amid on-going threats to media professionals and the limitations imposed by the industry's financial model, which must rely heavily on advertising revenue.

The government has been an advertising client for the media. Interestingly, money is employed as a censorship tool that brings gains for the corporate media. In doing so however it creates a rupture in the relationship with media consumers. The result of all this is an all-enveloping crises that is slowly killing the media. If we trace the role of the state we will find that since the broadcast liberalisation in 2002, the state has been one of the most important sources of funding for Pakistan's private media sector. On the other hand, government advertisements have acted as a backbone of the finances of both broadcasting and the printing press. We also see that the federal and provincial governments have often bought airtime on leading TV channels during prime time, subsidising their financial operations.

However, since the advent of a new government in the fall of 2018, government-advertising levels have gone down dramatically contributing to a new economic crisis against the backdrop of resurgence in censorship.[23] After the July 2018 elections, the provincial governments of Punjab and Sindh, the main contributors of advertisement revenues for the print and electronic media and the federal government in Islamabad, have slashed their advertisement budgets by 70 per cent, leaving the media industry in a precarious financial situation.[24]

The Government has also used a raft of draconian laws to dictate and suppress independent media. These include the Press and Publication Ordinance (PPO),

In PKR/billion

Annual Advertising Revenue Break Up					
Period	**FY16**	**FY17**	**FY18**	**FY19**	**FY20**
TV	38.0	42.0	38.0	28.0	26.0
Digital	4.5	5.5	8.0	10.5	13.7
Print	18.0	20.0	19.5	13.5	9.5
OOH	8.9	11.8	7.0	8.4	6.0
Brand Activation	4.0	5.0	6.0	4.5	2.3
Radio	2.8	3.0	2.5	1.8	1.0
Cinema		0.4	0.6	0.5	0.3
Total	**76.2**	**87.7**	**81.6**	**67.2**	**58.6**

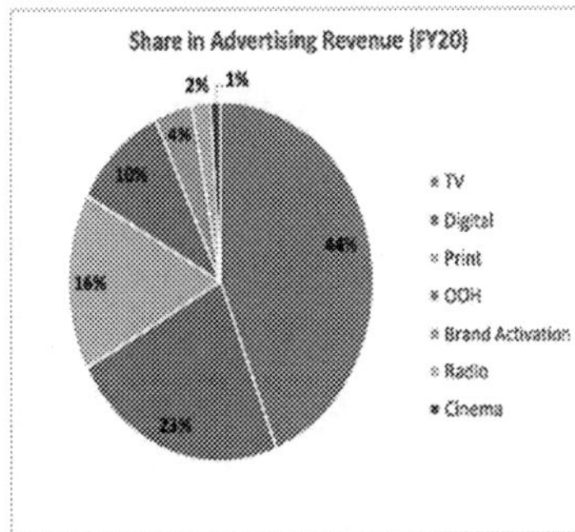

Latest Available figures: FY20 Source: Dawn

Source: Annual Advertising Revenue Break-Up, 2020, *Dawn*

Printing Presses and Publication Ordinance (1988), the Freedom of Information Ordinance (2002), the Contempt of Court Ordinance (2003), the Press Council Ordinance (2002), the Intellectual Property Organization of Pakistan Ordinance (2005) and the Access to Information Ordinance (2006). The Press and Publications Ordinance Law (1860) is a carry-over from the colonial era, while other undemocratic laws were put in place by military dictators to control the media and, as a consequence, public discourse.

Some of the most restrictive laws were introduced by General Musharraf in 2002:[25]

The Defamation Ordinance: It was 'supposed to protect people's reputations from unfair attack, in practice it has become a cruel tool to hinder free speech and protect powerful people from scrutiny.' The ordinance is said to ignore 'the standards set for freedom of expression slapping a legal straitjacket on the Press.

The Press, Newspapers, News Agencies and Books Registration Ordinance requires all publications and news agencies to register with local or provincial authorities. Failure to do so may lead to monetary imprisonment. In order to enhance the "controlling" effect of the ordinance, the military government also required the publishing entity to register an individual employee who could be held responsible for the contents of the material published.

The Pakistan Electronic Media Regulatory Authority (PEMRA): It was established in 2002 to regulate and promote broadcast media in Pakistan. The PEMRA Ordinance, 2002, allowed the private sector to own electronic media outlets like satellite TV and FM radio stations in Pakistan. The mandate of the authority was to:[26]

- Improve the standards of information, education and entertainment;
- Broaden the choice available to the people of Pakistan in the media for news, current affairs, religious knowledge, art, culture, science, technology, economic development, social-sector concerns, music, sports, drama and other subjects of public and national interest;
- Facilitate the devolution of responsibility and power to the grassroots by community level; and
- Ensure accountability, transparency and good governance by optimising the free flow of information.

PEMRA was set up and presented as a major step towards reforming the media. However, media observers soon discovered to their dismay that PEMRA actually masked a sharp regulatory ploy. Media practitioners view PEMRA as a licence-issuing office that mostly involves erecting regulatory hurdles in the way of broadcasters. Shutdowns of television channels, particularly during times of political tension, are used selectively to block the media from showing live coverage of key events and sensitive issues. PEMRA laws were utilised by Musharraf in his attempts to tame the media. Some stations were shut down and some were under severe harassment using these laws.

The 12-member authority is dominated by bureaucrats and ex-police officers. Media activists are not comfortable with the composition of the 12-member committee and they have stressed the need for a greater representation from the media itself.

The PEMRA has been used to silence the broadcast media by either suspending licences or by simply threatening to do so. In recent years, PEMRA has been tilting at those TV channels that had the temerity to fall out of line. The country's most popular TV channel 'GEO', has been smarting from suppressive PEMRA diktats. It was essentially targeted over the way it covered the lawyers' movement and its criticism of the government in power.[27] Hence, media freedom [is] constrained by the legal and regulatory framework, which despite promises has not yet been reformed by the new civilian government.

Under Strict Control

"The government and military now share the view that the media should support the Pakistani state, not criticise it. As a result, no one's left to put the brakes on measures, legal or extra-legal, taken against journalists whose reports news that authorities do not like. The military's in charge, without a coup"[28]—Steven Butler, Committee to Protect Journalists (CPJ) Report 2019.

The system of checks and balances in Pakistan remains beholden to military power, despite the constitutional roles of Parliament and the Supreme Court. The freedom of the media is further constrained as the power-holders of Pakistani state i.e. the military that controls and dictates to the media. As campaigner and journalist Munizae Jahangir stated, "You cannot critique the armed forces when, unfortunately, they have been at the heart of politics in Pakistan and the main decision-makers for most of our lives."[29]

More than any other state institution, the Pakistani Army has sought control over the country's privately owned media outlets as part of efforts to establish a narrative of national unification. As noted above, this narrative has frequently emphasised Pakistan's Islamic identity, identifying India as the greatest security threat against which Pakistani unity is a key defence. A similar dynamic arose in the army's efforts to influence the media debate around the country's controversial role in the global fight against terrorism. According to Pakistani political scientist Ayesha Siddiqa, the expansion in the media has allowed the military to systematically encourage a narrative that is not merely friendly in relation to the security establishment but has also allowed the military to develop "a new nationalist discourse to keep its institution relevant not only for the state but for society as well."[30] The Inter-Services Public Relations—the public relations wing of the Pakistani Army—was expanded and restructured to accommodate separate wings to engage with and monitor the print media, FM radio stations and privately-owned television channels.

As mentioned previously, various military regimes in Pakistan have had a special interest in intervening in the media realm. Following the first military coup in 1958 by General Ayub Khan, successful efforts were launched to buy the political allegiance of senior journalists. These trends were reinforced when General Muhammed Zia-ul-Haq imposed martial law in the country, leading to sharp divisions across the journalistic community throughout the 1980s.

Pakistan's deep state is implicated in stifling contrarian voices in the media. As CPJ in its report mentions that the military has quietly, but effectively, set restrictions on reporting: from barring access to regions including Balochistan where there is armed separatism and religious extremism, to encouraging self-censorship through direct and indirect methods of intimidation, including calling editors to complain about coverage and even allegedly instigating violence against reporters.[31] According to CPJ research, the military, intelligence, or military-linked and political groups were the suspected source of fire that resulted in half of the 22 journalist murders in the past decade.[32]

Recently in 2018 the Director-General of Inter Service Public Relations (ISPR) warned some journalists about their online anti-Army activities. He threatened them by stating that the secret agency was keeping an eye on them for spreading propaganda against the Army.[33] The military's widening reach is viewed as a source of intimidation. The military has clashed with Pakistan's elected government, which tried and ultimately failed to assert civilian control.

Not just the military but politicians have also influenced the media. There is a media-politician nexus that goes back some decades. Politicians have controlled the media content by bribing media houses and individual journalists through what is known colloquially as the *lifafa* (envelope) culture.[34] Such corruption persisted under the PPP-led coalition government, often at the highest levels. The Nawaz government offered all kinds of inducements ranging from bank loans to residential plots to unspoken lavish perks.

Also, an institutional form of control is the "press advice system", in which government officials constantly tell Pakistani newspaper publishers and editors how to behave and what to publish. The system was refined in the late 1970s under General Zia.[35] While it was supposed to disappear with Pakistan's return to democracy in 1988, its basic mechanisms seem to have been preserved and were perpetuated by federal and provincial information ministries a decade later.

In fact, radical organisations and militant groups have also grown strong enough to threaten violence with such leverage that the mainstream media often give in to their agenda. Radical groups and political parties such as the Jamaat-i-Islami, Sipahi-Sahaba and Pakistani Taliban, have infiltrated the mainstream media or strengthened and expanded their own media platforms. A survey by the Pakistan Institute of Peace Studies found that 69 per cent of 16 journalists and editors thought that radicalisation was crippling freedom of expression. Nearly 50 per cent found that the radical media had an impact on mainstream media, and 57 per cent thought that the media was concealing facts about radicalisation.[36]

As far as the investigations carried out by International Media Support (IMS) group are concerned, it very categorically highlights the leverage radical organisations might have with the mainstream media. The threats and intimidation that journalists are subjected to is alarming. The condition is so bad that the journalists acquiesce. It has been observed that when reporters are working on the ground for their stories, particularly in the frontier provinces, militants literally hinder this process and stop them from getting access to the local people.[37]

Silencing the Press–Journalists under the Surveillance State

"Journalists are shot like stray dogs in Pakistan—easily killed because their assassins sit at the pinnacle of power...Journalists have shown resilience, but it is hard to preserve when the state itself becomes complicit in the crime"—*Umar Cheema, an award-winning investigative reporter for the English-language News International in Islamabad.*[38]

Pakistan remains one of the most dangerous countries for journalists. The International Federation of Journalists (IFJ) has cited 138 journalist deaths between 1990 and 2020.[39] In its World Press Freedom Day 2021 report, media watchdog Freedom Network called Islamabad the "most dangerous" place to practise journalism. The report says 34 per cent of violations were recorded in Islamabad, including legal cases, threats, and detentions.

Journalists also face the threat of being labelled "anti-Pakistan", "enemy agent", and "pro-India", and sometimes are even labelled with allegations of blasphemy.

A CPJ report succinctly put a grim appraisal of the hostile environment Pakistani journalists face: "If you cover politics, corruption, or war, you're more likely than any of your colleagues to be victimized at the hands of the military or paramilitary or intelligence groups. You may also become a victim of one of the two sides in Balochistan's escalating ethnic strife or of militants operating in the Federally Administrated Tribal Areas, or of political factions, criminal groups, or feudal leaders vying for power. If threats and harassment don't force you to quit journalism, then perhaps you'll flee your home. If this fails, you may be killed. And if you are killed in the line of duty, it is likely that those who perpetrated the crime will walk away, given Pakistan's near perfect level of impunity."[40]

Intimidation, physical violence and arrests are used against journalists who cross the red line by trying to cover stories deemed off limits by the military. The taboo topics vary, but corruption, nepotism, cronyism, military business operations and extra-judicial killings by state security forces are a common foundation across the region.

Elizabeth Rubin who investigated the targeted killings of two journalists—Wali Khan Babar in Karachi and Mukkarram Khan Aatif in the tribal areas—has pointed out that there is an underlying culture of manipulation, intimidation, and retribution that has led to so many other killings. Her reporting also found out that:[41]

- An array of threatening actors that includes not only militants, criminals, and warlords, but also political, military, and intelligence operatives.

- A weak civilian government that acquiesces to the will of the intelligence services, the army, and criminal elements in the political parties.
- Intelligence services that aggressively pursue a political agenda; that pressure, manipulate, and intimidate news media.

Under the current regime of Imran Khan, the media's independence and freedom have been tested multiple times. First, the security and intelligence agencies declared some conflict-ridden areas in the northwest and southwest of the country off limits for journalists. Certain news topics, such as enforced disappearances and human rights violations in areas under military operations, went missing from news headlines and talk shows. Finally, news media was expressly told to stay away from criticizing vast swathes of state policies on national security, foreign relations and even financial and economic issues concerning the military and the China-Pakistan Economic Corridor (CPEC).[42]

Perhaps, nowhere in Pakistan, is the threat for journalists so grave as in Balochistan and Khyber Pakhtunkhwa. Balochistan has long been dangerous for journalists trying to report on the province's long-running independence insurgency and the military's determination to stamp it out—with both sides willing to act against the media. A 2011 ruling by the Balochistan High Court banned coverage of Baloch separatists or nationalist groups, stating that "If the electronic media and the Press publish propaganda reports out of fear and propagate the views of banned organizations, they are not acting as good and responsible journalists, but as mouthpieces for malicious and vile propaganda."[43]

Tilak Devasher in his seminal book, *The Balochistan Conundrum* underscores that there are multiple reasons for censorship and the targeting of journalists and newspapers in Balochistan. He points out that the army wants to conceal its ruthless suppression of Baloch activists and intense violations of human rights. In this context, they ensure that these violent activities are not reported, particularly in the international media. The army as pointed out by Devasher wants to control and manipulate the national narrative on Balochistan. He further elaborates that they have constructed a narrative that shows a small minority of 'miscreant' Baloch, by trying to seek 'provincial autonomy' and ownership of their natural resources, are succumbing into the hands of the 'enemies of Pakistan' and 'foreign agents.'[44]

Further Balochistan's Right to Information laws are considered the weakest in the country. The right of access to information remained a distant dream in the province as it has not yet reformed or replaced the Freedom of Information Act, 2005 in the aftermath of the 18th Constitutional amendment. In the light of the CPEC, the lack of access to the information of state bodies blocks any public oversight of projects being rolled out in Balochistan. Several journalists have criticised the lack of a new law, saying that it hampers their ability to report effectively in Balochistan. In the troubled frontier areas of Khyber Pakhtunkhwa, journalists also face similar security threats from both state and non-state actors. The convergence of various tension lines that run across a separatist movement, the resulting military repression and the presence of Taliban elements have created an extremely dangerous environment for journalists. In 2020 itself, four journalists were killed in connection with their reporting, especially investigative reporting, on corruption or drug trafficking.

Women journalists remain as an outlier in Pakistani media as they face multiple threats. They have to contend with social and cultural barriers, reputational harm, and sexual harassment in and outside the workplace. Digital violence against women journalists is also pervasive in Pakistan. Many women journalists have resorted to self-censorship to protect themselves against online harm and physical threats. Historically, women's access to and growth in media organisations has not been supported in Pakistan. According to an estimate, women journalists make up less than five per cent of Pakistan's news professionals. Newsrooms in Pakistan are male-dominated spaces, with few women journalists and little or no female representation in senior editorial positions.

Freedom Network points out that between the fall of 2019 and 2020, two women journalists have been killed for pursuing journalism careers—a first in the country's history.[45] The harassment of not just women journalists but also women civic and digital activists of Pakistan is an unfortunate constant pattern, as evinced in a 2019 study conducted by IMS partner, Digital Rights Foundation (DRF). The findings showed regular online harassment of women, with abuse being gendered and often aimed at Pakistani women on social media. A majority of the respondents in the study expressed distrust in government departments charged with helping them.

Under the current Imran Khan government, the threat to women journalists has intensified. In September 2020, over a dozen well-known women journalists issued a joint public statement detailing gross online abuse of a sexualized nature, including rape threats, often discernibly from ruling party supporters angry at their party being held accountable for its spectacularly poor governance.[46]

What is alarming is that there is a perfect record of impunity that perpetrators enjoy in Pakistan. It has fostered an ever-more violent climate for journalists. In the last two decades not one of those killings have seen a guilty conviction in the courts system. In 2020, Pakistan ranked ninth on the Committee to Protect Journalists' annual Global Impunity Index with at least 15 unsolved killings of journalists since 2010.[47] Further, the judiciary's indifference to media freedom is what journalists lament most in Pakistan.

However, to counter the censorship being imposed by the military, several prominent journalists have started broadcasting on YouTube. Some of the prominent journalists include Najam Sethi and Syed Talat Hussain who have started their independent shows on YouTube. However, this avenue is also on the verge of being closed. The government is proposing a measure to make the freedom to publish on social media contingent to obtaining a licence from the state. The widespread sense of intimidation, threat, abduction, and psychological trauma has pushed other prominent journalists like Taha Siddiqi and Gul Bukhari to seek refuge abroad.[48] However, Pakistani reporters overseas are not safe either. In Europe, the number of Pakistani journalists and bloggers under attack for criticizing authorities back home is increasing, according to Radio Free Europe.[49] One such example of horrendous treatment of journalists outside Pakistan is the death of Sajid Husain, the chief editor of *Balochistan Times*, in Sweden.

Succumbing to Silence-Self Censorship

Recently, the number of attacks on journalists in Pakistan has gone down, but the general state of media freedom gives credence to the assertion that this decline in attacks might not be because of an improvement of the security situation; it could be due to a growing trend of self-censorship among Pakistani journalists. According to Asad Baig, founder and executive director of Media Matters for Democracy the numbers of journalists killed are going down because the resistance from the media has lessened. And that is perhaps because of the very organized control mediums in place. And these are not just the journalists, but the media owners, editors and all the way up.[50]

It is also pertinent to see that self-censorship is something that is very pervasive. People are very careful on what to say, and what not to say, what are those clearly drawn red lines that they cannot cross. Words are silenced and things remain unsaid, untold and suppressed.

A survey published by Media Matters for Democracy found that 88 per cent of the 156 journalists who responded said they censored what they write or report. About 72 per cent said the trend had increased over time. Seven in 10 journalists said that censoring what they wrote made them feel safer. Six in 10 said they were very likely to self-censor information about the security establishment or religion and around 83 per cent stated "the media itself has become polarized and does not speak with one voice on issues related to freedom." Owais Aslam Ali, Secretary-general, Pakistan Press Foundation, said they would likely censor information about militancy and terrorism.[51]

Appalling State of Media under Imran Khan Government

The present government of the PTI led by Prime Minister Imran Khan is the third consecutive one coming into power as a result of general elections. However, rather than strengthening democratic institutions like the press, the government has adopted repressive policies to silence the media. In fact, under Imran Khan the clampdown on the Pakistani media had already reached a new level with restricting reports, shutting down programs, and job losses in the media industry. A Lahore-based media educator succinctly described the current state of affairs in Pakistan. She said that the country has come under martial law several times in the past but this time it is martial law under the garb of a democratic leader.[52]

The latest report of Reporters Sans Frontieres (RSF) has declared Prime Minister Imran Khan a "predator" of press freedom, describing him as having "dictatorial tendencies" and overseeing "brazen censorship" during the three years of his administration.[53] The report says that the PTI government is worse than military dictatorships in Pakistan when it comes to press freedom. The Human Rights Watch, Pakistan Press Freedom Report and Freedom Network Report have also pointed out that under the Imran Khan government, the worst crackdown on the media is happening, never seen in the history of the country. Pakistan also fares poorly in global press freedom rankings. Since Imran Khan has taken over as Prime Minister in 2018, it has fallen six places (to 145) in the Reporters Without Borders World Press Freedom Index.[54]

Pakistan under the leadership of Imran Khan, is known for taking sweeping U-turns. One such U-turn has been on the promises he made to ensure freedom of the Press. In its 'Naya Pakistan' poll manifesto, the ruling Pakistan Tehreek-e-Insaf (PTI) had stated that they are "committed to maintaining a vigorous free media, which will evolve its own rules to ensure responsible journalism, both in the electronic and print media." However, after winning the election, the PTI-led government first stopped state advertisements of two leading media houses, *Dawn* and Geo/Jang. Media groups that have questioned or critiqued the government were attacked. This led to a disruption in the home delivery of newspapers by spreading fear amongst the hawkers; government advertisements also disappeared from some media groups; cable operators were asked to either block channels or shift the location from their usual slot to the last numbers on the cable network to confuse viewers. Behind the scenes, the government and the military establishment exerted pressure on media houses not to report anything that showed the military in a bad light.[55]

Tactics of Intimidation used by the PTI Government

There seems to be an atmosphere of intimidation and fear. Various tactics have been used by the PTI government to muzzle the critical voices in the media. There are several cases of reporters being abducted and beaten, critical columnists being denied space, sackings of TV commentators and many other cases of self-censorship. In fact, over the past two years, journalists have complained about the curbs on their ability to do their job freely. The Pakistan Electronic Media Regulatory Authority (PEMRA) not only issued bundle of notices to TV channels unnecessarily but also barred some anchors from offering opinions on TV channels and talk shows. They were ordered not to discuss the issue pertaining to release of PML-N leader Shehbaz Sharif on bail. News channels were directed not to telecast live reporting of PML-N leader Maryam Nawaz's press conference and notices were issued to 21 news TV channels for non-compliance.[56] An interview of Asif Ali Zardari, former President of Pakistan and Co-Chairman of the Pakistan Peoples Party with host Hamid Mir was stopped from being aired shortly after it started on *Geo News* in July 2019. Due to its stories and content, *Dawn* came under severe attacks. Many journalists like Talat Hussain, Najam Sethi, Nusrat Javed and Murtaza Solangi have been forced out of their jobs.

The military and PTI government in most recent years have also widened the lines of what is acceptable. During the Balakot air strike in February 2019, coverage of Jammu and Kashmir was lauded as excellent news media coverage illustrating the grave injustices and human rights violations in the territory done by Indian military forces. A few months later, the news media was accused of pushing a "foreign agenda" in its coverage of the Pashtun Tahafuz Movement (PTM).[57] Social media and Internet outlets have been widely used as an alternative platform to harmonise pro-government voices in otherwise dominated television and print media. The latest tactic being followed by the Imran Khan Government is to use its army of sympathisers in the social media to troll journalists who are critical of the government. Further, information warfare campaigns against India are carried out on these social media sites. Pakistan has two main instruments working for the furtherance of this policy—the ISI and the Inter-Services Public Relations (ISPR).[58] The core Pakistani objective is to demolish "Brand India" by attacking its key components—an inclusive and secular society, democratic polity, decisive government, a developing economic powerhouse and strong foreign policy.[59] This is done through key social media sites like Twitter, WhatsApp, YouTube and Facebook. Further, a large number of fake social media accounts, especially on Twitter, have been created. The government wants to essentially institutionalise its ability to control narratives in the media.

The PTI government is further using draconian laws to stifle journalists and activists. In January 2019, the Imran Khan government, through a cabinet decree, approved the formation of the Pakistan Media Regulatory Authority (PMRA), a single body that is tasked with regulating all forms of the media, especially digital media platforms. Further, in 2019, the PEMRA issued a directive calling upon news channels [vide 6(d) of the order] to ensure that anchors "exclude themselves from their personal opinions, biases and judgments on any issue." The directive further stated that "anchors hosting exclusive regular shows should not appear in talk shows whether own and other channels as subject matter experts."[60]

The government also gained additional legislative authority to restrict information it deems "prejudicial" to the national interest. Authorities used these laws to prevent or punish media criticism of the government and the armed forces. To publish within Pakistan-Occupied Kashmir, media owners had to obtain permission from the Kashmir Council and the Ministry of Kashmir Affairs, and journalists had to depend largely on information provided by the government and the military. There were limitations on transmission of Indian media content.[61]

The PTI government also introduced the Criminal Law Amendment Bill 2020, which renders intentional ridicule and defamation of the armed forces a punishable offence liable to imprisonment of up to two years, or a fine up to five hundred thousand rupees, or both. There was vociferous opposition to the bill. However, the Standing Committee on Law and Justice only recently approved the Bill.[62]

After reining in the traditional media, the establishment has set about purging the Internet and social media of content not to its liking. To that end, the government is trying to step up online regulation. In February 2020, the Pakistan government passed a set of regulations to control the social media as well. The "Citizens Protection (Against Online Harm) Rules, 2020" mandates the social media platforms to remove or block content, which is considered objectionable by the government.[63] In October 2020, the government used those rules to briefly ban the TikTok application.

Recently another controversial media authority bill has been proposed by the government called the Pakistan Media Development Authority (PMDA). The PMDA has been conceived as a regulatory body that can "cater to the professional and business requirements of all forms of media and their users", according to a government proposal, and is meant to replace the current "fractured" regulatory environment and "fragmented" media regulation by multiple bodies.[64] This will be a new statutory institution established to regulate films, electronic, print and digital media in Pakistan in the age of meta data, digital and social media, and Internet-based content and advertisements. This proposed Pakistan Media Authority bill will be the last nail in the coffin of the dream of a free Press and freedom of expression in the country. There have been fierce protests by journalists against the proposed bill. The Pakistan Federal Union of Journalists (PFUJ), the All-Pakistan Newspaper Society, the Council of Pakistan Newspaper Editors, the Pakistan Broadcasters Association and the Association of Electronic Media Editors and News Directors have put up a united front rejecting the PMDA.

The PFUJ, Human Rights Commission of Pakistan (HRCP) and Pakistan Bar Council (PBC) have rejected the proposed Pakistan Media Development Authority (PMDA) Ordinance 2021 that the federal government intends to impose. 'The proposed law is draconian in scope and devastating in its impact on constitutional principles and guarantees for freedom of expression, media freedoms, and the right to information as well as the profession of journalism',[65] said the PFUJ, HRCP and PBC in a strongly worded joint statement. Human Rights Watch (HRW) has also denounced the proposed PMDA as a move to bolster the government's powers to control, censor and punish media outlets and journalists as part of an ongoing crackdown on freedom of expression in Pakistan.[66]

A Grim Picture

Imran Khan continues to say that there is no media crackdown in the country. In fact, he was audacious enough to say that the Pakistan media has more freedom than the British media. However, in reality, there is a strikingly different narrative.

According to a 2019-2020 report by the Freedom Network, there were 91 attacks against journalists across Pakistan in a one-year period, with the top three types of attacks being verbal or written threats of murder or 'dire consequences' (23 cases), off/online harassment (13 cases), and assassination attempts (11 cases), of which seven resulted in the actual killing of journalists.[67] According to available data, at least seven journalists, including Urooj Iqbal,

Mirza Wasim Baig, Muhammad Bilal Khan, Ali Sher Rajpar and Malik Amanullah Khan, were reportedly murdered during the year. The pathetic state of un-announced impunity for those who attacked the media can be perceived from the fact that not a single killer or attacker of journalists and media persons was brought to justice.

Further, the COVID-19 pandemic has exacerbated the violence against journalists as well as censorship and reprisals for questioning government policies in Pakistan.

CATEGORIES OF VIOLATIONS AGAINST MEDIA IN PAKISTAN (May 2019-April 2020)

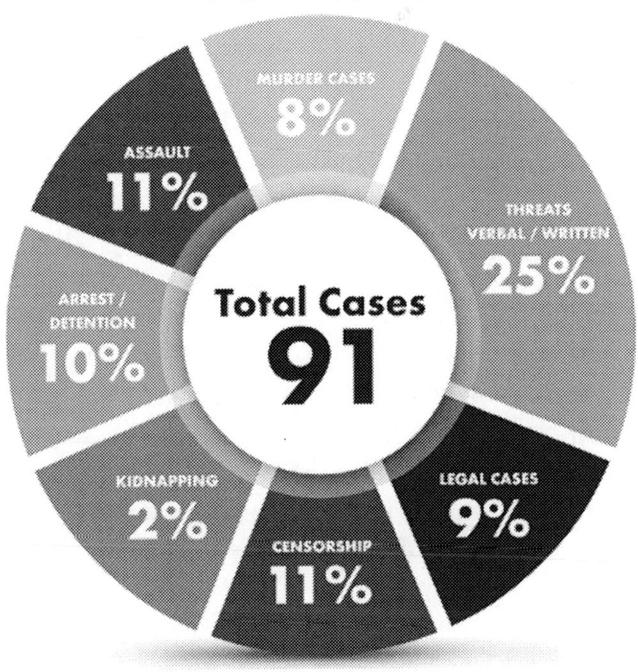

Source: Council of Pakistan Newspaper Editors (CPNE), Pakistan Media Freedom Report, 2020.

Some examples of what the media and journalists endured under the current government are enumerated in the following paragraphs:

- On July 21 2020, an unidentified assailant abducted journalist and outspoken critic of the military establishment, Matiullah Jan, in Islamabad the day before he was to appear before the Supreme Court for allegedly "using derogatory/contemptuous language and maligning the institution of the judiciary.[68]

- The Pakistan Electronic Media Regulatory Authority in January 2020 banned Kashif Abbasi, an anchor at ARY News television channel, generally considered a pro-government news outlet, for three months after the regulator said his programme sought to "debase and demean" the military.
- On April 20, 2021, an unidentified assailant shot and wounded Absar Alam, a television journalist, outside his house in Islamabad. Alam has been a prominent critic of the government.
- On May 25, 2021, Asad Ali Toor, a journalist, was assaulted by three unidentified men who forcibly entered his apartment in Islamabad. They bound and gagged Toor and severely beat him. Toor said that they identified themselves as being from a security agency, interrogated him about the "source of his funds", and took away his cell phone and other electronic devices. The authorities charged Toor with sedition for comments made on social media "maligning state institutions."[69]
- On 31 May 2021, senior Pakistani journalist Hamid Mir was told to stop hosting his talk show 'Capital Talk' by the Geo News channel after he critically talked about the military establishment. He accused them of censoring the media and persecuting journalists. Mir came under scrutiny after he delivered a fiery speech at a protest on May 28 in the wake of the attack on fellow journalist Asad Toor.

A media in chains cannot hold the powerful to account and serve public interest as it is meant to do. The people of Pakistan who are the consumers of the media are not getting a full or accurate picture of critical issues facing the country. The military and other powerful institutions have established lines of control to stifle the Press, by promoting people and issues considered favourable, and limiting the dissemination of content found objectionable. Pakistan's hypocrisy and the deep state are exposed time and again when brave journalists cross the red lines and speak against the military. When citizens are denied their right to information, it results in the crumbling of democracy. It gives an impetus to the state to propagate its own narrative without challenge. Under Imran Khan's government, freedom of the Press exists only on paper. This is a failure on the part of the state to honour its commitments to respect and uphold people's human rights to speak in a fearless manner. There is a dark future ahead. Reporter Azaz Syed rightly points out that the future generations will suffer the consequences of this crackdown. "When there's an entire era in which you haven't told the truth—it's like you've distorted history."[70]

ENDNOTES

1. Sadia Jamil (2020), *Handbook of Research on Combating Threats to Media Freedom and Journalist Safety*, IGI Global, USA, p. 13.
2. Adnan Rehmat, "Why is Pakistan media in crisis", *Dawn*, Islamabad, 21 July 2019.
3. Reporters without Borders, *World Press Freedom Index* 2020.
4. Between radicalisation and democratisation in an unfolding conflict: Media in Pakistan, International Media Support, 2009.
5. Roger D. Long, Dawn Delhi I: Genesis of a Newspaper, *Dawn*, Islamabad, 5 September 2017.
6. Huma Yusuf & Emrys Schoemaker, The media of Pakistan: Fostering inclusion in a fragile democracy? BBC Media Action, Policy briefing, September 2013.
7. Ibid.
8. Marco Mezzera & Safdar Sial, Media and Governance in Pakistan: A controversial yet essential relationship, Initiative for peacebuilding, October 2010.
9. Qaisar Abbas & Farooq Sulehria (eds.) (2021), *From Terrorism to Television: Dynamics of Media, State, and Society in Pakistan*, Routledge, London, p. 7.
10. Huma Yusuf and Emrys Schoemaker, The media of Pakistan: Fostering inclusion in a fragile democracy? BBC Media Action, Policy briefing, September 2013.
11. Fatima Salman, Evolving News Media Landscapes in India and Pakistan: Implications for regional peace and stability, South Asia Centre, August 2020.
12. Qaisar Abbas & Farooq Sulehria (eds.) (2021), *From Terrorism to Television: Dynamics of Media, State, and Society in Pakistan*, Routledge, London, p. 9.
13. Tilak Devasher (2018), *Pakistan at Helm*, HarperCollins Publishers, New Delhi,. p. 298.
14. Qaisar Abbas & Farooq Sulehria (eds.) (2021), *From Terrorism to Television:- Dynamics of Media, State, and Society in Pakistan*, Routledge, London, p. 9.
15. Ibid.
16. The Pakistan Credit Rating Agency Limited, Media Sector Study, June 2021.
17. Ibid.
18. Ibid.
19. Freedom House, Freedom in the World 2021 Country report–Pakistan.
20. Pakistan Bureau of Statistics (PBS), 2020.
21. Infoasaid, Media and Telecoms Landscape Guide, June 2012.
22. Ibid.
23. Who owns the media in Pakistan, Media Ownership Monitor.
24. Adnan Rehmat, "Why is Pakistan media in crisis", *Dawn*, Islamabad, 21 July 2019.
25. Marco Mezzera & Safdar Sial, Media and Governance in Pakistan: A controversial yet essential relationship, Initiative for peacebuilding, October 2010.
26. Tina Burrett & Jeff Kingston (eds.) (2020), *Press Freedom in Contemporary Asia*, Routledge, p. 331.
27. Ibid.
28. Committee to Protect Journalists (CPJ) Report, 2019.
29. Hasan Ali, Inside the fight for Press Freedom in Pakistan, *The Nation*, 5 August 2021.
30. Ayesha Siddiqa-Agha (2007), *Military Inc: Inside Pakistan's Military Economy*, Oxford University Press, London, p. 197.
31. "Acts of Intimidation: In Pakistan, journalists' fear and censorship grow even as fatal violence declines", CPJ Report, 2018.
32. Ibid.

33. DG ISPR Conference, PSEP TV, 4 June 2018.
34. Tina Burrett & Jeff Kingston (eds.) (2020), *Press Freedom in Contemporary Asia*, Routledge, p. 335.
35. Marco Mezzera and Safdar Sial, Media and Governance in Pakistan: A controversial yet essential relationship, Initiative for peacebuilding, October 2010.
36. Tina Burrett & Jeff Kingston (eds.) (2020), *Press Freedom in Contemporary Asia*, Routledge, p. 335.
37. Ibid.
38. Sherry Ricchiardi, Challenges for Independent News Media in Pakistan—A Report, Centre for International Media Assistance, 30 July 2012.
39. 138 journalists killed in Pakistan since 1990: IFJ, *Dawn*, Islamabad, 12 December 2020.
40. Sherry Ricchiardi, Challenges for Independent News Media in Pakistan—A Report, Centre for International Media Assistance, 30 July 2012.
41. Pakistan's Endangered Press and the Perilous Web of Militancy, Security, and Politics, CPJ Report, 2013.
42. Who owns the media in Pakistan, Media Ownership Monitor.
43. Acts of Intimidation: In Pakistan, journalists' fear and censorship grow even as fatal violence declines, CPJ Report, 2018.
44. Tilak Devasher (2019), *The Balochistan Conundrum*, HarperCollins Publishers, New Delhi, p. 479
45. Adnan Rehmat, Journalists in Pakistan push to end abuse of women in media, IMS, 2020.
46. Ibid.
47. Getting away with Murder, CPJ Global Impunity Index, 2020.
48. Tilak Devasher, Pak deep state war on media, *Tribune*, India, 4 May 2020.
49. Frud Bezhan & Daud Khattak, 'Victim of a sinister campaign': Pakistani Journalists face retribution even in European Exile, Radio Free Europe, 10 April 2020.
50. Surrendering to Silence An Account of Self-censorship among Pakistani Journalists, Media Matters for Democracy, 2018.
51. Ibid.
52. Raksha Kumar, As attacks against the press in Pakistan grow by 40% in a single year, journalists blame the West for not speaking up, Reuters Institute, 27 August 2021.
53. Prime Minister of the Islamic Republic of Pakistan since 18 August 2018, Predator since taking office, RSF report, 2021.
54. Reporters without Borders World Press Freedom Index, 2020.
55. Council of Pakistan Newspaper Editors (CPNE), Pakistan Media Freedom Report, 2020.
56. Ibid.
57. Fatima Salman, Evolving News Media Landscapes in India and Pakistan: Implications for regional peace and stability, South Asia Centre, August 2020.
58. Tilak Devasher, Pakistan Information war campaign against India needs attention, *The Indian Express*, 27 July 2020.
59. Ibid.
60. Nazir Ahmed Amir, Pakistan media under stress: Imran fails to walk the talk, IDSA comment, 17 January 2020.
61. 2020 country reports on Human Rights Practices, United States Department of State, 30 March 2021.
62. Pak parliamentary panel endorses jail for criticising armed forces; slammed for 'ridiculous idea', ANI, 10 April 2021.
63. Draconian internet laws, *Dawn*, Islamabad, 22 November 2020.

64. Explainer: What is the govt's proposed media authority and why has it invited criticism? *Dawn*, Islamabad, 2 June 2021.
65. PFUJ, HRCP, PBC to oppose muzzling of media, *The News*, 29 May 2021.
66. Patricia Gossman, Proposed Pakistan Authority seeks greater control of Media, Human Rights Watch, 23 August 2021.
67. Council of Pakistan Newspaper Editors (CPNE), Pakistan Media Freedom Report, 2020.
68. Journalist Matiullah Jan abducted in Pakistan 1 day before Supreme Court hearing, CPJ, 21 July 2020.
69. Pakistan Escalating attacks against Journalists, *Human Rights Watch*, 3 June 2021.
70. Hasan Ali, Inside the fight for Press Freedom in Pakistan, *The Nation*, 5 August 2021.

8

Pakistan's Foreign Policy: Chasing the Mirage

Amb Dinkar P. Srivastava

Foreign policy has enjoyed a large salience in Pakistan's national polity since its inception. This was unusual for a nascent country struggling with major internal issues. There was no external security threat to justify such an inversion of priorities. The 1947-48 war in Kashmir was launched by Pakistan. There has also been remarkable consistency in foreign policy followed by civil and military leaders alike. An alliance with the USA was concluded by a civilian government and continued under military leadership. The mutual defence pact with the USA was signed in 1954 when Ghulam Mohammad was the Governor-General. This was four years before Ayub Khan's military coup of 1958. The relationship with China has remained a cornerstone of its foreign policy regardless of the government in power. Pakistan displayed remarkable pragmatism in the choice of its foreign partners. The absence of democracy did not stand in the way of an alliance with America. Communist ideology was anathema to the Pakistani rulers. While they firmly grasped China's hands, they ruthlessly suppressed the left movement within Pakistan. Its foreign partners have been equally accommodative despite occasional criticism by the USA of Pakistan's human rights record.

Pakistan has followed a more complex pattern in its relations with its neighbours. There is an interplay of ideology and interests in its policies on J&K and Afghanistan issues. Kashmir is projected as an unfinished agenda of partition in a veiled reference to the Two-Nation theory. This goes beyond the pursuit of interests. Pakistan has made all other aspects of its relations with India hostage to the settlement of the 'Kashmir dispute.' In the case of Afghanistan, the Pakistan military has followed a policy of seeking strategic depth and promoted the Taliban to achieve this end. It has become difficult for both civil and military leaders to break out of these dogmas. This has imposed enormous costs in terms of unsustainable levels of military expenditure, which has impoverished the country. It has also given rise to the radicalisation of society.

Pakistan bases its claim on J&K on religion. Islam should not have been a factor in its relations with Afghanistan, a fellow Muslim country like Pakistan. However, its Afghan policy continued to be driven by religious ideology even after the withdrawal and collapse of the Soviet Union. Pakistan has continued to extend overt and covert support to the Taliban even though the latter has not disavowed its links with the al-Qaeda. It persisted with this policy despite the risk of falling out with America on whose help it is dependent.

Pakistan's foreign policy has been driven by its desire for parity with its larger neighbour to the east. This has led to the acquisition of nuclear weapons technology even at the risk of cut-off of military and economic assistance. Over time, its nuclear policy progressed from a 'credible minimum deterrence to 'full-spectrum deterrence. Pakistan's nuclear doctrine is based on First Use, which is inherently destabilising.

Pakistan has used religion as both ideological justification and a tool to implement its policy. Reliance on *jihadi* groups introduced new actors in the conduct of foreign policy. Foreign policy is no longer the domain of the GHQ and the Foreign Office only. Religious groups are now important stakeholders. This has a domestic fallout. It created a constituency that made it difficult to change external policy. Musharraf's perceived U-turn on Afghanistan produced a backlash by *jihadi* groups. There was an attack on the Indian Parliament by the Jaish-e-Muhammad in December 2001. There were attacks on various targets inside Pakistan, including an attempt on Musharraf's life on 25 December 2003. The launch of Operation Zarb-e-Azb in North Waziristan in June 2014 was followed by an attack on Army Public School in Peshawar in December of that year.

Jammu & Kashmir

Pakistan's foreign policy is characterised by the primacy of force over diplomacy. It launched a 'tribal invasion' in Jammu & Kashmir in 1947. It was India, not Pakistan that made the reference to the UN three months later. A corollary was that the military dominated in shaping foreign policy from the beginning. The tribal invasion of J&K was planned by GHQ in Rawalpindi and was led by

Col Akbar Khan, a serving officer of the Pakistani army. The role of Sardar Ibrahim Khan, who later became the first President of POK was to organise arms smuggling. This has been recorded in some detail by Akbar Khan. This pattern of force being the predominant feature of Pakistan's Kashmir policy would be repeated in 1965 when that country launched Operation Gibraltar. It would be demonstrated yet again during the Kargil war in 1999.

Pakistan always had an ambivalent position on the issue of the plebiscite. After the tribal invasion was launched, Mountbatten visited Lahore on 2 November and proposed a plebiscite under the aegis of the UN. Jinnah did not accept it. The tribal invasion was still going on; the atrocities committed by the tribal militia would not have endeared Pakistan to the people of J&K. The wishes of the people were incidental in Pakistan's decision-making. This would be repeated in 1950 when Pakistan rejected the proposal made by the UN mediator, Owen Dixon, to hold a regional plebiscite. Its stated ground was that this was a departure from the principle of a single plebiscite. However, it was willing to accept partition—also a departure from the principle of a single plebiscite provided it got the Valley. Pakistan rejected the plebiscite again in 1953 after agreeing to it in the Nehru-Mohammad Ali Bogra talks in Delhi. Prime Minister Bogra rejected it in a letter to Prime Minister Nehru in December 1953. The stated ground was the same as in 1950, which was less than convincing. The real reason was the military operation launched by the Pakistan army to quell the Sudhan revolt in POK that lasted for several years.[1] The unrest had started after Sardar Ibrahim, the first President of POK was sacked in April 1950 triggering a revolt by his tribesmen. Pakistan could hardly afford a plebiscite with such disturbing conditions in the area of J&K under its occupation.

All the UNSC resolutions on J&K were adopted under Chapter VI. These require the consent of the States to implement them. There are only two resolutions accepted by both India and Pakistan—the UNCIP resolutions of August 1948 and January 1949. The resolution of August 1948 asked Pakistan to withdraw all its troops and tribesmen from the territory illegally occupied by it, while India was asked to withdraw only the bulk of its forces. The plebiscite was to be held only after Pakistan had completely withdrawn its forces. This presented Pakistan with a dilemma—it did not want to give up the territory it had illegally occupied. Therefore, it went on dragging its feet on the issue of the plebiscite.

Pakistani commentators quote the subsequent UN Security Council resolution 98 of December 1952. A resolution adopted four years after the event cannot be used to rationalise its actions. Its chief merit in their eyes is that this did not ask Pakistan to withdraw from the territory illegally occupied by it. Interestingly, this also omitted reference to a plebiscite in the operative part. Pakistan does not seem to mind sacrificing plebiscite for retaining control over the territory.

The UNSC resolution 98 of December 1952 was a Chapter VI resolution, which was not accepted by India and hence not enforceable. It was adopted when the Cold War had shifted the balance in the Security Council in favour of Pakistan. If, however, the goalpost is moved, then the subsequent UN Security Council resolutions of 1965 and 1971 also need to be considered. They completely omitted reference to a plebiscite. The UNSC resolution 1172 adopted in June 1998 after the nuclear tests in South Asia included a passing reference to J&K in operative para 5. But this did not mention any of the previous resolutions on J&K.

Pakistan occupied the northern area in 1947. Major Brown, a British officer of Gilgit Scouts, led the mutiny against the Maharaja's government. It is unprecedented in the annals of any freedom fight that a representative of the colonial power leads the independence struggle. Brown has described his actions more accurately as a coup d'etat. The territory was thereafter placed under the NWFP administration, rather than being handed over to the provisional government of Jammu and Kashmir that had come into being.[2] Northern areas comprise 85 per cent of the territory of J&K State occupied by Pakistan. Pakistan in effect had changed the territorial *status quo* of the territory in its control without waiting for the plebiscite. Later, a secret agreement was signed in Karachi in April 1949 between the representatives of the Pakistan government, POK President, and Chairman of the Muslim Conference handing over the territory to Pakistan. This was a violation of the UN Security Council resolution as the POK High Court declared in its judgment in 1993. In his later life, Sardar Ibrahim, POK President, denied ever having signed the agreement.[3]

The Kargil invasion of 1999 followed the script of 1947. Pakistan had deployed the Northern Light Infantry, a unit of the Pakistani army though it was described as a Mujahidin action.[4] There was, however, a major difference. Pakistan had embarked on this adventure in a nuclearised environment. Both India and Pakistan had conducted nuclear tests in the previous year. This did not bring any moderation in Pakistani actions. It was willing to push the envelope despite the risk of escalation to the nuclear level. Implicit in this was the assumption that India would be restrained from taking any action, and Pakistan would be able to make territorial gains apart from 'unfreezing' the Kashmir issue. Its calculations went disastrously wrong. The Indian counter-offensive forced Pakistan to fall back. No help from 'all-weather friend', China, materialised. Nawaz Sharif landed in Washington on 4 July, a national holiday in that country, to seek President Clinton's mediation. Clinton asked for Pakistani withdrawal from the area occupied by it. The international community was not willing to reward irresponsible behaviour.

During the conflict, Foreign Secretary Shamshad Ahmad had made a statement on 31 May that 'We will not hesitate to use any weapon in our arsenal to defend our territorial integrity.'[5] This was a threat to use nuclear weapons in retaliation in a war, in which, Pakistan had until then, denied any official role. The threat, however, could not prevent India's conventional response. The lost war triggered a sequence of events that ended with Musharraf's coup against Nawaz Sharif. Pakistan had suffered both military defeat and an eclipse of democracy. The war had undermined Pakistan's credibility. It was launched after PM Vajpayee's visit to Lahore. There was a blame game in Pakistan. Though Nawaz Sharif's camp denied that he was fully aware of the scale of incursion, the prime minister had received some briefing at least.

While raising the J&K issue in every international forum, Pakistan has carefully avoided talking about the part of the state it has illegally occupied. It claims a mandate to administer POK and Gilgit-Baltistan on the basis of the UNCIP resolution of August 1948. Some commentators have supported this claim citing a reference to 'local authority' in the UNCIP resolution. The resolution had in fact asked Pakistan to withdraw all forces under its control. This cannot be cited to justify its continued occupation. The UNCIP resolution of August 1948 stated that the 'local authorities' on the Pakistani side would function under the UN's surveillance, not Pakistani control.

The Northern Areas have been re-named 'Gilgit-Baltistan.' Prime Minister Imran Khan announced in November 2020 that the territory would be given 'provisional provincial status.'[6] The announcement was made during the election campaign and was criticised by the opposition parties as an attempt to influence the outcome of the elections in favour of the PTI. If and when this change is affected, it will be an overt admission that Pakistan has integrated that territory in a departure from its own official position rendering plebiscite irrelevant. Both POK and Gilgit-Baltistan are already integrated in Pakistan in effect.

Afghanistan

Pakistan justifies its Afghan policy in terms of seeking strategic depth against India. This implies that the country faces a threat from India. All four wars were initiated by Pakistan. The policy defies logic. Pakistan has to use its military assets to fight the war against India, rather than withdraw them westward leaving its major population centres undefended. The strategic depth is to be achieved at the cost of Afghanistan's sovereignty. This is an attempt to disguise an inherently expansionist policy in defensive terms. The policy also has the paradoxical result of providing Taliban strategic depth. They are now embedded in Pakistan society. The Tehrik-i-Taliban in Pakistan has challenged Pakistan's writ not only in remote regions of South and North Waziristan but in the heart of the national capital. This was illustrated by the Lal Masjid episode in 2007 where a group of radicals challenged the state's writ.

From Afghanistan's perspective, the threat comes from Pakistan, not India. Pakistan's policy seeks to involve Afghanistan in an unnecessary confrontation with a friendly country. If at all Pakistan needed strategic depth against India, it could have sought to achieve it by developing friendly relations with Afghanistan. This, Pakistan has never attempted.

The policy of seeking strategic depth involves permeable borders and represents a departure from the British policy that Pakistan claims to have inherited. The Durand Line was finalised in 1893-96. A decade later, the Anglo-Russian Convention of 1907 established Afghanistan as a buffer state. This helped cool the great power rivalry. The British were thereafter content with maintaining the *status quo* as long as their Indian empire was safe. Immediately, after the partition, Pakistan tried to continue this policy. Indeed, it went further and claimed that the Durand Line was the international border. This changed in the Eighties. Pakistan became the springboard for *jihad* against Soviet presence in Afghanistan. This required porous borders to allow the free flow of arms and Mujahidins into Afghanistan.[7] Encouraged by the Soviet withdrawal, Pakistan tried to expand its presence in Afghanistan and establish its influence in Central Asia in the name of Islam.

The Soviet withdrawal from Afghanistan following the Geneva Accords changed the geo-political context. But there was no change in Pakistan's policy. It was no longer acting as a proxy of external powers. The ISI organised the Jalalabad offensive. Despite the failure of the offensive, Pakistan continued its attempt to install a pro-Islamabad regime in Kabul. It successfully used Benon Sevan, the UN mediator, to persuade Najibullah to step down before agreement on an interim government was reached. Pakistan used the power vacuum to install a coalition of Peshawar-based Mujahedin parties in Kabul. Pakistan's constant interference, and attacks by the Hikmatyar on the Rabbani government, plunged the country into civil war.

Benazir Bhutto was to later blame Zia's Afghan *jihad* as having brought drugs and Kalashnikov culture to Pakistan. While in power, she continued Zia's forward policy in Afghanistan. The Taliban was created during Benazir's second term as Prime Minister in 1994. The rise of the Taliban is sometimes credited to an attempt to open a trade route to Central Asia, which was being blocked by tribal leaders. The narrative also includes an incident where a band of religious students led by Mullah Umar killed the tribal chief who had kidnapped and raped minor girls. Trade has never played a major role in Pakistan military's calculus. This account underplays the strategic considerations.

The Taliban did not represent a spontaneous movement. The cadre of students (Taliban) came from a madrassa in Pakistan. Their mentors were Maulana Fazlur Rehman, the head of the JUI(F), and General Nasrullah Babar, the Interior Minister in the Benazir Bhutto government. Later, the Taliban also had the support of a section of the State Department led by Robin Raphael, the US Assistant Secretary of State. UNOCAL, an American oil company, was backing an oil pipeline project through Afghanistan and lobbied for the Taliban in Washington. However, this phase ended with bombings of US missions in Tanzania and Kenya in 1998. Pakistan however, continued to support the Taliban until 9/11.

The impressive continuity in Pakistan's Afghan policy is rooted in its domestic politics as much as its regional ambitions. Pakistan has used religion to undermine Pashtun nationalism in NWFP. Under the Khan brothers, the province wanted to join India at the time of partition. While in other provinces the state legislatures decided the issue of accession, the British insisted on organising a referendum in the NWFP. The decision by Badshah Khan to boycott the referendum swung the outcome in favour of Pakistan. After partition, the ANP remained the dominant political force in the province. This changed after the rise of *jihadi* groups in the Afghan war of the Eighties. This was repeated after 9/11, when Islamabad used these groups to undermine the ANP's influence.

Pakistan supported the Taliban, which gave shelter to the al-Qaeda. After 9/11, Musharraf made a tactical peace with the USA. But at home, he allowed the MMA, a coalition of religious parties, to form governments in the two key provinces bordering Afghanistan—NWFP and Balochistan. After Musharraf's departure, the ANP and PPP staged a comeback. The Muttahida Majlis-e-Amal

(MMA), which had secured 68 seats in 2002[8] was reduced to 4 seats in 2008.[9] This showed that the sweeping victory of religious parties in the 2002 elections was contrived. However, the ANP faced constant onslaughts from the establishment keen to accommodate *jihadi* groups. Pakistan signed the Waziristan accord while Pakistan was part of the international coalition against terror. This allowed the Afghan Taliban to gain sanctuary in Pakistan and continue attacking coalition forces.

Pakistan facilitated the Doha Accord between the USA and the Taliban. The elected government was kept out of the Doha talks, where the USA was negotiating with the Taliban whom it did not officially recognise. While the USA had distanced itself from the Afghan government, Pakistan continued full support to the Taliban. This allowed the Taliban to gain legitimacy and secure American withdrawal. They showed no interest in intra-Afghan dialogue and rejected a cease-fire. Prime Minister Imran Khan in an opinion piece in the *Washington Post* on June 22, 2021, stated that 'In the past, Pakistan made a mistake by choosing between warring Afghan parties, but we have learnt from that experience.'[10] The thrust of Pakistan's actions and diplomacy belies this claim. Pakistan has been most consistent in giving sanctuaries to the Taliban even when Pakistan was officially aligned with the USA in the war on terror. Admiral Mike Mullen in his testimony to the US Congress had stated, 'With ISI support, Haqqani operatives planned and conducted that truck bomb attack, as well as the assault on our embassy.'[11]

Speaking at the international conference on 'Central and South Asia Regional Connectivity: Challenges and Opportunities' in Uzbekistan, President Ghani said: 'Intelligence estimates indicate the influx of 10,000 *jihadi* fighters from Pakistan and other places in the last month, as well as support from their affiliates and the transnational terrorist organizations.'[12] He added:

> "Contrary to repeated assurances by Prime Minister Khan and his generals that Pakistan does not find a Taliban takeover in Afghanistan in Pakistan's interest, and short of the use of force will use its power and influence to make the Taliban negotiate seriously, networks and organizations supporting the Taliban are openly celebrating the destruction of the assets and capabilities of the Afghan people and the State."[13]

The collapse of the Ghani government after the American withdrawal brought the Taliban to power. This was not a military victory against the USA. The withdrawal of American forces was linked to US domestic politics. The US forces had ceased combat operations in 2014, except for counter-terrorist strikes. It was the Afghan National Army (ANA), which bore the brunt of the fighting. The ANA must have been demoralised by the spectre of US 'engagement' with the Taliban, while the Afghan Government was excluded from the discussions.

Soon after the Taliban captured Kabul, the highest-ranking foreign dignitary to visit Afghanistan was Lt General Faiz Hameed, the ISI chief. His visit underlined the locus of power. The announcement of the Taliban Cabinet bore the ISI's stamp with the Haqqani faction being given the most important posts. The emergence of a hard-line government made it clear that Taliban 2.0 was no different from the Taliban of the Nineties.

With the Taliban's capture of power in Afghanistan, Pakistan has achieved a major foreign policy goal. Has this given her the strategic depth? The Taliban have still not recognised the Durand Line. Their success would surely inspire those who dream of establishing an Islamic Emirate in Pakistan. Whether the Afghan Taliban sacrifice their links to the Pakistan Taliban remains to be seen. The TTP remains a threat to Pakistan. This may not have been Pakistan's agenda, but ideology does not always follow national boundaries. If, however, the Taliban represent Pashtun nationalism, as many of their apologists claim, this would have a fall-out in Khyber-Pakhtunkhwa.

Pakistan has not officially recognised the Taliban regime. Nor has it been able to win recognition for its creation from other countries. Pakistan's double game in Afghanistan has also strained its relationship with the USA—its long-time benefactor. The Biden Administration's decision to release $ 7 billion of Afghan funds in the USA to the victims of 9/11 may reflect the USA's view of the future of this relationship.

Nuclear

The quest for nuclear power status has been an important dimension of Pakistan's foreign policy since the 1970s. Bhutto had announced that Pakistanis would eat grass but will have a nuclear weapon. This statement heralded a policy of seeking nuclear material and technology clandestinely. A.Q. Khan, who worked for a Belgian company, managed to steal blueprints for advanced centrifuges and escape to Pakistan. This was the beginning of the Pakistani nuclear programme. Pakistan, in turn, proliferated nuclear technology to Iran, Libya, and North Korea.

These activities were exposed following Gaddafi's decision to open up Libya's nuclear programme and surrender the material and equipment to America in 2005. The media has focused on the A.Q. Khan network. Khan was indeed one of the important players in the drama. But the Pakistani nuclear programme is tightly controlled by the army. It is inconceivable that activities on this scale could have been carried out for an extended period without the active support of the Pakistani civil and military establishment at the highest levels. Obviously, the narrative of Khan's culpability was carefully built up to shield the Pakistani state. A.Q. Khan soon received a Presidential pardon from Musharraf. I was Indian Ambassador to Libya at that time. I was told by a key Western envoy that Pakistan received more than ten billion dollars of financial gains from Libya. The Libyan exposure led to a temporary rupture in Libya-Pakistan relations.

Pakistan's proliferation activities have created a major headache for the international community. In the case of North Korea, Pakistan embarked on an exchange of nuclear technology against missiles. This was initiated during Benazir Bhutto's visit as Pakistan's Prime Minister to North Korea in 1994. She proudly acknowledged her role in subsequent interviews she gave. The nuclearisation of the Korean peninsula has resulted in a major security threat to South Korea, Japan, and the USA. It must have also caused some consternation to its all-weather friend, China, which does not want to see a nuclear-armed neighbour in its backyard. Its discomfort with the North Korean programme is evident from the fact that it went along with the UN Security Council resolutions against that country.

Pakistan had to be mindful of US concerns about its proliferation activities. In the 1980s, the US Congress passed a series of legislation to strengthen the non-proliferation regime. However, their effect was to simply raise the threshold for executive action against proliferating countries from checking the process to the actual conduct of the nuclear test. This enabled Pakistan to continue her enrichment programme. The USA must have been aware of Pakistan's nuclear programme, but chose to turn a blind eye. Pakistan was a useful ally in the *jihad* against the Soviet Union in Afghanistan. This phase came to an end with the Soviet withdrawal from Afghanistan, which was completed in 1989. The following year, President Bush refused to certify that Pakistan did not possess a nuclear weapon, a requirement under the Pressler amendment. This led to the disruption of American military and economic assistance to Pakistan. This caused a lot of resentment in Islamabad. Pakistan, however, continued its proliferation activities in other regions.

The acquisition of nuclear capacity, even though it was at a nascent stage of development in the Eighties, led to greater risk-taking on the part of Pakistan. A.Q. Khan gave his interview to Kuldip Nayar in 1987 claiming that Pakistan had developed a nuclear weapon. This was at a time when Pakistan's official position was that it did not have nuclear weapons. The statement was timed to coincide with the exercise, Operation Brasstacks.[14] If it was a signal to the Indian side as General Kidwai, former Head of Pakistan's Strategic Plans Division, claims, it had no effect. By the time Kuldip Nayar published the interview on 1 March 1987, the crisis had already blown over. Pakistan, however, had underlined its willingness to indulge in nuclear blackmail. Its behaviour was contrary to the normal paradigm where nuclear weapons states avoid any action that may lead to escalation to the nuclear level. It used the fear of nuclear exchange to draw international attention to the Kashmir issue. Kashmir as a nuclear flashpoint became a standard mantra of Pakistan's foreign policy in the Nineties. Pakistan also used the nuclear dimension to encourage *jihadi* activities. This policy reached its climax in the Kargil war in 1999. The war had followed nuclear tests in the sub-continent in the previous year. Unfortunately, for Pakistan, the Kargil adventure backfired against it. The international community refused to sanction Pakistan's illegal acquisition of territory. The Indian military pressure forced it to withdraw. It is unclear, however, if Pakistan has seriously reviewed its policy.

The nuclear 'assets' have assumed a mythical quality in the Pakistani mindset. After 9/11, President Musharraf decided to join the international coalition against terrorism. In his speech of September 2001, he explained to the Pakistani public the abrupt turnaround in Pakistan's policy in Afghanistan with reference to preserving the safety of Pakistan's strategic assets, a reference to nuclear weapons that it possesses.

Pakistan's risk behaviour has generated proliferation activity and undermined international peace and security. This is compounded by blocking negotiations on the fissile material cut-off treaty (FMCT) in Geneva. The continued production of fissile material shows that Pakistan is expanding its armoury. It is not content with 'credible minimum deterrence.' It claims to have 'Full Spectrum Deterrence' capacity as General Kidwai boasted in a talk in the International Institute for Strategic Studies (IISS) in London in 2020.[15]

USA

Pakistan's relations with the USA have been for long the most important facet of her foreign policy. It began soon after the country was created after partition. Jinnah hinted to a US diplomat that Pakistan would be a useful foil against communist expansion in the Middle East. Raymond A. Hare, a US diplomat, reported to the US State Department about his meeting with Jinnah on 2 May 1947. Jinnah had told him that the "establishment of Pakistan is essential to prevent 'Hindu Imperialism' from spreading into the Middle East; Muslim countries would stand together against possible Russian aggression and would look to the USA for assistance."[16] Jinnah was talking of 'Hindu Imperialism' and the Russian aggression in the same breath, and claiming for Pakistan the leadership of the Muslim countries. Jinnah had also taken it upon himself to organise Muslim countries against Russian aggression and obtain US assistance in their name! Prime Minister Liaquat Ali Khan visited the USA in May 1950. Pakistan was cultivating the USA as a source of military aid against India. The USA saw Pakistan as a potential partner in its global fight against communism. The objectives of the two countries did not coincide, but the USA chose to ignore this divergence in perception.

Pakistan signed the Mutual Defence Assistance Pact with the USA in 1954 and joined the Baghdad Pact and CENTO. The policy of alignment with the West came naturally to the Muslim League leadership that had grown up under British patronage in pre-partition India. Independent India chose non-alignment. The first phase of the USA-Pakistan relationship lasted till the early 1960s. Ayub Khan received the Chinese Ambassador soon after his return from Washington. China wanted Pakistani support on her admission to the United Nations. Ayub wanted China's support against India. China was non-committal at that stage. Both sides got over their hesitations soon. Pakistan signed a boundary agreement with China soon after the Sino-Indian war of 1962. The timing underlined that the alliance was aimed against India.

The next phase of the USA-Pakistan relationship began in July 1971, when Kissinger made a secret trip to Beijing from a base in Pakistan. This relationship was cemented during the 1971 war when the USA sent the 7th Fleet to the Bay of Bengal. This was a signal that there was a convergence in US and Chinese interests in South Asia. Before returning to Pakistan after his UNGA speech in 1971, Bhutto met President Nixon and profusely thanked him for help during the Bangladesh war. However, relations between Pakistan and America soured soon over the question of Pakistan's quest for nuclear weapons. Bhutto had initiated the programme and sworn that Pakistan would develop nuclear weapons even if the people of Pakistan had to eat grass. He claimed from his prison cell that his nuclear policy was the reason for his downfall.

There was a lull in Pakistan's relations with America following the military takeover by General Zia in October 1977. This changed soon after the Soviet intervention in Afghanistan. Pakistan had emerged as a frontline country. Under the Reagan Administration, Pakistan benefited from a large amount of American military and economic assistance during the Afghan *jihad*. The USA also acquiesced to Pakistan's nuclear programme. Not only did it turn a blind eye, but legislation framed by the US Congress also changed the threshold for imposing sanctions for proliferation activities from process to possession of the nuclear device. This allowed Pakistan to continue its programme without fear of sanctions till it tested the device. In 1990, finally, President Bush refused to give certification that Pakistan did not possess a nuclear device. This led to the suspension of military aid to Pakistan. Pakistan saw the development as an American betrayal. It was actually Pakistan that had exploited the relationship to extract military aid as well as tacit acquiescence to Pakistan's clandestine nuclear programme.

The nuclear tests of 1998 brought international focus on South Asia. America imposed sanctions on India and Pakistan after the tests. It soon lifted sanctions against Pakistan on humanitarian grounds. Pakistan has successfully exploited the belief held in the West that a nuclear-armed country could not be allowed to collapse fearing that this would lead to the fall of nuclear weapons in the hands of mullahs. Pakistan managed to secure US intervention during the Kargil war to secure a face-saving exit.

9/11 inaugurated a new phase of the USA-Pakistan relationship. It was to bring intense US engagement in the region. However, this was qualitatively different from the collaboration between the two countries during the Cold War when both countries saw a positive convergence. Pakistan was now required to forsake the al-Qaeda and Taliban, which were essentially its creations in order to ensure the survival of its strategic assets. Musharraf had to accept an alliance with the USA under the threat that a refusal would result in the USA taking out its nuclear assets. In his address of September 2001, he likened his decision to the episode in the Holy Quran where Prophet Mohammad had made his peace with the Jews. He was underlining the tactical nature of the relationship. This indeed reflected the equation between the two countries during the next decade. Pakistan had once again emerged as a recipient of large-scale US military and economic assistance. However, it did not want to sacrifice the Taliban, which is regarded as a strategic asset to seek dominance over Afghanistan. Musharraf had promised to support America's war on terror but continued to harbour Taliban and al-Qaeda leaders. In the post-9/11 phase, America failed to check Pakistan's duplicity. After 2005, as US attention was diverted to the worsening situation in Iraq, the Taliban began to re-group and attack coalition forces in Afghanistan.

Musharraf's ouster in 2007 was followed by a new gift to Pakistan in the shape of the Kerry Lugar Act in 2009, which restored assistance to Pakistan after a brief hiatus. Pakistan until now had received almost $ 15 billion of assistance from the USA since 2001. The Act had provisions to check the military's interference in civilian politics in Pakistan. This drew a sharp reaction from the military. Eventually, the provision proved harmless. Not only did it not check the military's role in politics, but it also failed to induce it to extend support to the USA for extricating itself from Afghanistan. The sanctuaries enjoyed by the Taliban in Pakistan ensured that the military surge undertaken by Obama in 2011 did not bear fruit.

Osama bin Laden was killed by American commandos in an operation in May 2011. The discovery that he was living in Abbottabad, near the Pakistan military academy, exposed Pakistan's duplicity. There was an outburst of emotions at a popular level against American action. There followed an upsurge of violence against American targets in Afghanistan. Admiral Mike Mullen in a testimony to the US Senate Armed Forces Committee in September 2011 stated that the Haqqani network was a veritable arm of the ISI. This was a reference to an attack by the Haqqani network on high-profile US targets including the US embassy in Kabul.

Pakistan started on the wrong wicket with the inauguration of the Trump presidency in 2016. The relations reached their lowest point in 2018 January when President Trump ordered the stopping of American aid to Pakistan. The US policy was, however, soon reversed. In July of that year. President Trump wrote a letter to Prime Minister Imran Khan seeking his help to secure a safe exit from Afghanistan. Prime Minister Imran Khan received an invitation to visit Washington. The visit in July 2019 drew assurance from President Trump for US mediation over Kashmir. Pakistan had once again become a key partner for the USA. It obliged the USA by releasing Mullah Baradar for beginning the Doha dialogue with the USA. The Doha Accord with the Taliban has not produced peace in Afghanistan. The Biden Administration set a deadline of September 2021 to complete the withdrawal of American troops from Afghanistan. The withdrawal has been completed ahead of schedule in August. The American departure could result in Pakistan losing a source of aid in the long run. The American concern is to avoid any precipitous turn of the event, which would be embarrassing to it. It may not have any long-term interest in the Af-Pak region.

Pakistan has been remarkably successful in maintaining the autonomy of its decision-making on core issues despite the USA being the largest aid-giver to that country. The USA could not restrain Pakistan from edging closer to China at a time when America's relations with that country were strained. During the next two decades, the USA failed to check Pakistan's nuclear programme. The

Administration was aware of Pakistan's attempt to acquire nuclear material and technology clandestinely. However, Pakistan was a useful ally in a covert war against the Soviet Union in Afghanistan.

Pakistan, a Moderating Influence?

At the height of the Gulf war, General Mirza Aslam Beg gave a call on 1 February 1990 for strategic defiance of the West. This went against the assumption underlying British and American policy for more than five decades that Pakistan would help moderate Arab countries. Pakistan army chief made the call when America was engaged in Operation Desert Storm to vacate Saddam's invasion of Kuwait. Not only had Pakistan ignored American interests, but also the Saudi's. Prime Minister Nawaz Sharif was supportive of the Saudi request. The army chief's statement was hugely popular with the public. The episode showed the latent anti-Americanism in Pakistan at the popular level, and within the army, which was considered its primary constituency.

China

Pakistan signed a border agreement with China in 1963. The negotiations had begun much earlier. This was just after Ayub Khan's visit to Washington in 1961. The agreement coincided with the worsening of relations between India and China. 'The Sino-Pakistan agreement, in principle, on the demarcation of the border was announced on 27 December 1962, the day the first round of Indo-Pakistan talks on Kashmir opened in Rawalpindi.'[17] It symbolised the Sino-Pakistan coalition against India and this indeed is the reason for its durability. Pakistan ceded 5,180 square kilometres of the area of POK to China. This was a Pakistani attempt to draw China into South Asia. It also brought in a recognition of the Pakistani position in POK which otherwise had no legal basis. This was a violation of UN Security Council resolutions on Jammu & Kashmir because Pakistan had changed the territorial *status quo* without plebiscite. This was probably the reason why the agreement was not notified to the United Nations, which is the repository of international treaties. The Chinese motivation was to establish a foothold south of the Karakorum in Kashmir. This amounted to breaching the watershed principle and undermining India's position on border negotiations.

The agreement between the two countries was signed at a time when Pakistan was a member of SEATO and CENTO and undermined its fundamental objective of containing communism. Pakistan was soon to discover the limitations of the new relationship. In the final phase of the 1965 war, Ayub Khan accompanied by Bhutto, made a secret visit to China to ask for Chinese assistance. The Chinese leaders advised Pakistan to be prepared for a long war of attrition. Prime Minister Zhou en-Lai suggested to Ayub that he should be ready to lose some major urban centres. Ayub was not prepared to sacrifice Lahore. He came back empty-handed and accepted the UN Security Council resolution 211 on a cease-fire. The resolution caused considerable embarrassment to the Ayub regime. It neither mentioned the previous UN Security Council resolution on J&K nor plebiscite.

The next stage of the Sino-Pak relationship started with Kissinger's secret trip to Beijing from a Pakistani airbase in 1971 to prepare for Nixon's visit. Nixon's visit to Beijing in the following year was aimed at weaning away China from the communist bloc. The rift had already taken place seven years earlier. This put an official stamp on a *fait accompli*. Pakistan sought to benefit from this relationship in South Asia.

The Sino-American rapprochement initiated by Nixon's visit to China was based on America's global calculations. The USA wanted to neutralise China in its confrontation with the Soviet Union. The immediate objective was to get Chinese support for America's exit from Vietnam. The Chinese pressure on North Vietnam was critical in securing 'Peace with Honour' for America. Pakistani calculations were rooted in sub-continental politics. Pakistan was soon to discover once again the limits of its relationship with China. China did not come to Pakistan's rescue in the 1971 war. It contented itself with making some strong statements but took no action on the ground to relieve pressure on the Pakistani Army in East Pakistan. China, however, vetoed Bangladesh's admission to the UN in 1972. This was the first time China had exercised its veto soon after replacing Taiwan in the UN Security Council.

There were two major developments in the Sino-Pak relationship in the 1980s. China built the Karakorum highway in 1986. There was very little trade between the two countries, certainly none through the overland route. The exercise only underlined the strategic relationship between them. China had developed an overland route to supply Pakistan in case of need. The second development during the 1980s was the beginning of Chinese technology transfer for Pakistan's nuclear programme. This has remained shrouded in secrecy but China signed an agreement to supply to the civil nuclear reactor Chashma-I in 1992. This was just after China had joined the NPT that year.

In the 1990s, the Chinese focus shifted somewhat. After the collapse of the Soviet Union, China was adjusting to the realities of the unipolar world. Its efforts were limited to safeguarding the domestic system. The vulnerability of the Chinese Communist Party was underlined by the events of Tiananmen Square in 1989. After the Soviet collapse, the balance in the United Nations had also shifted. China needed India's support in the UN Commission for Human Rights to defeat the resolution on the Tibet situation. China also signed a confidence-building agreement with India in 1996. However, it maintained its relationship with Pakistan. The Pokhran-II nuclear tests by India in 1998 were soon followed by nuclear tests by Pakistan. This is believed to be based on a Chinese cold-tested device in Lop Nor.

China played a critical role in the drafting of UN Security Council resolution 1172, which was adopted after the nuclear test of 1998. Its task was facilitated by the fact that China assumed the presidency of the UN Security Council in the critical month of June immediately after the nuclear test. China presided over a meeting of P-5 Foreign Ministers held in Geneva on 4 June, which came out with a hard-hitting statement. Unlike the initial statements of the Security Council, which had condemned both India and Pakistan, this was tilted more in favour of Pakistan. This was a direct result of Chinese intervention. This became the basis for UNSC resolution 1172 adopted two days later on 6 June. China tried to bring a reference to the Kashmir issue in the resolution. Russia managed to dilute the reference. The final text adopted does mention the previous UN Security Council resolutions on Kashmir.

During the Kargil war in 1999, Pakistan discovered the limits of its relationship with China once again. At the height of the war when Pakistan had begun to lose ground, Nawaz Sharif and Musharraf made two separate visits to Beijing to seek Chinese support. Only after they drew a blank did Pakistan turn towards the USA. Nawaz Sharif's visit to America on 4 July was an immediate sequel to his visit to Beijing on 1 July. China did not help in terms of military intervention. It had even more limited capacity to mediate; China had no leverage on India. This forced Pakistan to turn towards America. The American statement brokered by President Clinton called for the return of Pakistani forces to its side of the line of control. This gave Pakistan a fig leaf to cover its retreat. Pakistan was not allowed to retain the territory it had occupied illegally. It is unlikely that the Pakistani rulers have missed out on the implications of the Chinese silence for Pakistan.

China announced an investment in Pakistan under the China-Pakistan Economic Corridor (CPEC) in 2013. One of the flagship projects was Gwadar port. It is located in Balochistan away from all major Pakistani population centres. It has no commercial value for either Pakistan or China. It is essentially a naval base. The Chinese presence would help consolidate the Federal Government's hold on the restive province. Gwadar is close to the Gulf region, which still provides a substantial chunk of China's oil supply.

Chinese investment in Pakistan under the CPEC is part of the larger Belt and Road Initiative (BRI). Unlike projects in other countries, the Chinese involvement in Pakistan is driven almost entirely by geopolitical considerations. There is very little likelihood of China being able to realise its return from Pakistan, which is facing a major economic crisis. Under the CPEC, China had announced an investment of 46 billion dollars in Pakistan over a period of ten years. This figure has been downsized and the actual investment is unlikely to exceed 23 billion dollars, which is roughly half the figure cited initially. Most of this amount is credit given to the Chinese companies executing the project in Pakistan. The grant element or equity is minimal. The actual implementation of projects will be done by companies in the private sector. However, re-payment is backed by a sovereign guarantee by Pakistan. China has also secured a commitment by the Pakistan Government to ensure that Chinese companies get a 17 per cent post-tax return on investment in dollar terms. This arrangement has ensured that all the risks are transferred to Pakistan.

Pakistan faces a major power deficit. Most of the Chinese credit under the CPEC will flow into the power sector. This includes coal-based power plants, which will come under increasing pressure on account of environmental concerns. Most of the international credit agencies will stop investing in thermal power plants. The bulk of Chinese investment under the CPEC will go to PoK and Gilgit-Baltistan. PoK is to receive 5.6 billion dollars in terms of Chinese credit and investment, while the corresponding figure for Gilgit-Baltistan is 14 billion dollars. This includes an agreement for Chinese credit of 12 billion dollars for the Daimar-Bhasa dam. In addition, China is going to invest in infrastructure projects worth more than 2 billion dollars in the region. The Chinese credit and investment in POK and G-B is many times more than an investment of $ 900 million in Gwadar. This will strengthen the Chinese presence in a strategic area. After the events of last year in Ladakh, consolidation of the Chinese presence in the region has a strategic significance for India.

The Sino-Pakistan relationship is devoid of any ideological basis. Pakistan has kept quiet on the question of the human rights of the Uyghur Muslims. China, however, is concerned about the export of radical Islam from the Af-Pak region to Central Asia. China has also conducted military exercises with Central Asia countries, especially Tajikistan, to counter terrorism.

Middle East

The British encouraged Pakistan to establish close relations with the countries of West Asia since the emergence of Pakistan. Their thinking was that Muslim Pakistan would help influence Arab countries in favour of the West. 'Bevin did ask Liaquat Ali Khan to get in touch with the Arabs.'[18] Bevin was the British Foreign Secretary at the time. Jinnah had written to Hassan Banna, the founder of the Muslim Brotherhood, assuring him that his government 'shall assume a purely Islamic character and work in close cooperation with the other strong international Islamic organizations, which are headed by your Ikhwan-al-Muslimun society [the Muslim Brotherhood].'[19] Jinnah's letter showed an attempt to exploit Pakistan's Islamic identity in its relations with the Arab countries.

In the beginning, it was Iran, not Saudi Arabia that was the fulcrum of Pakistan's policy in the region. Iran was quick to recognise Pakistan. The Shah of Iran visited Pakistan in 1950. The two countries signed a border agreement in 1958-59. This helped Pakistan to consolidate its hold on Balochistan where both the Ruler and the people had opposed accession to Pakistan in 1947. Iran under Shah was the largest bilateral donor to Pakistan, providing US$ 800 million in loans and credits between 1974 and 1975.[20]

Pakistan was also keen to create a constituency amongst the oil-rich countries of the Middle East as this gave it importance in the West. However, in the initial stage at least, its perceived proximity to the Arabs was an exaggeration. It did not receive much of a response from Saudi Arabia under King Saud. The King visited India and Pandit Nehru visited Saudi Arabia in 1955. In the summer of 1956, Chaudhry Muhammad Ali, Pakistan's Prime Minister, visited the Saudi Kingdom. Pakistan's approach to these Middle Eastern countries was supported by Britain to counter Nasser's influence. It was also helped by the rift between Egypt and Saudi Arabia over Yemen, which underwent a revolution in 1962. This was the beginning of a civil war in that country fuelled by two Arab protagonists.

Pakistan's relationship with Saudi Arabia deepened after Faisal became King in 1964. He saw the security of his Kingdom based on pan-Islamism. This suited Pakistan also, which had adopted solidarity with Muslim countries as a major plank of its foreign policy. 'This commonality of purpose resulted in the 1967 Saudi-Pakistan mutual defence agreement.'[21] The Pakistan Army's presence in Saudi Arabia was initially limited to the training mission. Their presence expanded after the Iranian revolution and the siege of Mecca of 1979. As sectarian tension rose, the Saudi search for security brought more Pakistani soldiers to the Kingdom. 'In 1983 there were approximately 13,000 Pakistani military personnel in the Kingdom.'[22]

Saudi Arabia was not the only conservative regime Pakistan cultivated. A contingent led by then Brigadier Zia-ul-Haq participated in crushing Palestinian opposition to King Hussain in Jordan in 1970. The event came to be known as Black September and had an important fall-out in Pakistan's domestic politics. Some years later, King Hussain of Jordan placed a phone call to Bhutto recommending Zia for the post of Army Chief. Bhutto made the fateful choice, which eventually cost him his life.

Pakistan was also keen to create an identity that was anchored in the Middle East rather than South Asia. The trend was accentuated after the break-up of Pakistan in 1971. Pakistan hosted the second OIC Summit in Lahore in 1974. This coincided with the first oil price shock of 1973 that brought enormous wealth to Gulf countries and Iran. Pakistan had found generous benefactors.

Pakistan's policy in the Middle East was centred on developing relations with the conservative, pro-West regimes. It revolved around relations with Iran, Saudi Arabia, and Turkey in the first few decades. All three were part of a US-led military alliance. This helped Pakistan to maintain close relations with all three. With the Iranian revolution of 1979, the context changed. Sectarian tension was added to traditional Arab-Iran rivalry. The Iranian revolution coincided with Zia's policy of encouraging greater Islamisation at home. Its concomitant was a preference for the Sunni version of the Sharia. This was not simply a reaction to the events in Iran; Zia was searching for legitimacy for his military regime. The ideological affinity with Wahabi Islam was cemented by Saudi funding of Afghan *jihad.*

Four decades later, sectarian tensions have risen, further complicating Pakistan's choices. Not only has Saudi-Iranian rivalry intensified, but there is also a sharp difference amongst the Sunni powers with Erdogan's backing of the Muslim Brotherhood, which is an anathema to Saudi Arabia, the UAE, and Egypt. This made Pakistan's choices difficult. Saudi Arabia had requested Pakistani troops for the Yemen war. Nawaz Sharif referred the issue to the Pakistan National Assembly, even though foreign policy is part of the domain of the Executive. The Parliament rejected the proposal. Saudi Arabia and the Gulf States were not happy with Pakistan's choice. Saudi Arabia established the Islamic Military Counter Terrorism Coalition (IMCTC), the Islamic NATO, on 15 December 2015. Pakistan joined the initiative, though it was initially given the cold shoulder. If Pakistan refused to support Gulf countries in Yemen, will it stand by it in other situations?

Saudi Arabia placed $ 3 billion in the State Bank of Pakistan and provided an extended credit facility of $ 3 billion for oil purchases to Pakistan in 2018. This helped rescue Pakistan's tottering economy. Saudi Crown Prince Mohammad Bin Salman visited Pakistan in February 2019.[23] Though he promised $ 20 billion of investment in Pakistan, including an oil refinery in Gwadar, nothing has materialised. The souring of relations may be linked to a development that came towards the end of the year. In December 2019, Mahatir Mohammad offered to host an Islamic Conference in Kuala Lumpur. Pakistan, along with Indonesia, Turkey, and Iran, decided to join the meeting. The meet was seen by Saudi Arabia as a challenge to the OIC, and the Saudi leadership of the Muslim world. Prime Minister Imran Khan's decision to attend the conference triggered an angry Saudi response. Though Imran Khan backed out of the meet, this left a bad impression on the Saudis.[24] The situation has been made worse by Pakistani Foreign Minister Qureshi's outburst against the Saudi refusal to call an OIC Foreign Ministers' meet on J&K. PM Imran Khan visited the Saudi Kingdom in May 2021 on the occasion of Lailat-al-Qadr. He returned empty-handed.

There is rivalry between Iran and Pakistan over Afghanistan. This has been accentuated by Pakistan's lurch towards the Saudi Kingdom. At home, there is a strong trend towards Islamic Sunni identity since Zia's period, at least. Both these factors make Pakistan suspect in Iranian eyes. Pakistan signed the Iran-Pakistan pipeline deal during Zardari's visit to Tehran in 2013. Since then, Pakistan went back on it. The absence of substance in the relationship is reflected in the trade figures. Pakistan's two-way trade with Iran stood at a paltry $ 358.64 million in 2016. The same year, its trade with the Saudi Kingdom stood at $ 2.243 billion—six times higher than trade with Iran. The next year (2017), trade with Iran remained at around the same level—$ 357.71 million. However, trade with Saudi Arabia went up sharply to $ 3.064 billion—more than eight times trade with Iran.

Just three days prior to the Saudi Crown Prince's visit to Pakistan on 17 February 2019, there was a terrorist attack on a bus carrying IRGC soldiers in the Sistan-Balochistan province of Iran on 14 February. The attack resulted in the killing of 27 IRGC soldiers. The suicide attacker was later identified as a Pakistani national. Major General Qassem Soleimani, the Commander of the Quds Force of Iran's Islamic Revolution Guards Corps (IRGC), said, "It worries Iran that the Pakistani nation and government allow Saudi money to end up in the hands of these Takfiri terrorists."[25] The Taliban's advance in Afghanistan has caused concern in Iran. The Iranian Foreign Minister Zarif described it as an existential threat to Pakistan and a security threat to India and Pakistan. Since then, the Taliban have reached Islam Qila on Iran's border near Herat.

Pakistan has had in the past a measure of success in playing on the sympathies of Muslim countries. It has misused the OIC platform for criticism of India. At the same time, it has hedged its position on issues of core interest to Saudi Arabia and the UAE. Ironically, it has lost credibility with the Arabs as well as Iran. Its friends like Turkey and Malaysia are neither willing nor able to replace Saudi Arabia as the banker of last resort for Pakistan. The law of diminishing returns has come to haunt Pakistan's Middle East policy as well.

Central Asian Republics (CARs)

The emergence of the Central Asian Republics following the disintegration of the Soviet Union in 1992 coincided with a triumphal mood in Pakistan. Pakistan saw the Soviet withdrawal from Afghanistan as a vindication of its policy of supporting *jihad* in that country. It assumed that the new Republics would follow its lead into an Islamic bloc. The perception of the Central Asian Republics was different. They were more advanced than Pakistan in terms of every index of social development. They had no desire to follow Pakistan's lead.

The Central Asian Republics were very wary of the spread of Islamic extremism from Afghanistan. The Tajik-Afghan border continued to be manned by Russian troops even after the collapse of the Soviet Union. Soon thereafter, Tajikistan along with Kazakhstan and Kyrgyzstan joined the Collective Security Treaty Organisation, which was floated by Russia in 2002. The emergence of new security architecture was in a sense a continuation of old equations. They acted to check Pakistan's dream of discovering a natural hinterland in Central Asia. By 1995, the Central Asian Republics had joined China in issuing the Shanghai Declaration. The Pakistani ambition of heading an Islamic bloc of Central Asian Republics had found an unexpected challenge from its 'all-weather friend.' China wanted to spread its influence in the space vacated by the erstwhile Soviet Union. To some extent, there was a convergence of interests between Russia and China—both were averse to the spread of Islamic extremism in this region. While Russia was concerned with the spread of extremism in the Central Asian Republics, China was concerned about the situation in Xinjiang.

The opening of the Central Asian Republics had presented Pakistan with an excellent opportunity for trade and transit. Pakistan wasted them. Trade with the Central Asian Republics presumed access to the Indian market. Pakistan was averse to providing this. The Pakistani market by itself was not a sufficient attraction for these Central Asian countries. This is mentioned by Riaz Mohammad Khan, a senior Pakistani diplomat, in his book '*Afghanistan and Pakistan: Resistance to Modernity.* Transit through the Af-Pak region could have earned handsome revenues for both Afghanistan and Pakistan. But this required stability in Afghanistan. Pakistan's policy of seeking dominance instead of letting Afghans decide their own fate had plunged the country into a prolonged civil war. This blocked any chance of substantially expanding trade.

Pakistan's trade with Central Asian countries is negligible. Tajikistan is one of the closest neighbours. Its two-way trade during the January-June period was 38.6 million dollars in 2018, accounting for a mere 1.9 per cent of its global trade figure. On an annualized basis, this might be around $ 77.2 million. This has kept dropping in subsequent years. The corresponding figure for 2019 was 35.3 million dollars, amounting to 1.7 per cent of the two-way trade. In 2020, this came down to 12.5 million or 0.6 per cent of Tajikistan's global trade.[26] Even discounting last year's trade on account of the pandemic, the trade turnover is not impressive. In the case of Kazakhstan, bilateral trade for the quarter of January to April 2021 was a paltry 15.63 million dollars or around $ 60 million on an annualized basis.[27] Pakistan's trade with Uzbekistan was $ 68 million in 2017, $ 50 million in 2018, and around $ 81 million in 2019.[28]

Trade and economics have influenced the foreign policies of major countries. This is not only true of the West but is reflected in the rise of modern China. This, however, has never figured very high in the calculations of the Pakistani leadership. Immediately after the partition, Britain devalued the pound by nearly 40 per cent. Indian and Pakistani currencies were part of the Sterling area. India followed suit by devaluing the Indian rupee. Pakistan refused. This created a major anomaly and disrupted trade. The immediate impact was on jute growers in East Pakistan. Their main market was in the jute processing industries of West Bengal. They lost the Indian market, which could not absorb over-valued jute exports from East Pakistan. Whether this was an unintended consequence is difficult to say. The only beneficiary was West Pakistan, which was a net importer.

Pakistan refused to extend Most Favoured Nation (MFN) status to India. This essentially means non-discrimination and formed part of GATT and WTO. Pakistan had created a roadblock to normal trade on the bilateral level. It replicated this within SAARC. Bilateral trade remains marginal. In 2018-19, Indian exports to Pakistan were $ 2.06 billion, while Pakistan's exports to India were $ 495 million. Pakistan's share in India's total exports was 0.60 per cent, while India's share in Pakistan's total exports was 2.20 per cent.[29]

Trade ties could create a constituency for peace. The founding of the European Community was based on this idea. There are lobbies within Pakistan that are opposed to trade normalisation with India. Recently, Pakistan's Finance Minister, Hammad Azhar, had announced that Pakistan would import sugar and cotton yarn from India. Pakistan faces a sugar shortage; Indian sugar is cheaper than that from other countries. Pakistan's Commerce Ministry had recommended the import of cotton yarn from India for Pakistan's textile industries. The decision of the two key ministries was reversed the next day, April 1, 2021, by the Imran Khan government.[30] Pakistan has stuck to its ideological position even where Pakistani consumers and industry stand to benefit from it.

Conclusion

Pakistan's foreign policy has occupied an outsized role in that country's national life. It continues to chase the mirage of 'parity' with India. This has trapped it into seeking a role beyond its means. The military culture has not been sensitive to developmental issues. Pakistan is on its 23rd IMF bail-out. Yet it seeks to dominate Afghanistan in the name of strategic depth. It is still not reconciled to the territorial *status quo* that resulted from the partition of 1947.

ENDNOTES

1. UN Security Council document S/PV.762 Add 1, as cited in *Forgotten Kashmir: The Other Side of the Line of Control* by Dinkar P. Srivastava, p. 78.
2. *Forgotten Kashmir: The Other Side of the Line of Control* by Dinkar P. Srivastava, p, 31.
3. Dr. Shabir Choudhury as cited in *Forgotten Kashmir: The Other Side of the Line of Control* by Dinkar P. Srivastava, p. 50.
4. *From Kargil to the Coup—Events that Shook Pakistan* by Nasim Zehra, p, 117.
5. Zehra, N., 2018. *From Kargil to the Coup: Events that Shook Pakistan*, Sang-e-Meel Publications, p. 188.
6. Mehdi Hasan Khan, Towards a Constitutional Provincial Status for G-B, *Express Tribune*, 9 November 2020.
7. Farzana Sheikh as cited in the Durand Line by S. K. Lamabah, p. 51.
8. NWFP Speaker's Slot Goes to MMA, *Dawn*, 22 November 2002.
9. ANP, PPP dominate in NWFP Assembly, *Dawn,* February 2008.
10. Imran Khan: Pakistan is ready to be a partner for peace in Afghanistan, but we will not host U.S. bases, *The Washington Post.*
11. Pakistan's Spy Agency Is Tied to Attack on U.S. Embassy, *NYT,* 22 September 2011.
12. Ghani at Int'l Summit Blasts Pakistan for 'Supporting' Taliban, *Tolo News*, 16 July 2021.
13. Ibid.
14. Pakistan's Policy of 'Quid Pro Quo Plus': Remarks by Lt Gen Khalid Kidwai (retd.) at the IISS London, 6 February 2020.
15. Ibid.
16. US FR 1947, Vol. III as cited in *The Shadow of the Great Game: The Untold Story of India's*

Partition by Narendra Singh Sarila, p. 310.

17. Ayub Khan: Pakistan's First Military Ruler, p. 140.
18. The *Untold Story of India' Partition* by Narendra Singh Sarila, p, 383.
19. A Friendship Fit for a King by Dr. Ayesha Siddiqa, *The Friday Times* https://www.thefridaytimes.com/a-friendship-fit-for-a-king/
20. Ammar Ali Qureshi, Neighbours of many surprises, *TFT*, 2 December 2016.
21. A Friendship Fit for a King by Dr. Ayesha Siddiqa, *The Friday Times*, https://www.thefridaytimes.com/a-friendship-fit-for-a-king/
22. Ibid.
23. Saudi Crown Prince's Visit, 19 February 2019.
24. K L Summit, *Dawn*, 23 December 2019.
25. Source: Iran's Soleimani warns Pakistan against Saudi attempts to destroy it', Press TV, 21 February 2019.
26. Embassy of the Republic of Tajikistan in the Islamic Republic of Pakistan.
27. Embassy of the Republic of Kazakhstan in the Islamic Republic of Pakistan.
28. https://wits.worldbank.org/CountryProfile/en/Country/PAK/Year/2019/TradeFlow/Import/Partner/UZB/Product/all-groups
29. Department of Commerce, Government of India, International Trade Centre Database, The Observatory of Economic Complexity.
30. Cabinet rejects ECC summary to import cotton, sugar from India, sources, *The News*, 1 April 2021.

9

Pakistan Nationalism and Identity: Effect on Pakistan Army's War-Fighting Doctrine

Lt Gen Rakesh Sharma (Retd)

Introduction

After Pakistan was created, the Army usurped the role of custodian of Pakistan's nationhood and identity. Its primary constitutional mission of ensuring national security and national unity of Pakistan has driven its overreach, by overthrowing elected civil governments, enforcing martial law, and dismissing Parliament on multiple occasions. The idea of Pakistan, then *begs the most fundamental question*—is Pakistan the land and people inside a certain geographical boundary or, a nation-state? As a corollary, what is the inter-relationship between the idea of Pakistan and the role of the Pakistan Army, as evident over the last seven decades. It is apparent that to foster its control on national polity, even with elected governments in the saddle, the Pakistan Army honed in its interpretation of nationalism and identity.

Is Pakistan a theological Islamic state, an ideological state, a sham democracy, a national security, paranoid, state or a failed State? Pakistanis are still struggling with the elemental question—who are we? Arabs or South Asians? Muslims first or Pakistanis first? Is there such a thing as Pakistani culture? Can Hindus, Christians, Parsis, Ahmadis, and other non-Muslims be equal to Pakistanis? Or is Pakistan only for Muslims? The common perception rests with the monolithisation of Pakistan based on Islam as a factor.[1] Obviously, the 'idea of Pakistan' since the time it was first conceived, is in a flux, essentially in the manifestations of its identity—the debate of what it means to be a Pakistani, the special difficulty of reconciling this identity with Islam and regional and internal challenges.

'Nation' means a form of cultural or social community whose members share an identity, mental makeup, sense of history or common ancestry, parentage or descent. By this definition, Pakistan is not a nation. Its people are too disparate and divided, have too little trust in those whom they perceive as outsiders, and identities of tribe and ethnicity are strong. This is painfully apparent in Karachi—Pakistan's megacity of nearly 17 million—which is frequented by violent ethnic and religious clashes. And, while the flag is saluted with great fervour in Punjab, it does not fly at all on schools in Balochistan where the national anthem is also not sung. Islam, hostility to India and the Urdu language were identified as the cornerstones of Pakistan's national ideology. Emphasis on Islamic unity was seen as a barrier against the political tide of ethnic nationalism, which could undermine the integrity of the nation.[2] Pakistan is divided, disorganised, economically backward, corrupt, violent, unjust, often savagely oppressive towards the poor and women and home to extremely dangerous forms of extremism and terrorism—'yet it moves.'[3] Islam is not only the basis of the country's identity and source of much of Pakistani culture; for Pakistani soldiers it is also a defining aspect of the profession of arms.[4]

In this context, the all-importance of the Pakistani Army is evident. The best case example is that in a court case in 1997 on corruption and the ISI's funding of anti-Benazir Bhutto politicians from slush funds, ex-COAS, Gen Beg told the court that, "*...he was not answerable (to the court) regarding his actions as COAS, and the sitting army chief was the only competent and proper person*" to ask what he did and why![5] Indeed, the so-called "institutionalized decision making" from the military's viewpoint implies civilian politicians, including the current PM, Imran Khan, could hold office as long as they ensured continuity in policies preferred by the military. With continuity in the Pakistani polity by direct or indirect control, the Pakistan Military retained and strengthened its role as guardians of the ideological frontier. Since the Pakistan Army is the only permanent custodian of the nation in all manifestations, the identity of the institution *willy nilly* becomes analogous to that of Pakistan, as a State.

A study of the Pakistani Army, its past, current manifestations, and its perceived future role, its India-centric nature and the impact on Pakistani nationhood, has to be contextualised against this background. The central theme of this chapter is to develop the argument that the question of Pakistani nationhood stands unresolved. It is also essential to highlight that it is not the madrassas alone, the national education curriculum in Pakistan is also institutionalised and fans hate-India and *shahadat/jihadi* narratives.

Pakistan–Nationalism and National Identity

The view that nationalism and national identity are rooted in a broad civilisational framework should not make us oblivious to the role of the ethnic, religious, and regional identities. One of the remarkable achievements of the Indian civilisation lies in its tolerance and accommodation of diverse identities as well as the facilitation of a creative synthesis of these identities. This has been one of the major hallmarks in the continued survival and resilience of Indian civilisation, despite that there have been disagreements between the over-arching national identity and sub-national identities.

In the case of Pakistan, the differentiation of the state and nation and the issues pertaining to nationalism and national identity are singularly relevant. The fundamentally different nature of state and nation, the first, a politico-legal entity, and the second, a psychological one creates a disjunction, which can be the cause of great tension. The linkage between the two has been recognised by many philosophers and social scientists as national *identity*—which can be subjective. National identity can be defined as a process of collective self-awareness, having boundaries, having continuity in space and time, being in communication and in communion internally and externally, feeling responsible for actions carried out collectively and individually, and holding others responsible for theirs and with the end product being successful adaptation and survival.[6]

Pakistani nationhood—the myth of its so-called idea or ideology that had been created and nurtured by the Military-Politicians (the Military Presidents), cannot be divorced from its contemporary nature. The Pakistan Army exhibits a deep-rooted lack of trust on nearly everything, history of continuing crises, sponsorship of proxy wars in the West and East and perpetual blame-game. The situation offers little hope to overcome the perpetual turmoil. If the boisterous statement of PM Imran Khan at the 76th session of the United Nations General Assembly in September 2021 is any indicator, and with total support evident to the Taliban government in Afghanistan, there is no likelihood of any ideological makeover of Pakistan.

Religion as Pakistan's National Identity

In the Lahore Resolution of 1940, Mohammed Ali Jinnah had demanded a separate Muslim state:

> The Mussalmans are a nation by any definition.... The Hindus and Muslims belong to two different religious philosophies, social customs, literatures...indeed, they belong to two different civilisations which are based mainly on conflicting ideas and conceptions.

The lack of nationhood can be traced to the genesis of Pakistan and the single factor that drove it—religious identity. Since inception, Pakistan's leaders have played upon religious sentiment as an instrument of strengthening identity. In a 1960 article in *Foreign Affairs*, Ayub Khan wrote "*...till the advent of Pakistan, none of us was in fact a Pakistani, for the simple reason that there was no territorial entity bearing the name.*"[7] It was rightly felt even in 1960, that "*...it is doubtful that either Islam or threat of an external enemy can generate sufficient cohesion for a national orientation and the government after all is the most comprehensive organisational structure on a country-wide scale.*"[8] Indeed post the break-up of East Pakistan, this debate of identity was even more profound. "*...what are the links that bind us? What is our national identity and the peculiar oneness that makes us a nation apart from others?... If we let go the ideology of Islam, we cannot hold together as a nation by any other means.... If Arabs, the Turks, the Iranians, God forbid, give up Islam, the Arabs yet remain Arabs, the Turks remain Turks, the Iranians remain Iranians, but what do we remain if we give up Islam?*"[9]

The fear of dilution of the Muslim identity became the new nation-state's identity, reinforced over time through the educational system and constant propaganda.[10] Under pro-Western rulers, Islam has been a rallying cry against perceived Indian threats. Islamist groups have been sponsored and supported by the state machinery at different times to influence domestic politics and support the military's political domination.[11] Pakistan's state institutions, especially its national security institutions, such as the military and the intelligence services, have played a leading role in building Pakistan's national identity on the basis of religion. Emphasis on Islam created a nexus between the 'custodians of Islam' and the country's military establishment, civilian bureaucracy and the intelligence apparatus. During its history, the greatest threats to Pakistan's central authority came from groups seeking regional autonomy, ethnic rights or political inclusion. However, successive governments linked these threats to either an Indian-inspired plan to weaken Pakistan or communists.[12]

Mr. Z.A. Bhutto reopened the debate on national identity, emphasising the Islamic roots, with scholars declaring Pakistan as the 'Kingdom of God' in a Muslim territory behind the demand of Pakistan.[13] Gen Zia-ul-Haq created a new Pakistani Army's credo—*Iman, Taqwa, Jihad fi Sabil Allah* (Faith, piety and jihad for the sake of God),—and stated that "*...this country can only be kept together by the Armed Forces and not by politicians.*"[14] Gen Zia hated India and sought national unity in the name of Islam. The Islamisation of Gen Zia was "*...being described as essential therapy to resolve a longstanding national crisis of identity.*" This Islamisation pushed by Gen Zia is having a telling effect in contemporary Pakistan, as it emphasised sectarian differences, created societal cleavages and plunged society in violent turmoil. As the Pakistan Armed Forces officer corps became lower middle class, it became less 'Americanised,' which was its hallmark in the first 30 years of its existence, and turned religious. Gen Zia's measures to make the Army more Islamic, may have pushed in many officers who wanted to ride to higher promotions, to adopt an Islamic façade! Indeed, Islam is a powerful motivating force in the Pakistan Army.

India and Kashmir Centricity

From Independence itself, the focus on rivalry with India as an instrument of securing legitimacy and authority defined political power in Pakistan, and influenced the relationship between the state and the citizens. Protecting Pakistan's nationhood by military means took priority over all else, conferring a special status upon the national security apparatus. Inflexibility in relations with India and the belief that India represented an existential threat led to maintaining a large military, which in turn helped the military assert its dominance in the life of the country. India had to be painted as an enemy of Islam in order to bolster Pakistan's self-image as a bastion of Islam.[15] This characterization of India as a Hindu state and Hindus as irreconcilable enemies of Islam and Muslims overlapped with the ideas of the religious and political leaders. Gen Ayub Khan wanted Pakistani nationalism to reflect pan-Islamic aspirations and a fear of Hindu and Indian domination.[16] Anyone calling for regional autonomy or ethnic identity was identified by the generals as pro-India. The institutional hatred of the Pakistan military for Hindu India increased phenomenally post the 1971 war, because the military now sought to avenge its humiliation in Bangladesh. Later, Mr. Bhutto projected India as an enemy of Islam and Muslims and therefore an inveterate foe of Pakistan.[17] This is despite the fact that he could have worked to redefine the basis of Pakistani nationalism.

Passion over the injustice of Kashmir has, ever since Independence, been central to the Pakistani identity. Grievances over the partition of Punjab and Bengal, and the loss of Kashmir, were fuelled by the sense that India, rich and powerful, could with impunity seize what rightfully belonged to Pakistan. Anger over the fate of Kashmir, the most painful issue of all throughout Pakistan's existence, was one of the issues that bound the nation together.[18] As Jaffrelot puts it: *"Pakistan, as a state, relies more on anti-Indian nationalism than on national integration. To put it in a nutshell, this is a case of nationalism without a nation."*[19] Jean-Luc Racine argues that anti-Indianess keeps the country together, and that the "*persisting tension with India is not without its advantages: in the context of the multiplicity of dissensions which plague Pakistan, India and the question of Kashmir offer an invaluable subject on which a near consensus prevails.*"[20]

Systematic Indoctrination of Public in Pakistan

Pakistan's public education system has an important role in radicalising Pakistan. A key requirement of education is that children learn to understand and cherish the values of truthfulness, honesty, responsibility, equality, justice, and peace that go with it. Children's identities and value systems are strongly shaped by the national curricula and textbooks in Social Studies, English, Urdu and Civics from Classes I to XII. The responsibility for designing them in Pakistan lies with the curriculum wing of the Federal Ministry of Education and the provincial text book boards.

Initially, President Ayub's regime had prescribed and mandated grade 1 to college levels textbooks, to create a standard narrative of history. Pakistan's educational system underwent significant changes during Gen Zia's years, with an Islamist ideological agenda. These textbooks were replete with historic errors, had prescribed myths, and aimed at supporting military rule in Pakistan. These inculcated hatred for Hindus, gloried wars and distorted the pre-1947 history of the area constituting Pakistan. This tendentious teaching of history continues describing communal riots at the time of partition as "Hindu and Sikh massacres of unarmed Muslims, and that the 1965 war a Pakistani victory that ended only when "India sued for peace" because it was "frightened of the Pakistan army and the people of Pakistan." The separation of East Pakistan was explained as collaboration between "external and internal enemies" and "Indian aggression."[21] Such teachings and texts attempt to depict the invincibility by false bravadoes of the Pakistan Army!

Madrassas in Pakistan have been a focus of world attention for creating this kind of exclusionary and sectarian worldview. The religious education mixed with militancy is supposed to be a deadly mix, giving rise to the narrow vision that breeds hate and irrationality and results in international *jihad.* This however is not entirely true. The madrassas are not the only institutions breeding hate, intolerance, a distorted worldview, etc. The educational material, as per the "The Subtle Subversion: The State of Curricula and Textbooks in Pakistan Government

Run Schools" do much more than the madrassas. The textbooks tell lies, create hatred, inculcate militancy, and much more.[22] The themes that emerge most strongly as constituting the bulk of the curricula and textbooks of the three compulsory subjects are:

- That Pakistan is for Muslims alone.
- That Islamic teaching, including a compulsory reading and memorisation of the Holy Qur'an are to be included in all the subjects, hence to be forcibly taught to all the students, whatever their faith.
- That the ideology of Pakistan is to be internalised as faith, and that hate be created against Hindus and India.
- Students are to be urged to take the path of *jihad* and *shahadat*. A few examples of anti-Hindu teachings in the curriculum documents state the following as specific learning objectives:
- The child should be able to understand the Hindu and Muslim differences and the resultant need for Pakistan. (p. 98).
- Develop understanding of the Hindu Muslim differences and need for Pakistan. (p. 99).
- Hindu-Muslim Differences in Culture. India's evil designs against Pakistan (the three wars with India). (p. 100).
- Identify the events in relation to Hindu-Muslim differences, which laid the foundations for Pakistan. (p. 101).
- The Hindu has always been an enemy of Islam. (p. 102).
- Hindus did not respect women. (p. 103).
- The religion of the Hindus do not teach them good things—Hindus worship in temples which are very narrow and dark places, where they worship idols. Only one person can enter the temple at a time. In our mosques, on the other hand, all Muslims can say their prayers together. (p. 104).
- '... the social evils of the Hindus.' (p. 105).[23]

Against this backdrop, with the primacy of the institution in one and all spheres, it is essential to examine the contemporaneous nature of the Pakistan Army's thoughts on war-fighting against its sole and sworn enemy—India.

Pakistan Army's Obsession and Threat Theory

The Pakistan military, more than most militaries, sees itself as a breed apart, and devotes great effort to inculcating in new recruits the feeling that they belong to a military family different from and vastly superior to Pakistani civilian society.[24]

Whatever the feelings of the population later, military coups in Pakistan when they happened, were popular with most Pakistanis, including the Pakistani media, and were subsequently legitimized by the judiciary.[25] Its discipline, efficiency and solidarity have repeatedly enabled it to take over the state, and dominate it from behind the scenes with a civilian government at the helm.

Pakistan Military's Economic Empire

The Pakistan military's success as an institution and power over the state comes from its immunity to kinship interests and the corruption they bring with them.[26] Pakistan's economy is controlled by a ruthless business conglomerate—the army that owns everything in the country, from factories and bakeries to farmland and golf courses. Many of Pakistan's largest corporations are also controlled by the military, thanks largely to an opaque network of powerful 'foundations' originally set up to look after the pension needs of army personnel. The largest three—the Fauji, Shaheen and Bahria foundations under the Army, Navy and Air Force, respectively, control more than 100 separate commercial entities involved in everything from cement to cereal production.[27]

In 2009, the Fauji Group had assets worth Rs. 125 billion and the Fauji Foundation Rs. 44 billion. While its 13 hospitals, 69 medical centres, and mobile dispensaries, 93 schools, 2 colleges, and 77 technical and vocational centres are admirable, its spending is tax-exempt and gets unfair commercial advantages by subsidies. The military leadership justified its power and privileges and ever-increasing perquisites as just rewards for its labour in the course of building a Pakistani nation and state. Many of Pakistan's own intellectuals accuse the Army of being more interested in making money than in defending the state. They describe the military as parasitical, insisting it grabs the best land—both agricultural and commercial—monopolises large areas of the country's economy and seizes the most lucrative state contracts. They argue that the ills that beset Pakistan are the result of a corrupt and predatory Army.[28] The Pakistan Army presents itself as a reluctant coup-maker, and its ability to execute a military takeover is often attributed to having contingency plans. Closer scrutiny reveals a pattern of careful planning including disorder on the streets orchestrated with the help of the reliable street power of Islamist political parties.[29]

The Pakistan Army is the greatest organisation for social advancement in the country with officers recruited from lower middle classes moving into the educated middle classes. In this context, the organisation is changing, and is changing faster than the rest of the nation. These days many of the generals are the sons of clerks and shopkeepers or, if they are from military families, they are sons of *Havildars.*[30] Indeed, the Pakistan Army has been a nationalist Army with an Islamic look.[31] It neither runs Pakistan effectively nor allows any other organisation to do so while its domination has eroded the capacity of the Pakistan State. Pakistan's political pattern has been an alternation between weak, unstable democratic governments and an authoritative and power-hungry Army. The military's role has been central, in which one province, Punjab, is grossly over-represented.

Bharat—the Omnipresent Threat

Officers and men of the Pakistan Army speculate endlessly on Indian intentions and capabilities. India, most men in uniform believe, is implacably hostile to the country's existence and intent on absorbing Pak territories into its own republic. Hindustan opposed partition, and as Pakistanis constantly recall, snatched Kashmir. In 1971, India contributed to the breakup. The Indian national anthem refers possessively to Sindh, which is entirely Pakistani territory. Pakistani thinking on Afghanistan is governed by the conviction that the Indians are plotting to encircle them.[32] When terrorist groups attack India...their actions enjoy a degree of instinctive, gut sympathy from a majority of Pakistanis....[33] Even in 1999, the imposition of martial law was not contested by any civilian group.[34] However, between 2004 and 2007, there were a number of instances of mass desertions and refusal to fight against militants, albeit more so in the Frontier Corps units. By early 2010, more than 2000 soldiers had been killed.

The Pakistan Army suffers from an obsession with India in general, and Kashmir in particular. Kashmir is not, however, specifically a military obsession. It is widely shared in Punjab, and to a lesser extent in NWNP and FATA, far less in Karachi, Sindh and Balochistan. Indeed it is not Islamist in origin, but a Pakistani nationalist issue. Zulfiqar Ali Bhutto once said, *"Kashmir must be liberated if Pakistan is to have its full meaning."* Speaking of an average Pakistani officer, Gen Naqvi said, "*He has no doubt in his mind that the adversary is India, and the whole raison d' etre of the Army is to defend against India. His image of Indians is of anti-Pakistan, anti-Muslim, treacherous people.*"[35] In fact, the 1971 War had scarred the Pakistani officer cadre, creating a way of thinking that seeks retribution in vengeance.

The 1990s near-anarchy of Karachi has been explained in several dimensions as issues of ethnicity (Muhajirs, Pathans, Afghans, Sindhis and Biharis pitted against each other), sectarianism (Sunni versus Shias), Islamic fundamentalism versus secularism, economics, struggle for power and absence of power-sharing and drugs and drug-trafficking.[36] However, the military saw the violence in

Karachi as India's retaliation for its troubles in Kashmir. President Musharraf also made it plain that he did not trust or like India, thought India wanted to "destabilise Pakistan" and "to isolate Kashmir and crush whatever is happening with all their force." Asked if India wanted "...a stable modernizing Pakistan as its neighbour", he replied, "Not at all. They want a subservient Pakistan that remains subservient to them."[37]

Pakistan Military's Warfare Doctrines

In examining the Pakistan Army's basic character and warfare doctrines, it is essential to fathom what it considers for itself as the challenge from India. "*At the conventional level, despite the current disparity in size and growing disparity in the nature of conventional weaponry available to India that promises to give it overwhelming superiority over time, Pakistan operates on the assumption of "strategic equivalence." Loosely translated, this means that Pakistani forces can blunt any conventional Indian attack and respond effectively by undertaking its own offensive actions into Indian territory. All under a nuclear overhang. Pakistan's new army doctrine recognises a wider spectrum of conflict that includes sub-conventional warfare in addition to conventional warfare that, in turn, includes low-intensity operations, conventional war and nuclear warfare. The latter is aimed at complementing comprehensive deterrence and adding to the combat potential of the regular forces, leading to a potentially heavy cost for any aggressor. Nuclear war is seen "only as a last resort.*""[38] As a contrary opinion, Pakistan's nuclear doctrine is grossly belligerent, with 'First Use' as its basis and tactical nuclear weapons bandied about in conventional war-fighting.

The Evolution of Pakistan Army Doctrine

Pakistan's military doctrines have been evolving over the last seven decades. In 1947, the Pakistan Army's war strategists developed a combat doctrine, called 'The Riposte.' It featured a strategy of 'offensive-defence.' Later, the swagger of the American ethos crept into the doctrine, leading to a concept, which concluded that only an offensive approach could bring victory. A strong offensive was the overriding strategy in 1965—India was seen as a minor power. Until 1986, 'offensive' remained Pakistan Army's major strategic concept. The 1947-48 war, which is referred to as the first Kashmir war, brought out the concept of war by proxy.[39]

The war of 1965 revealed Pakistan's offensive expansionist strategy. First was Pakistan's understanding, based on its intelligence from the hinterland of Kashmir, that the Muslim population was in support of a takeover by Pakistan and would partake effectively in neutralising the Indian Army. Second was the 1962 India-China war, which suggested that the Indian Army was in a poor state and would not withstand an offensive by the Pakistanis. Third was Pakistan's success in the Rann of Kutch action where the Indian higher command and control had shown distinct signs of weakness.[40]

The strategy of the 1971 war was a riposte from West Pakistan into Indian territory, seeking to forestall an Indian decision in East Pakistan and draw international intervention. In 1986, India conducted a war game, Operation Brasstacks, which demonstrated a full-fledged war as opposed to a limited war with decisive victory for the Indian forces. This seemed to rattle the Pakistan Army. So, they conducted Operation Zarb-e-Momin with the aim to send a message to the Indians that Pakistan had the capability and resolve to carry out effective defence against Indian aggression, and carry the fight into Indian territory.

For the first time, the 'defence' component of Pakistan's 'offensive defence' strategy became larger and an understanding came within the Pakistani security establishment that India was not a minor threat—a conventional offensive into India would lead to disaster.

Since the Nineties, Pakistan began to compress the conventional war sphere, aiming to avoid a conflict. To do so, they enlarged their unconventional sphere (hybrid war) and expanded the nuclear threat by reducing their threshold and introduced the threat of tactical nuclear weapons. Kargil was the unfinished operation of the Siachen loss of 1984. The strategy of proxy war was adopted. While mujahedeen from Pakistan and Afghanistan were brought in to occupy the heights in Kargil, the command and control remained with the Pakistan Army that also involved a fair number of regulars. The strategy was brilliant, but failed because the basic presumption that the Indians would not fight proved wrong.[41]

Pakistan Army and India's Cold Start Doctrine

In response to India's Cold Start doctrine, Pakistan devised a new concept of warfare, which brings out an even increased defensive mindset of its military leadership. It concedes that although some territory will be lost, the Pakistan Army must fight with all it has and achieve parity with India. They suggested that even a stalemate with India will be considered a victory.[42]

It is most relevant to follow the changed doctrinal thought processes post the nuclear blasts of 1998 and the Kargil War in 1999. The region has retained an ugly stability, with a continual proxy war by Pakistan against India, more specifically Jammu and Kashmir. Pakistan also was strongly convinced post Op Parakaram, that a conventional war with India as the aggressor has not taken place due to the shadow of nuclear weapons, especially the tactical nuclear weapons. Pakistan not only drafted its nuclear doctrines, operationalised C4I2SR (command, control, communications, computers, intelligence, information, surveillance and reconnaissance) capabilities, and openly threatened the use of TNWs in response to the Indian conventional superiority and offensive plans under the Cold Start Doctrine. It was again a non-linear, irregular war in Jammu and Kashmir blended with the nuclear threat and strong conventional defensive and nuclear posturing. A strong relationship and military-civilian assistance from China suited this environment perfectly for Pakistan, with India's perception of a two-front war scenario putting asymmetric force postures before her. China may not have overtly supported Pakistan in the past Indo-Pak conflicts, including the Kargil War, but this may not be the case presently, because of its physical presence in Pakistan through the CPEC and the tensions on the Line of Actual Control in Eastern Ladakh since 2020.

As argued above, Pakistan and Indian mutual relationship has remained in everlasting succession of antagonism, under a nuclearised environment. The Pakistan Army proclaims that Pakistan is continually faced with an existential security dilemma from a perceived threat from a much larger and more resourceful India. It is also claimed that this threat and instability is increasing due to existing and projected asymmetries and disparities in conventional forces and high-technology hardware inductions and ballistic missile nuclear submarines.

Pakistan's Army Doctrine: Comprehensive Response

Pakistan's Army Doctrine, called Comprehensive Response, was enunciated in 2011. In response to India's proactive military operations strategy, commonly dubbed Cold Start, Pakistan overhauled its conventional war-fighting with a nuclear deterrent strategy. Later, Pakistan practised its Comprehensive Response in four major military exercises under the Azm-e-Nau series near Sialkot, Cholistan, and Sindh. The larger objective of the exercises was to recover lost territory. Pakistan would aim to take the battle into its enemy's territory before the Indian military advances with offensive operational plans.

Pakistan also sought full-spectrum deterrence against widening force asymmetries in conventional war-fighting capabilities with India. In this effort, Pakistan conjoined conventional and nuclear deterrence to opt for 'strategic equivalence' with India. Pakistan's full-spectrum deterrence is dependent upon nuclear artillery shells, tactical nuclear weapons, Nasr (HATF9) of range 60 km and Shaheen III of range 2,750 km. The concept of full-spectrum deterrence has vague thresholds, and this, Pakistan felt, has deterred conventional war. It must be stated, however, that Pakistan has yet to travel on course for the naval leg of the strategic triad to achieve full-spectrum deterrence.

Pakistan Military Modernisation

Global Firepower that issues the National Power Index has issued rankings, utilising over 50 individual factors.[43] For 2022, Pakistan is ranked 9 out of 140 countries ranking above Turkey, Australia, Brazil and Canada. Pakistan has increased its defence allocation to 1.37 trillion Pakistani rupees ($ 7.8 billion) for the fiscal year 2021-22, an increase of 6.2 per cent. In October 2021, Pakistan's Chief of Army Staff, General Qamar Javed Bajwa, reiterated that the focus of the army was on enhancing conventional capability including "Intelligence, Surveillance, Reconnaissance, air defence and cyber and mechanization."[44]

China has long supplied Pakistan's armed forces. The relationship has deepened in recent years with Pakistan making major purchases of top-of-the-line Chinese export equipment. Five major arenas are:

- **Nuclear Weapons Programme.** It is widely said that China provided significant assistance to the Pakistani nuclear weapons programme. China is alleged to have provided missile components, warhead designs, and even highly-enriched uranium. The political motive behind this is clear. Pakistan acts as an effective foil against growing Indian regional ambitions. However, it is clear that nuclear assistance is the most deadly example of Chinese/Pakistani defence cooperation.
- **JF-17 Fighter.** The JF-17 fighter is the new premier multi-role fighter of the Pakistan Air Force, supplanting the position previously held by American F-16Cs. Featuring integration with a wide variety of air-to-air and air-to-ground munitions, including active radar air-to-air missiles and air-launched cruise missiles, the JF-17 brings a lot of modern capability and modern ergonomics for its cost.
- **A-100 Multiple Rocket Launcher.** Multiple rocket launchers (MRLs) are some of the deadliest artillery systems on the battlefield. The A-100 is one of the latest MRL systems, reaching an operational capability of around 2,000. The first units were sold to Pakistan by China around 2008; since then, Pakistan has built facilities to indigenously produce rockets for the system.

- **VT-1A.** The VT-1A, alternatively known as the Al-Khalid or MBT-2000, is one of the more capable tanks. It has been designed as a joint project between Pakistan and China with thermal gunner's sights, a panoramic commander's sight, and a 125 mm gun. Pakistan is considering acquiring the VT-4, China's further development of the VT-1A design.
- **HQ-16.** The Pakistan Army has acquired the Chinese HQ-16 medium-range surface-to-air missile (SAM) for the defence of its formations on the ground. A deep modernization of the Russian Buk SAM, the HQ-16 utilizes vertical launch and containerized missiles to enhance reaction time. HQ-16 batteries are also said to be highly mobile, allowing them to avoid artillery and SEAD/DEAD attacks. Pakistan is also in negotiations to buy the longer ranged Chinese HQ-9 system, a Chinese analog to the Russian S-300 long-range SAM.[45]

Pakistan, despite the dire financial straits it is in, is continuing focused military modernization. Some of Pakistan's latest armour developments were witnessed during the 9 November 2021 visit by Army Chief Gen Qamar Javed Bajwa to state-owned armoured fighting vehicles manufacturer, Heavy Industries Taxila, including newly developed protection measures and remote weapon stations for main battle tanks.

- An indigenously developed 155 mm artillery gun barrel.
- Ballistic and improvised explosive device protection for armoured fighting vehicles.
- Programmes to manufacture, rebuild and upgrade armoured personnel carriers and tanks.

The visit shows the indigenous Viper infantry fighting vehicle and a modernised version of the Type-85APII main battle tank. At one point, a Type-85APII turret is visible with an exposed composite armour module, possibly indicating replacement with a new type. Major modernisation projects available in open source information are:

- Efforts toward improving armoured capabilities include finding substitutions to component imports and indigenous development, specifically, the manufacturing of auxiliary power units for the Al-Zarrar and T-80UD tanks.
- The development and trials of a sabot FSDS-T round.
- The development of a driver's thermal imaging/night vision periscope.
- The assembly of engines for the Al-Khalid and T-80UD tanks.

- The rebuilding and upgrading of 160 Type-85IIAP main battle tanks between 2019-2020 and 2021-2022.
- A pilot effort to rebuild T-80UDs (completed in August 2019).
- The continued rebuilding of M113-series armoured personnel carriers.
- The continued upgrade of Type-59 main battle tanks to the Al-Zarrar version.
- The low-rate production of 20 Al-Khalid I tanks, plus the final-stage development of the Al-Khalid II (featuring an enhanced power pack and fire-control/gun-control system).

Pakistan has also shown keen interest in buying Turkey's autonomous rotary-wing attack "Kargu" Kamikaze drones, which have a range of 10 kilometres (6.2 miles) and can carry six rockets at a time. The Pakistan Air Force is acquiring two Chinese Wing Loong-II unmanned aerial vehicles, one ground control station and associated equipment worth $ 44.4 million.

Conclusion

The Pakistani national identity, so carefully constructed over the years by the Pakistan Army to its benefit, has largely failed to find any large-scale acceptance to bridge regional differences and shape that nation into one. It is hardly news to anybody that the people of Balochistan and interior Sindh feel alienated from the idea of Pakistan.

In sum, the developed and demystified DNA of the Pakistan Army exhibits its exploitation of religion, hate-India, Kashmir bogey and nuclear flash point, as binding factors for the nation, and projects to the world the inherent instabilities, to become a permanent rentier State. It is apparent that even the future generations are being gravely poisoned with anti-Indian sentiments. The anti-India, and existential threat hate-speeches constantly pedalled to its own populace, and to military personnel has facilitated the Pakistan Army to remain on the top pedestal.

Even after seven decades, the Pakistani Army is indeed still obsessed with India as it suits its ambition of being the sole power and indispensability to the nation, and it assists it in retaining the corporate control it has over businesses. To that end, the Inter-Services Intelligence (ISI) and its espionage, subversion and sabotage, and public relations and propaganda division (ISPR) provide the requisite support. All attempts to bank on economic trade and interaction and people-to-people contacts, to begin rapprochement between India and Pakistan will remain at nought, until the Pakistan Army is reined to its constitutional role, divested from the corporate structures, and that over-arching role in national polity called THE ESTABLISHMENT! Such an overhaul is not foreseeable, and if it happens it will be with attendant internal turmoil. Until then, the Pakistan Army will continue with pumping in nationalism with anti-Indianism and Kashmir centricity.

ENDNOTES

1. Ashok Behuria, Myth of the Monolith: The Challenge of Diversity in Pakistan, *Strategic Analysis* Jan-Mar 2005, IDSA, New Delhi, p. 61.
2. Husain Haqqani, *Pakistan Between Mosque and Military*, The Brookings Institution Press, 2005, p. 15.
3. Anatol Lieven, *Pakistan A Hard Country*, Penguin Group, 2011, p. 4.
4. Carey Schofield, *Inside the Pakistan Army*, Pentagon Press, 2011, p. 31.
5. Husain Haqqani, *Pakistan Between Mosque and Military*, The Brookings Institution Press, 2005, p. 219.
6. Brewster Smith, *The Metaphorical Basis of Selfhood*, 1985, pp. 1053-54.
7. Mohammed Ayub Khan, Pakistan Perspective, *Foreign Affairs*, vol. 38, no. 4, July 1960, p. 547.
8. Karl Von Vorys, *Political Development in Pakistan*, Princeton, Princeton University Press, 1965, p. 27.
9. Waheed-uz-Zaman, in his editorial note, "In Quest of an Identity, Proceedings of the First Congress on the History and Culture of Pakistan", held at University of Islamabad in April 1973, quoted in Edward Mortimer, *Faith and Power: The Politics of Islam*, London, Faber and Faber, 1982.
10. Husain Haqqani, p. 14.
11. Ibid, p. 3.
12. Ibid, p. 16.
13. Richter, *Political Dynamic Islamic Resurgence in Pakistan*, p. 549.
14. Husain Haqqani, p. 128.
15. Husain Haqqani, p. 16.
16. Ibid, p. 42.
17. Anwar H, Syed, "Z A Bhutto's Self-Characterisations and Pakistani Political Culture, " *Asian Survey*, vol. 18, no. 12 (December 1978), p. 1260.
18. Carey Schofield, p. 46.
19. Christophe Jaffrelot in *Pakistan: Nationalism without a nation?* Christophe Jaffrelot (ed.), New Delhi: Manohar, 2002, p. 42.
20. Ibid, p. 207.
21. K.K. Aziz, *The Murder of History in Pakistan*, Vanguard Books, Lahore, 1993, pp. 188-205.
22. A.H. Nayyar & Ahmad Salim, The Subtle Subversion The State of Curricula and Textbooks in Pakistan, Sustainable Development Policy Institute, Islamabad, 2002, p. 17.
23. The excerpts have been taken from National Curriculum, Social Studies for Classes I-V, Government of Pakistan, Ministry of Education (Curriculum Wing) Islamabad, March 2002, Social Studies Class VI-VIII, Punjab Textbook Board, Lahore, March 2002.
24. Anatol Lieven, p. 163.
25. Anatol Lieven, p. 164.

26. Ibid, p. 167.
27. *The Times of India*, New Delhi, Pakistan's economy controlled by a ruthless conglomerate – The Army, 12 November 2020.
28. Carey Schofield, *Inside the Pakistan Army,* Pentagon Press, 2011, p. 2.
29. Husain Haqqani, p. 255.
30. Anatol Lieven, p. 182.
31. Ibid, p. 184.
32. Carey Schofield, p. 19.
33. Anatol Lieven, 2011, p. 5.
34. Hasan-Askari Rizvi, *Military, State and Society in Pakistan,* Sang-e-Meel, Lahore, 2003, p. 8.
35. Anatol Lieven, p. 186.
36. La Porte, *Pakistan in 1995: The Continuing Crisis*, pp. 182-183.
37. Steve Coll, Excerpts from President General Pervez Mussarraf's Interview, *Washington Post,* 25 May 2002.
38. Shuja Nawaz, *The Battle for Pakistan: The Bitter US Friendship and a Tough Neighbourhood,* Penguin Random House India, 2019, accessed at https://scroll.in/article/939003/what-is-the-view-of-the-pakistan-army-about-the-possibility-of-a-nuclear-war-with-india#:~:text=At%20the%20conventional%20level%2C%20despite,assumption%20of%20%E2%80%9Cstrategic%20equivalence% E2%80%9D
39. Amarjit Singh, It took Pakistan three defeats to understand the flaw in its war strategy against India, *The Print*, 20 October 2020, accessed at https://theprint.in/opinion/it-took-pakistan-three-defeats-to-understand-the-flaw-in-its-war-strategy-against-india/527531/?amp
40. Ibid.
41. Ibid.
42. Ibid.
43. Refer Global Fire Power Rankings at https://www.globalfirepower.com/countries-listing.php
44. Hanan Zaffar, After Taliban Takeover, Pakistan Focuses on Military Modernization, 25 November 2021, accessed at https://www.thedefensepost.com/2021/11/25/pakistan-military-modernization/#:~:text=Focus%20on%20Modernization%20and%20Procurement, an%20 increase%20of%206.2%20percent
45. Charlie Gao, China Boosted Pakistan's Military with These Five Weapons Systems, *National Interest*, 28 November 2021, accessed at https://nationalinterest.org/blog/reboot/china-boosted-pakistan%E2%80%99s-military-these-five-weapons-systems-197110

10

Pakistan and the Taliban Takeover of Afghanistan and its Aftermath

Amb Gautam Mukhopadhaya

Introduction

Pakistan's role in raising, nurturing, promoting and providing shelter, safe havens, training and logistics for the Taliban is an open secret acknowledged by just about everyone except Pakistan. Not so obvious or well realised is the covert hybrid war it has conducted against Afghanistan over 20 years from the end of 2001 until the eventual military takeover by the Taliban with barely concealed Pakistani military, technical, logistical, intelligence, satellite and other assistance, and the participation of Pakistani and foreign/regional *jihadi* outfits at key stages, most visibly by Pakistani regulars in the Panjsher operation.

What defies belief is that such a vast operation executed over 29 years (if we include the first phase of the Taliban since they were raised in Afghan refugee camps in Pakistan from 1992), but particularly since 2002, should have gone un-noticed by Western intelligence or un-censured by Western governments, who turned a veritable blind eye to it. That involvement has not ended with their takeover of Afghanistan. The Taliban '*jihad*' against 'foreign occupation' is not over. It is only mutating. It is turning inwards against freedom-loving Afghans and outwards against the region.

As China, Russia, the USA and the West need Pakistan once again as a frontline or ringside state for their varying interests—geo-political, economic or humanitarian—the danger that Pakistan's role in investing in not just the Taliban but a whole consortium of associated radical extremist groups active in the region from the Caucasus to Xinjiang in Central Asia, will remain shrouded in the shadows with no one willing to reveal a dirty family secret, remains. This is likely to have profound consequences for not only the region but also Russia and China and the West.

In addition, how the Russia-Ukraine war affects East-West and US-Russian relations could also have a bearing on what happens in Afghanistan. On the one hand, it could marginalise Afghanistan in international attention further with serious consequences for the humanitarian situation in Afghanistan, drug trafficking, arms proliferation and regional and global terrorism. On the other, it could become a secondary theatre for a new Cold War and covert operations against Russian interests in Central Asia once again.

Evolution of the Taliban from Taliban

To understand what future direction the Taliban and allied groups are likely to take and Pakistan's possible role in it, it is instructive to trace how the Taliban has evolved from its origins in the madrassas and refugee camps on the Pakistani side of the Durand Line between 1992 and 1996 through its rule in Afghanistan from 1996 to 2001 (Taliban 1.0), to its relocation in Pakistan after they were driven out of Afghanistan by the USA and the Northern Alliance post 9/11 from 2002-21 where they regrouped as a radicalised insurgency using suicide and other forms of terrorism (Taliban 2.0), to their new incarnation as a victorious force and new 'government' in Kabul in August-September 2021 (Taliban 3.0).

Briefly, Taliban 1.0 was basically an ultra-conservative, mainly Pashtun, Sunni religious militia reared in neo-Deobandi seminaries (such as the Haqqania madrassas, Maulana Sami-ul-Haq and others) on the Pakistan side of the Durand Line and organised and placed under a pious religious preacher, Mullah Omar, who imposed harsh and repressive religious codes over an ethnically diverse population by force between 1996 and 2001 with the help and tutelage of Pakistan, over all but 10 per cent of Afghan territory held by the Northern Alliance. This was reversed with 9/11 and the US support for the Northern Alliance in taking back Afghanistan from the Taliban as part of the war on terror, the Bonn Accord, and 20 years of the US-backed Islamic Republic of Afghanistan.

In contrast, Taliban 2.0 were resuscitated after its ouster from Afghanistan, once again in Pakistan, as a radicalised army recruited and trained with the help of the ISI into a potent insurgent force using terrorist techniques using country-made Improvised Explosives Devices (IEDs), suicide terrorism, and more sophisticated commando operations to gradually occupy Afghanistan until their final push in tandem with the departure of US troops from Afghanistan.

Taliban 1.0 was a repressive but not yet terrorist force. Taliban 2.0 was however a full-fledged militant outfit using terrorism as its primary weapon of choice with several of its key operatives sanctioned by the United Nations Security Council although the USA never proscribed the Taliban as a terrorist organisation viewing its post 9/11 'war against terror' as primarily against the al-Qaeda. Many Taliban figures were however kept in detention in Guantanamo for alleged terrorist associations during Taliban 1.0 and released conditionally as part of the Doha 'peace' process. Several Taliban figures still remain in the UNSC's Sanctions list although they were to be de-listed as part of the US-Taliban Doha Accord.

Now that it is in power, the new Taliban rulers should be seen not as Taliban 2.0 as they were during their terrorist insurgency phase against the USA and the Islamic Republic, but as Taliban 3.0 with a new agenda. What could be that agenda and what kind of relationship can we expect between Taliban 3.0 and Pakistan?

Taliban 2.0: The Insurgency Phase, 2002-2021

It is unlikely that the Taliban takeover was a planned operation hatched by the ISI into its eventual form from the outset. Rather, Taliban 2.0 certainly grew in scale, ambition and sophistication with covert Pakistani help since about the mid-2000s when the US interest in Afghanistan started wavering in favour of the remaking of the Middle East starting with Iraq by the so-called 'Neo-cons.' The ISI knew that all it had to do was play a double game to harass and outlast the USA, ensure that Afghanistan could never stand on its own feet and become strong enough to threaten or resist Pakistan, and terrorize the Afghan population into submission through a violent war of attrition by the time the USA left. It worked for that end. It was a complex operation with several components executed with patience to a near-perfect demonstration of Sun Tzu's maxim of 'winning a war without fighting' with one difference; Pakistan's trademark use of terrorism. It was very much a work of the Mullah-Military combine.

Islam has been part of Pakistan's foreign policy toolkit vis-à-vis Afghanistan with a view to capitalising on their common religious identity and affinity and attenuating their long-standing differences over the sanctity of the Durand Line from at least the 1960s when Pakistan started promoting Islamic education and culture among Afghan youth in universities. This got a serious fillip with President Zia-ul-Haq's agenda of Islamisation of the Pakistani army and society and the anti-Soviet *jihad* led by the Afghan Mujahideen with US, Pakistani and Saudi backing with Islam as a rallying point.

It got a further boost with the religious indoctrination of madrassa students that had commenced in nascent form in the refugee camps and orphanages that mushroomed on the Pakistani side of the Durand Line and into Afghanistan with the help of radical Gulf charities, and raised as 'Taliban' from the mid-1990s. These madrassas were re-purposed post 2001 as recruiting grounds for Taliban insurgents and suicide squads, organised into cells, and mobilised both as militants and suicide bombers into Afghanistan. Even a back-of-the-envelope calculation of the numbers of suicide bombers that would be required to staff such an operation on the scale it achieved would run into the thousands, if not tens of thousands.

This indoctrination was accompanied by a radicalisation of religious teachers and preachers in Pakistan and Afghanistan fusing Afghanistan's Sunni Hanafi Islamic traditions with Pakistani 'neo-Deobandi' Islam and Wahabism and Salafism imported from Saudi Arabia and the Arab world to radicalise Afghans and prepare the ground for Islamism over what we may call 'Afghaniyat' or a more catholic and composite Afghan nationalism encapsulating various ethnic, sectarian and political strands symbolised today in the 'war of flags' between the tri-coloured Afghan flag and colourful women's dresses representing Afghanistan's national diversity, and the black-and-white Taliban flag and black robes of Taliban women representing a puritanical uniformity.

Pakistani Objectives in Promoting the Taliban

One of the primary objectives behind Pakistan's formation and backing of the Taliban was to confuse their Afghan, Pashtun and Islamic identities and enlarge their base within Afghanistan and to submerge them within a larger radical Islamist identity of the Ummah under an 'Emirate' headed by an 'Amir-ul-Momineen' (leader of the faithful) to serve several Pakistani ends.

First, it helped undercut and eclipse pan-Pashtun nationalism (and later, irredentism) represented by politically and culturally important figures like Khan Abdul Ghaffar Khan, Daud Khan and others in the past.

Second, it helped turn Pashtun nationalism away from the Durand Line to foreign occupation whether it was the Soviets in the past or the USA-led coalition until recently using Islam as a rallying point unifying all Afghans.

Third, it helped the Taliban and Pakistan to extend their influence over diverse Pashtun tribes, both Ghilzai and Durrani in the south and east (although some like the Alokazay have remained resistant) and those dispersed in enclaves in the north and west (since Amir Abdul Rehman's time) extending into non-

Pashtun majority areas of Afghanistan. In the process, the words 'Afghan', and 'Pashtun' were conflated to signify a primarily Pashtun Afghan identity that is being heatedly debated in Afghan social media as subordinating Afghanistan's other ethnic and composite identities to the Pashtun and becoming a highly divisive issue.

Fourth, Taliban Islamism and its association with other Islamist ethno-religious outfits in Central Asia and beyond have helped blur ethnic and territorial boundaries bringing both other Afghan ethnicities and the wider Islamic population in the region extending from Central Asia to South Asia under its umbrella and potentially setting the stage for their expansion into these areas.

Modus Operandi

The radicalisation of Afghan religious students and teachers in Pakistan and Afghanistan was followed by a planned programme of infiltration, sleeper cells and shadow governments built over a period of time to develop intelligence and strengthen its grip over areas increasingly out of government control. It used information warfare and social media internally and externally on a massive scale capitalising on the mistakes and excesses of the USA and the weak, corrupt and predatory government of the Afghan political elite.

Second, the Taliban's ultra-conservative, puritanical and hybrid interpretation of the *Shariat* as the basis of governance was projected as a sign of its ideological integrity and steadfastness and used to target and discredit what it regarded as the fickleness and 'moral corruption' of past communist, Mujahideen ('warlord'), technocratic or democratic governments based on leftist, ethnic, egotistic or republican foundations that were viewed as insufficiently Islamic, inherently corrupt and essentially ungodly because they are man-made, and therefore flawed, selfish and deviant. Western influence and the role and status of women played a particularly neuralgic part in this. The misrule, corruption, mistakes and external dependence of the past are seen as perverse deviations from Afghan honour and the virtues, values and fundamentals of the holy injunctions of the *Shariat* and other Islamic codes of conduct that the Taliban supposedly reflected.

But the most potent instrument in the armoury of the Pakistani ISI and the Taliban was their very sophisticated psychological operations using escalating levels of terrorism to create an image of invincibility and inevitability and wear down resistance among the Afghan people already tired of 40 years of foreign intervention, internecine fighting, repressive Taliban rule and Pakistani-sponsored terrorism. This applied both in the countryside where identification with the corrupt political elite was limited to tribal or ethnic ties, and towns, particularly Kabul, that were special targets for suicide attacks and complex operations against hospitals, schools, mosques, civil society and media, so that there was virtually no resistance to the Taliban when they moved in for the kill. Even foreign embassies, especially the Indian Embassy, was not spared such attacks that were attributed to the Haqqani Network at the bidding of the ISI.

Combined with this were assassinations targeting those most capable of leading a resistance against the Taliban and Pakistan starting with Ahmad Shah Massoud himself two days before 9/11 but including such figures as former President of Afghanistan, Burhanuddin Rabbani, Police Chief and later Governor of Kandahar, Gen Abdul Raziq, doughty fighters like Mutalib Bek in Taloqan, Abdul Jabbar Qohraman in Helmand, and countless others including unsuccessful ones like the ones against one-time intelligence chiefs, Amrullah Saleh and Assadullah Khaled. Khaled survived but was wounded for life.

All these strategies were deployed within a skilful diplomatic and political strategy that too had many components. It deceived the USA in its war on terror by cooperating with the USA in allowing its territory to be used for ground lines of communication and intelligence operations for the US war on terror for which it was compensated, while simultaneously using the Taliban as a proxy force to attack US forces and target killing close to 2,500 US troops, and eventually forcing and shaping a withdrawal deal between the USA and the Taliban that virtually enabled Pakistan to wait for the final stages of the US withdrawal for the Taliban to take over Afghanistan by force. It also used Russia and China in various ways to reinforce President Trump's decision to exit Afghanistan, legitimize the Taliban, keep India out, and shape an outcome to its liking.

An equally important part of Pakistani strategy was to use all the instruments at its disposal including blackmail and victimhood, to reinforce the USA's own definition of its intervention in Afghanistan purely in terms of its counter-terrorism objectives against the al-Qaeda, to limit US investment in Afghanistan to a CT role, without corresponding investments in building institutions, trade, economy, mineral wealth and even a national army capable of defending its territory that could have allowed Afghanistan to stand on its own feet. It ensured that a discredited Afghan state shorn of resources would collapse the moment the USA left.

Every time the USA had an epiphany that Pakistan was indeed the source of the problem as it happened under President Obama when he launched his 'Af-Pak' diplomatic strategy and President Trump with his South Asia strategy,

Pakistan used the UK, which had its own reasons to be soft on Pakistan to good effect behind the scenes to confuse the Americans and relieve pressure on Pakistan. It did this partly by bringing India and the Kashmir issue as the reason for the Pakistani obsession with Afghanistan, effectively externalising a bilateral problem between India and Pakistan into Afghanistan, that too using terrorism as a tool of its foreign policy.

This discreet role came out in the open when UK Defence Chief Nick Carter accompanied Pakistani Army Chief Gen Qamar Bajwa to Kabul to meet President Ghani to press for a transitional arrangement bringing in the Taliban after its May 2021 offensive.

Politically, it also expended a fair amount of energy in reaching out to ethnic and political forces in Afghanistan to get them to join or at least reconcile them to a Taliban government, and even inviting many of them to Pakistan with the promise of representation, posts and power-sharing to make the new Taliban dispensation more internationally acceptable, but also possibly as a means of reining in Taliban irredentism over the Durand Line.

Pakistan failed in this. The composition of the Taliban Cabinet through its phases of expansion remains a hard-line conservative and *jihadi* grouping that combines Taliban 1.0 and Taliban 2.0 and is 'inclusive' only to the extent that it co-opts various factions of the Taliban and the odd minority face without real power. Faced with Taliban intransigence over the Durand Line, Pakistan continues to reach out through the ISI to non-Pashtun leaders who have little stake in the Durand Line and press for inclusivity to mitigate Taliban Pashtun nationalism, without much success.

Deception was a key part of the Taliban and Pakistani strategy at the negotiating table and the battlefield right through the 20-year operation. It was deployed most critically in the final stages of the takeover when according to reliable reports, elements in President Ghani's establishment in touch with the Taliban or ISI issued instructions to Governors and commanders on the field to surrender or retreat without fighting on the understanding that there would be a transitional government, and when the Taliban entered Kabul before the US August 30 deadline effectively surprising and snubbing it.

Finally, Pakistan's role in planning the Taliban military strategy in Afghanistan especially its final push from May to September including its almost open involvement in the operations in the Panjsher valley also needs to be investigated. There can be little doubt that such a sophisticated military and diplomatic strategy that first took control of the unprotected countryside to convey a picture of inexorable advance, then captured border check and customs points and neutralised threats from the north and west, then mopped up the south and east that it had softened over the years, and finally moved swiftly to capture Kabul catching even the USA that was in the midst of a major evacuation effort and final phases of its troop withdrawal by surprise, could not have been planned by religious 'mullahs' albeit militant ones.

The open and triumphant presence of the then Pakistani ISI chief, Lt Gen Faiz Hameed, in the final stages of the military operation in Panjsher and Taliban government formation packed with figures from the Haqqani Network that the US Joint Chief of Staff, Mike Mullen, once described as a veritable arm of the ISI, should set at rest any doubt that the Pakistani GHQ in Rawalpindi did not need to hide its fingerprints any more. They had won.

Taliban 3.0

Having achieved victory, what then does Taliban 3.0 mean for the region and the world? Does the Pakistan-Taliban 'project' end with the Taliban running Afghanistan or is this the beginning of a new chapter for the region and the world? The situation in Afghanistan (and the world) is still too fluid and political forecasting too risky for clear answers. However, a few trends can be noted.

First, if the Taliban Cabinet with Guantanamo returnees and 17 designated terrorists, many with known ties to the al-Qaeda and other regional extremist outfits is anything to go by, there is every likelihood that Taliban 3.0 will mark an 'export' and regionalisation of *jihad* with the Taliban providing a base for operations for a range of *jihadi* outfits of diverse persuasions from the Caucasus to Central Asia and Pakistan that have been fighting together in the trenches against the USA and NATO and the ANDSF for the last 20 years.

Of particular concern amongst these are the Haqqani Network who arguably occupy pole position in the Taliban power structure today holding charge of the Ministries of Interior (that controls security, intelligence, and the issue of passports and IDs), Communications, Refugees & Repatriation and Education, are known to have ties with the al-Qaeda, the ISI and elements of the IS-K, have expressed the ambition of establishing a Caliphate over Muslim lands from North Africa to South Asia, and have the organisational ability and financial muscle to attempt it. Melissa Skorka[1] points out how the West, despite ample evidence, has consistently underestimated the potency and international links and alliances of the Haqqani Network and has no strategy to contain it. On the contrary, there are signs that not just Pakistan, but also the USA and other major powers have been cultivating the Haqqani Network, Sirajuddin Haqqani and Anas Haqqani in particular, for a larger political role in future.[2]

Second, post-August 2021, the Taliban are now trying to establish a new theocratic state based on their fundamentalist ideology. In an instructive article in the website of the Middle East Institute, Atlantic Council scholar, Javid Ahmad[3] has detailed how the Taliban is now using its Islamic morality based on a hybrid mixture of Hanafi, neo-Deobandi, and puritanical customs, mores and beliefs "wrapped in Islamic *Shariat*" (including some Salafist elements imbibed from the al-Qaeda and foreign fighters), to "re-Islamize" Afghanistan around revivalist principles similar to those of the Muslim Brotherhood, and channelize Afghan and religious nationalism into an official religious ideology of the Islamic Emirate of Afghanistan. Ironically, this is precisely the agenda of the revived and re-energized Tehrik-e-Taliban Pakistan (TTP) for Pakistan that the Pakistani army opposes.

Third, Ahmad also shows that although the Afghan Taliban remain true to its Hanafi core and its *jihadi* ambitions and is still essentially confined to Afghanistan and not 'internationalist' in character, it has been sufficiently influenced by the Muslim Brotherhood and Salafist ideas brought in by the Arabs (in addition to their own Pashtun traditions of hospitality that led them to host and shelter the al-Qaeda in the 1990s) to continue to host the al-Qaeda and ethnic or sectarian regional Islamist outfits with whom it has forged international alliances and fought shoulder to shoulder for more than two decades to enable them to pursue their agendas outside Afghanistan without directly having a hand in it.

Resistance and Complications

Yet, not everything is working according to the Pakistani plan; nor is Taliban rule bringing it any greater legitimacy or the consent of the Afghan people. However much the West may highlight the very real and severe humanitarian, financial and economic crisis that Taliban Afghanistan is going through that is almost entirely the creation of its military takeover of Afghanistan at least partly to salve their conscience and compensate for their political, military and strategic failures and responsibility for this situation, the reality is that the Taliban are an alien ideology to most Afghans; that they took over and continue to rule Afghanistan by force; that they have not really changed ideologically from the 1990s (if anything, they have hardened); that they are not accepted by the vast majority of the people of Afghanistan many of whom have voted with their feet to leave Afghanistan (and many more would if they could); and that they are unlikely to be able to provide the stability and governance that Afghanistan needs.

Nor can the international community brush away the daily word-of-mouth, social media and other reports of denial and suppression of political and human rights of women, minorities and the general population, evisceration of the media, beatings, abductions and disappearances including of women activists, house-to-house searches, confiscation of possessions especially arms and vehicles, that they fear could be used for an armed resistance, the torture and killing of former ANDSF officials or those suspected to be so, and dispossession of and brutalities against minorities ranging from Panjsheri Tajiks to Hazaras and others that have now largely disappeared from the international media and the political agenda of the West, to become the preserve of activists and conscience keepers. The Ukraine crisis is magnifying the double-standards of the West on this. The fact remains that there is a huge gap between the Taliban and the Afghan people, especially non-Pashtuns, and this is being aggravated every day.

For various reasons, however, it has become difficult for even relatively liberal Pashtuns opposed to the Taliban ideology to openly challenge them politically or militarily. As a result, though there is very little evidence to suggest that the Taliban is amenable to ideological compromise, to a very great extent, even Pashtuns opposed to the Taliban ideologically continue to believe that the latter can be softened and changed (including on neuralgic issues like women's right to education and work), through persistent dialogue, reform and persuasion, and oppose armed struggle and advocate pursuing that approach over armed struggle.

Beneath the larger Taliban-anti-Taliban divide, it is separating the large majority of Pashtuns who favour a peaceful approach towards reform of and accommodation with the Taliban, and non-Pashtuns, especially Tajiks and Hazaras, who believe that the Taliban is a Pashtun supremacist, anti-women, anti-minority and extremist force backed by Pakistan who has to be resisted at all costs, including armed struggle.

This opposition to the Taliban is likely to erupt at the first sign of a credible resistance and could also take a north-south, Pashtun-non-Pashtun turn. The very public praise by figures like Sirajuddin Haqqani and raising of suicide brigades like the Badr, the house-to-house searches, especially in the Tajik areas of Kabul, Panjsher and northern provinces, and reports of mobilisation of Taliban forces towards the Tajik border are likely intended to pre-empt, forestall and fight any possible 'spring offensive' on the part of the armed resistance.

Within the Taliban and other *jihadi* forces and the ISI, serious contradictions have also emerged between the traditional Kandahar and Helmand-based Taliban *shuras* closely affiliated to Mullah Omar and those of the Haqqani Network dominant in the eastern provinces backed by the Pakistani ISI over power and influence; between the Taliban, the al-Qaeda and more nihilistic outfits like the Islamic State of Khorasan, elements of which have been documented to have shady links with the Haqqani Network, Lashkar-e-Taiba, and the ISI over leadership over the Islamist agenda; and between the Afghan Taliban and Pakistan over the latter's management, tutelage and control over the former, their relationship with the TTP (that one effort at mediation by Sirajuddin Haqqani failed to resolve), and the Durand Line, where there were clashes in December 2021 between the Afghan Taliban and the Pakistani frontier forces and official statements revealing historic differences between Afghanistan and Pakistan over the Durand Line.

Each of these can seriously complicate the Pakistani agenda in Afghanistan, but the case of the Durand Line suggests that Pakistani efforts to dilute Pashtun nationalism and Afghan irredentism over the Pakistan-Afghanistan boundary by promoting Islamism over Afghan nationalism and fencing the boundary, is not working. If anything, the fencing and release of TTP prisoners from Afghan jails with the Taliban military takeover of Afghanistan, may have exacerbated it. So long cross-border movement was not restricted, Pashtun objections to the Durand Line did not come to a head. The fencing, and periodic Pakistani cross-border shelling and operations against TTP elements sheltering in Afghanistan are aggravating latent Taliban resentment against Pakistan and giving rise to sentiments expressed by Afghan Taliban spokespersons of the Durand Line 'dividing the Pashtun nation.'[4] Some have even argued that it is Pakistan that does not recognise the Durand Line by its continuing interference in Afghanistan and its treatment of the latter as a fifth Pakistani province.

Even today, Pakistan needs to keep the Afghan pot boiling lest it be turned on Pakistan for a variety of reasons: diverting attention from the Durand Line and the Pashtun question on both sides including the challenge posed to it by the Tehrik-e-Taliban Pakistan on the violent side and the Pashtun Tahafuz movement in the pacifist direction; preventing deep anti-Pakistani sentiment in Afghanistan from being directed against Pakistan physically; externalising its own *jihadi* problem towards the region; and preventing India from playing any role in Afghanistan.

The contradictions in Pakistani policy towards Afghanistan and the Taliban are also evident in what passes for its economic policy towards Afghanistan. One of the objectives behind imposing the Taliban into Afghanistan in 1995-96 was simply to keep Afghanistan backward and isolated, push it socially and economically into the dark ages in the name of Islam, and bring Afghanistan and Central Asia under Pakistani sway. During that period, there was no sign even of reconstruction of the massive damage done to Kabul during the intra-Mujahideen fighting of 1992-96 that helped bring them into power as an ostensibly stabilising force, let alone 'development.' Even the Gulf charities present only promoted their conservative religious and social agenda to keep Afghanistan blinded by religion.

That phase did not last owing to the resistance put up by the Northern Alliance, 9/11 and the US-led intervention, but it was not accidental that only three countries recognised the Taliban government from 1996 to 2001. Pakistan was quite happy that it was that way because it helped keep Afghanistan away from international attention and under its tutelage and use it as a backyard for its destabilising designs.

Today, the Taliban talk of international recognition, aid, trade and foreign investment, Pakistan talks about 'geo-economics' while its own economy is in a state of shambles, and China talks about expanding its BRI into Afghanistan. In principle of course, this should be welcomed. However, one has to question Pakistan's policies even here. The Taliban cannot change overnight from a *jihadi* force to a development state. Today, Pakistan is trying to project its interests in Afghanistan and Central Asia not in terms of 'strategic depth' but in terms of 'geo-economics.' This is but a thinly-veiled attempt to use China's strategic ambitions and heft, economic muscle, and Belt and Road Initiative, to 'stabilise' Afghanistan under its political tutelage. In reality, it is one more attempt to use Afghanistan for its strategic depth couched in 'geo-economics', limit, and if possible, sever Afghanistan's historic trade and cultural ties with India, and reorient it towards Central Asia and China. This is misguided and futile if not delusional.

Any ambitious economic activity requires security and stability. Pakistan's obsessive-compulsive investment in instability in Afghanistan through religious extremism runs counter to China's need for stability to pursue its BRI. Sooner or later, China will have to come to grips with the fact that it cannot stabilise Afghanistan by simply taming the ETIM and other Uighur independence or Islamist groups. It will have to take on the entire associated conglomerate of violent, extremist outfits that use Afghanistan as their base including the al-Qaeda and Islamic State. China may be tempted to fill the vacuum left by the US strategic and military withdrawal from Afghanistan to secure its vulnerable western frontier and fulfil its strategic ambitions towards Iran, the Persian Gulf and the Arab world, not least to escape US and Asian pressure on the Indo-Pacific, but it will be wary of being drawn into the quicksand of Afghanistan as other imperial powers like Britain, the Soviets and the USA have done.

Conclusion

Cumulatively, the post-2021 situation in Afghanistan presents a far more complicated picture of Afghanistan in 2022 of a fractured political and military landscape and multiple conflict fault lines than the simple Taliban-Northern Alliance contest of the 1990s or the Western gamble that the Taliban will be able to provide stability and governance in Afghanistan at the very least to alleviate human suffering, control drug trafficking and arms proliferation, and prevent large-scale displacement and refugees from reaching Europe if not to provide prosperity under an Islamic theocracy rather than a failed attempt at democracy. If anything, we may be looking at a Syria-Iraq-Libya scenario in the region.

The Russia-Ukraine crisis may complicate this further. There are credible grounds to believe that one of the motives of the Doha Accord with the Taliban, and the US departure from Afghanistan, was to hand over Afghanistan to extremist forces under the umbrella of the Taliban to destabilise China and Russia at their weak underbellies in Central Asia and Xinjiang, put Pakistan on notice, and complicate things for Iran. The new Russia-West Cold War being fought in Ukraine is likely to add to the temptation to use Central Asia as another theatre in this war. One has to wonder if the sudden public appearances and conciliatory statements of the little seen or photographed Sirajuddin Haqqani, the leader of the Haqqani Network, with a bounty of US$ 10 million on his head, has something to do with this.

ENDNOTES

1. Melissa Skorka, 'Afghanistan's Most Dangerous Threat', *Foreign Affairs*, 24 January 24, 2022, https://www.foreignaffairs.com/articles/central-asia/2022-01-24/afghanistans-most-dangerous-threat
2. Notably Opinion/PR pieces in the *New York Times* during the Doha Process.
3. Javid Ahmad, 'The Taliban's Religious Roadmap for Afghanistan', MEI@75, 26 January 2022, https://www.mei.edu/publications/talibans-religious-roadmap-afghanistan
4. See Umair Jamal, *The Diplomat*, 11 January 11, 2022, 'Taliban Pakistan Ties Run into Trouble', https://thediplomat.com/2022/01/taliban-pakistan-ties-run-into-trouble/;
   Kunwar Khuldun Shahid, 'Afghanistan and Pakistan's Troubles Won't End with a Taliban Victory, *The Diplomat*, 26 January 2022, https://thediplomat.com/2022/01/afghanistan-and-pakistans-troubles-wont-end-with-the-taliban-victory/;
   Raza Khan, 'Is a Rift between Pakistan and the Afghan Taliban Imminent'? *Al Jazeera*, https://thediplomat.com/2022/01/afghanistan-and-pakistans-troubles-wont-end-with-the-taliban-victory/

11

The Road Ahead

Tilak Devasher

Where will Pakistan be a year from now?

Predicting Pakistan is always fraught with risk, given the number of moving parts. Time and again, a sudden international event had made Pakistan an important player on the regional stage leading to its tattered economy being bolstered yet again while an out-of-the-box initiative by an Indian or Pakistani leader has paved the way yet again for a thaw in relations. Yet, at the time of writing, the portents do not look very bright for any of this happening.

Leaving aside the unexpected, three trends, in particular, are noteworthy and could resonate in the year ahead—the precarious economic situation, civil-military relations and the survivability of the Imran Khan government; and developments in Afghanistan that are impacting Pakistan.

Pakistan continues to be in dire economic straits; the stop-go IMF bail-out as well as aid received bilaterally has kept Pakistan afloat but has not enabled it to make structural changes that could resuscitate the economy on a long-term basis. These structural issues would include a low tax-to-GDP ratio, low savings rate, low investment to GDP ratio, circular debt, slow GDP and job growth, huge debt and low innovation and competitiveness. Neither would Pakistan be able to enhance spending on socio-economic development given the large outlays for debt servicing and defence.

According to the Pakistan Economic Survey, the provisional GDP growth rate for FY2021 was estimated at 3.94 per cent, higher than the targeted growth of 2.1 per cent, for the outgoing fiscal year. Many observers had however, expressed scepticism over the figure. There was widening fiscal deficit, revenue collection shortfalls and the Pakistan rupee depreciated from Rs. 123 against the USD in August 2018 to Rs. 177 in December 2021. This has resulted in an increase in the debt servicing cost as well as inflationary pressures.

Pakistan has had to accept tough conditions of the IMF in order to get approval for a $ 6 billion Extended Finance Facility (EFF) in July 2019. While this enabled Pakistan to partially stabilise the economy, it had to undertake numerous strategic, technical, and legislative changes. The programme has led to enormous hardships for the people due to substantial increases in the rates of electricity and gas and withdrawal of subsidies. With exports stagnant, high imports, inelastic revenue collection and growing inflation, Pakistan faces an uphill task in steadying its economy.

Add to this, Pakistan has been on the Financial Action Task Force (FATF)'s 'grey list' since June 2018 for its failure to curb terror financing and money laundering. While Pakistan has made progress in fulfilling some of the action points it was mandated to do, it is likely to languish on the list given its failure to get its anti-terror financing and anti-money laundering laws and practices completely in line with international standards.

Against such a backdrop, Pakistan, a year later, is probably going to be in similar dire economic straits, if not worse. Acknowledging this, Pakistan has projected a shift in emphasis from 'geo-politics' to 'geo-economics', an articulation that was evident in the Islamabad Dialogue in 2021. This was reiterated in the first ever National Security Policy 2022-26 (NSP) that held: "Pakistan's vital national security interests are best served by placing economic security as the core element of national security." It remains to be seen in the year ahead whether this gets translated into action or, like other high-sounding policies, remains on paper. However, putting economic security as the core element of national security is indeed a belated recognition of the abysmal state of the economy that required urgent remedial measures.

Not only is the economy in a precarious position but politically, too, the leadership has failed to demonstrate either vision or maturity to take the country out of the morass it finds itself in. The prognosis in 2019[1] and 2020[2] had been that having 'selected' Imran Khan, the army was unlikely to pull the rug from under his feet soon. Thus, civil-military relations in the short-term were likely to be smoother than they had been for a long time with the caveats that Imran Khan did not start getting ideas of being the effective chief executive of Pakistan and started performing, especially in the economic sphere. Unfortunately for him, Imran Khan has failed on both counts. He tried to interfere in the selection of DG ISI, something that the army considers its preserve. Curiously, such interference was apparently done on grounds not purely professional. Moreover, his performance on the economic front has been dismal, making even the army chief talk about geo-economics, the new buzz word in Pakistan. As a result, 'being on same page' narrative has receded into the background. Given the no-confidence motion submitted by the Opposition and the way the numbers seem to stack up in the National Assembly, at the time of writing, it would be a miracle of sorts if Imran Khan were to survive in power the next year, let alone come back to power in the 2023 elections.

The Establishment has several instruments to destabilise the government. For one thing, Imran Khan's thin majority in parliament is dependent on the support of smaller parties that the army had stitched together. It will take only a phone call to get these parties to withdraw support overnight. The Opposition has got its act together once the army signalled that it would be 'neutral' and so introduced a No-Confidence Motion in the National Assembly. There are also plans to undertake 'Long Marches' in various parts of the country. In addition, the foreign funding case against the PTI is coming to a head and most analysts are agreed that the evidence is strong and would have adverse consequences for Imran Khan. What would be interesting to see is what instrument is ultimately used to get rid of Imran Khan.

Two areas of concern would be Balochistan and KPK. The former is likely to simmer with incidents like the ones in Panjgur and Nushki in February 2022, taking a toll on the security forces. In KPK, the Tehrik-e-Taliban Pakistan (TTP), bolstered by unification of splinter groups, the presence of the Taliban in Afghanistan and their release of TTP members from Afghan prisons, would pose a continuing threat to the security forces. While one attempt of the army at talks failed in November 2021, further talks cannot be ruled out though the conditions laid down by the TTP would be difficult for the army to accept.

In addition, two different kinds of movements would have implications for the future. The first is the Tehrik-e-Labbaik that since 2017 has signalled the rise of Barelvi assertion. It was used as a tool of political engineering during the 2018 national elections to dent the vote bank of the PMLN. The Barelvis have now sensed power and influence and they are likely to use it effectively both electorally and on the streets. The second is the rights movement of the Pashtuns spearheaded by the Pashtun Tahafuz Movement. The Pashtuns, especially the youth, have been at the receiving end of violence and dislocation for decades in furtherance of the army's foreign policy agenda in Afghanistan. They are now asking for an end to being treated as cannon fodder and demanding rights as Pakistani citizens under the constitution. This movement is extremely uncomfortable for the army that has traditionally been suspicious of ethnic movements, seeing them as challenging the sovereignty of the state.

Beyond the day-to-day issues, there are the serious long-term challenges that Pakistan faces—Water, Education, Economy, and Population—collectively that I had termed as the WEEP factors.[3] Continued neglect of these elements would work to Pakistan's detriment, negating advances in other areas. Among the most critical ones are the declining water availability and its cascading effects on availability of food, employment, and exports. A key reason for this state of affairs is that the leadership in Pakistan has not taken a long-term view of the situation and instead of investing in the real sinews of power like human capital to build a stable Pakistan, it has focused on military power. In the process, development of human capital has suffered that, in turn, has adversely impacted the overall development of the country. For example, according to the UN Commission on Sustainable Development, 200,000 children die annually from diarrhoeal diseases alone. The total number of civilians, security force personnel, and terrorists who died between 2003 and September 2017 was 62,483.[4] Those figures alone should give the leadership of every government pause for thought and reorient their policies. However, it has not been done so far and is unlikely to be done in the year ahead.

Bigotry and extremism is likely to grow. The lynching of the non-Muslim Sri Lankan manager of a Sialkot factory on alleged blasphemy charges and the killing of a Christian clergyman in Peshawar graphically highlighted this. In reality, such outcomes were the result of the state policy of appeasement of religious elements for narrow political gain. Added to this was the forced conversion of minor girls from the minorities. It is estimated that hundreds of girls are abducted and forcibly converted every year while the state looks on as a mute spectator. This is likely to continue.

While Imran Khan had come to power on the promise of ending corruption and bringing the corrupt to justice, the reality is quite different. Transparency International's Corruption Perception Index (CPI) ranked Pakistan 140 out of 180 countries, indicating a drop of 16 places from its previous ranking. It had a low CPI score of 28 during 2021. So much for Imran Khan's rhetoric.

Unlike the National Action Plan (NAP), the National Internal Security Policies (2014 & 2018) and Vision 2025 formulated by the PML-N government, the National Security Policy (NSP) mentioned earlier, did not consult either parliament or the opposition parties and neither were the provinces taken on board during the formulation process. This has made the NSP partisan from the start. Moreover, while it identified internal security fault lines like terrorism, violent extremism, and sectarianism and organised crime as being serious issues, it failed to provide a roadmap for upholding the rule of law and countering terrorism and violent extremism. It is noteworthy that according to the World Justice Project, Pakistan ranks 130 out of 139 countries on rule of law. Imran Khan, too, was forced to acknowledge in a recent article that the "most urgent of all challenges facing our country" was the "struggle to establish the rule of law."

Foreign policy would continue to pose challenges. The changing geo-politics alignments find Pakistan in the China camp, where it is likely to remain. The fact that Pakistan's priority in foreign relations is to seek bilateral and multilateral financial aid and bailouts for its economy, also does not help in furthering its interests.

Its relations with the USA have plummeted, not the least because of undiplomatic comments made by Imran Khan on the relationship. The American snub of epic proportions of President Joe Biden not having made a phone call to him has rankled Imran Khan personally and hurt his ego. Pak-USA relations have been transactional, focused on a single point agenda of Afghanistan. With the pullout from Afghanistan, the central pillar of Pakistan's relations with the USA has eroded. The USA no longer has much need for a Pakistan that most US analysts blame for the resurgence of the Taliban and the US defeat. Pakistan is likely to continue to chaff at being downgraded but does not have the heft to broad base its relations with the USA. There would continue to be a narrow focus on counter-terrorism, especially if there is a major resurgence of the ISKP and/or the al-Qaeda and the safety of Pak nuclear assets.

The China-Pakistan Economic Corridor (CPEC) would continue to be the pivot for relations with China. However, the bills for repayments of loans/ investments will accumulate that Pakistan will find increasingly hard to settle. This will make it even more dependent on China that is unlikely to provide easy bail-outs while the Chinese will increasingly find Pakistan's inability to re-pay loans and interest to be a major constraint. Two other troubling aspects need to be factored in. One is the protests in Gwadar over Chinese practices in the area. Led by the Jamaat-i-Islami, Balochistan, a movement titled '*Gwadar ko haq do*' (Give Gwadar its rights) was launched on 16 November 2021. The key demand was the banning of illegal fishing by Chinese trawlers off the Makran Coast in order to protect the rights of Gwadar fishermen. The second issue is the security of Chinese workers in Pakistan on CPEC. In 2021, the TTP had targeted such workers who were deployed on the Dasu dam, leading to the death of nine of them. Further targeting of Chinese workers, would strain the 'all-weather' relationship.

The initial euphoria of the Taliban take-over in Kabul on 15 August 2021 has gradually given way to concern, a concern that is likely to grow in the future. Two issues are at the forefront: The Taliban have controversially questioned the validity of the Durand Line, calling it an unresolved issue, dividing a nation and declaring that they will not allow further construction. This has come as a shock to Pakistan though it has tried to underplay it by calling it a localised problem. The second issue is the Taliban not being more helpful vis a vis the TTP. Pakistan had expected that the Taliban would ensure that the safe havens and sanctuaries of the TTP in Afghanistan would not be permitted and the Taliban would help in defanging them. This has not happened for a variety of reasons, not the least because of Pakistan not appreciating fully the nature of the relationship between the two. Both these issues will continue to have resonance in the year ahead.

With the Islamic world, especially Saudi Arabia and the UAE, Pakistan's relations have cooled down considerably. This has been largely due to Pakistan trying to align itself with Turkey, Malaysia, and Iran to form an alternative Islamic block. In the process, Pakistan was in danger of losing the support of its greatest benefactor, Saudi Arabia, that has frequently bailed it out with financial aid, deferred payment for energy and for providing employment to millions of its workers. Saudi Arabia has now stipulated that the $ 3 billion cash deposit that it gave Pakistan for a year in November 2021 would have to be returned anytime on a three-day notice as and when the Saudis wanted it. What will continue to rankle Pakistan is the lack of interest shown by Saudi Arabia and the UAE on Kashmir.

With India, Imran Khan has taken the untenable position that without a repeal of the revision of the temporary Article 370 and Article 35-A pertaining to Jammu and Kashmir, there can be no forward movement in Indo-Pak relations. Since this is not happening, the bilateral relationship is in cold storage and likely to remain there until Imran Khan is at the helm or he does one of this famous U-turns. His persistent personal tirade against PM Modi has made matters worse. Even the NSP is littered with an anti-India tirade: India is accused of "military adventurism", "non-contact warfare", "arms build-up", "belligerence towards Pakistan" and policies of "exceptionalism that undermine the global non-proliferation regime."

Given the above scenario, what Pakistan leaders need to do is serious introspection about where they are and how they have got there. However, given the political polarisation and the economic situation, it is unlikely that this will happen in the near term.

ENDNOTES

1. *Pakistan Insights 2019.*
2. *Pakistan Insights 2020.*
3. Please see the author's '*Pakistan: Courting the Abyss.*'
4. The big problem with water, Editorial, *The Express Tribune*, 27 September 2017, https://tribune.com.pk/story/1517024/big-problem-water

Index

*